GLOBAL POLITICS
IN THE HUMAN INTEREST

Explorations in Peace and Justice:
New Perspectives on World Order

GENERAL EDITORS
Elise Boulding
Richard Falk
Samuel S. Kim
Saul H. Mendlovitz
R. B. J. Walker

GLOBAL POLITICS
IN THE HUMAN INTEREST

MEL GURTOV

with the assistance of
Dariush Haghighat

LYNNE RIENNER PUBLISHERS • BOULDER & LONDON

Published in the United States of America in 1988 by
Lynne Rienner Publishers, Inc.
948 North Street, Boulder, Colorado 80302

and in the United Kingdom by
Lynne Rienner Publishers, Inc.
3 Henrietta Street, Covent Garden, London WC2E 8LU

Library of Congress Cataloging-in-Publication Data

Gurtov, Melvin.
  Global politics in the human interest.

  (Explorations in peace and justice)
  Bibliography: p.
  Includes index.
  1. International relations.   2. International
  economic relations. 3. World politics—1945–
I. Title.   II. Series.
JX1391.G87   1988   327.1′1   87-27504
ISBN 1-55587-098-4 (lib. bdg.)
ISBN 1-55587-099-6 (pbk.)

British Library Cataloguing in Publication Data
A Cataloguing in Publication record for this book
is available from the British Library.

Printed and bound in the United States of America

The paper used in this publication meets the requirements of the American National
Standard for Permanence of Paper for Printed Library Materials Z39.48-1984. ∞

For my daughters

Alia, Marci, and Ellene

" . . . in the bloom of life, like the sun

at eight or nine in the morning.

Our hope is placed on you."

Contents

Charts

Preface

Teaching world politics has made me acutely aware not only of the limited perception most U.S. students have of other societies. That is hardly a novel discovery. But I have also become more aware of, and concerned about, the direction most studies of world politics seek to take students: away from recognition and appreciation of the world's diversity; away from an understanding of how closely interlinked peoples and societies really are—that what happens "out there" really does affect what happens at home; toward acceptance of conflict and violence as the unalterable pattern of state politics; and toward embracement of the "American way" as the only reasonable path toward a satisfactory world order.

Hence this book, the chief purpose of which is to propose a relatively new way of looking at world politics. It challenges conventional thinking and hopes to awaken readers to a global crisis that directly affects them. My approach is not merely to define the dimensions of this crisis but to redefine national and global security in ways that promote the human interest. By "the human interest" I mean satisfaction of the basic material and nonmaterial needs of the overwhelming majority of the planet's people, especially in the underdeveloped countries but also in the so-called developed world.

Two contrasting global trends also motivated my writing: profound inequalities between and within nations whose fates are increasingly interdependent; and the emergence of projects and ideas at many levels that have the potential to move human society toward greater equity and sustainability. The first of these trends is, of course, dominant in world politics, and as such is a principal cause of dangerous instabilities: arms races, state as well as group terrorism, war, revolution and counterrevolution, resource and ecological crises. Yet, if we can understand how all these forms of violence—to ourselves, to others, to the environment—are structured into political-economic systems and into the international behavior of states, we have the conceptual basis for transforming the rules in humane ways. And as the rules change, a new global agenda is fashioned for restoring security at every level of human activity.

Underlying my analysis is a set of values, identified as Global Humanist (see Chapter 3), that distinguishes my approach from most other studies of world politics. Human-centered values, such as peace and social justice, are increasingly being recognized as important tools for defining, analyzing, and resolving the great world-scale problems of our time—and doing so while avoiding becoming captive to particular political institutions and ideologies. But to emphasize values, as Saul Mendlovitz reminds us, is to cut against the grain of the social sciences, which traditionally have been biased "against work that explicitly utilizes preferences and values as a way of defining problems to be investigated, and as a standard to be used for what will be considered an adequate solution to the problems."[1] My own personal and political evolution leads me to conclude that the credibility of social science research rests to an important degree on the explicitness with which we identify our own values and how they affect what and how we analyze.[2] There is simply no such thing as value-free research.

Some years ago, in a process that began with rethinking U.S. intervention in Indochina, I gradually moved away from a traditional, U.S.-centered conception of international politics. This book is a road stop on that continuing journey of personal and political renewal. I owe a profound intellectual and emotional debt to a rather diverse group of contemporaries, including Carl Rogers, Paolo Friere, Ram Dass, George Kennan, and Richard Falk. And by their example as well as their written work, Gandhi, Martin Luther King, Jr., John Vasconcellos, and Daniel Ellsberg have also inspired and changed me. I doubt that any of these people would reflect on world politics in the same way I do. But I would like to think that they would regard what I have written as a contribution to making the world a little bit better.

I also wish to thank Dariush Haghighat, a doctoral student from Iran, for his skillful research on several of the case studies in this book. He has been a joy to work with. We both are grateful to the University of California, Riverside, for an intramural research grant and the opportunity to travel to Washington, D.C., during 1986. At that time I interviewed key people in several of the globalist organizations mentioned in Chapter 7, and I would like to express my appreciation for their help: John Marks of Search for Common Ground; Nancy Graham of the Institute for Soviet-American Relations; and Mark Rilling of the U.S. Institute of Peace.

The manuscript profited from the counsel of Ray Maghroori, Elise Boulding, and Sam Kim, each of whom read it in its entirety and offered valuable suggestions for improvement. I thank them as well as several anonymous reviewers. Of course any errors or omissions are my responsibility alone. Finally, the actual production of the manuscript could not have been accomplished without the wonderful skills of Aline Messer in Riverside and Peggy Tombleson in Portland.

My final words of thanks are for my family: my wife, Leigh Anne, and my daughters, Ellene, Marci, and Alia. Their love and gentleness are a constant inspiration to work harder at being a global citizen.

Mel Gurtov

GLOBAL POLITICS
IN THE HUMAN INTEREST

CHAPTER ONE

Crisis and Interdependence in Contemporary World Politics

This dominant culture set the tone and standard for most of Shikasta. For regardless of the ideological label attaching to each national area, they all had in common that technology was the key to all good, and that good was always material increase, gain, comfort, pleasure. . . . And all this time the earth was being despoiled. The minerals were being ripped out, the fuels wasted, the soils depleted by an improvident and short-sighted agriculture, the animals and plants slaughtered and destroyed, the seas being filled with filth and poison, the atmosphere was corrupted. . . . These were maddened creatures, and the small voices that rose in protest were not enough to halt the processes that had been set in motion and were sustained by greed. By the lack of substance-of-we-feeling.

—Doris Lessing, *Re: Colonised Planet 5, Shikasta*

The splitting of the atom has changed everything save our mode of thinking, and thus we drift toward unparalleled catastrophe.

—Albert Einstein

GLOBAL INSECURITY

Someone once defined fanaticism as "redoubling your efforts when you have lost sight of your original objective." The blind pursuit of national security fits this definition of fanaticism perfectly. As state leaders invest more and more political, human, and economic resources in weapons, aid programs, alliances, and the exploitation of resources, the security of persons, societies, and the planet as a whole actually seems to decline. In the industrialized, technologically advanced countries of

1

the First and Second Worlds,* insecurity is mainly reflected in acute anxiety about the arms race and frustrations about the ability of capitalism or socialism to deliver the "good life" except at very high social and ecological costs. In the underdeveloped countries of the Third World, where three-fourths of the world's population of about 5 billion people live, insecurity takes a more basic form: the daily quest for survival.

The causes and consequences of this pervasive insecurity, and the extent to which its different forms are interrelated and mutually reinforcing—the degree, for example, to which the quest for security in the First and Second Worlds takes place largely at the expense of the Third World, yet also has profound economic and social impact on their own societies—are the principal subjects of this study. The reasons are simple: The human costs of global insecurity are staggering; the narrow understanding of "national security" by most state leaders keeps these costs high and mounting; the penetration of every aspect of world politics (such as alliances, the ecosystem, global finance and trade, and people's movements and exchanges) by this global crisis has created great foreboding but equally great hesitancy to take remedial action; and, as a result, the prospects for planetary survival itself are not optimistic.

State leaders everywhere invariably seek to put the best possible face on their own situations, and many serious scholars persist in arguing that humankind will resolve today's problems just as it resolved yesterday's. But the contention here is that the present global crisis is unprecedented and beyond quick technological fixes. Time and opportunity may be running out. As U Thant, the former secretary-general of the United Nations, forcefully put the issue in 1969:

> I do not wish to seem overdramatic, but I can only conclude from the information that is available to me as Secretary-General, that the

---

*The definitions of First, Second, and Third Worlds used throughout this book differ from those commonly employed. "First World" here designates the superpowers—the United States and the Soviet Union. "Second World" refers to the advanced economies of Europe, East and West, Japan, Canada, Australia, and New Zealand. "Third World," as discussed in chapter 4, embraces a wide spectrum of economically "underdeveloped" (even if rapidly industrializing) societies, including not only those in Asia, Africa, Latin America, and the Middle East, but also several in Europe (namely, Portugal, Spain, Greece, Turkey, Albania, and Bulgaria). No categorization is entirely satisfactory; the main virtues of this one are that it sets the two superpowers, with their unparalleled global influence, apart from the other industrialized and politically influential states of the Second World, and that it draws attention to how much Second World states have in common despite evident differences in their social systems.

Members of the United Nations have perhaps ten years left in which to subordinate their ancient quarrels and launch a global partnership to curb the arms race, to improve the human environment, to defuse the population explosion, and to supply the required momentum to development efforts. If such a global partnership is not forged within the next decade, then I very much fear that the problems I have mentioned will have reached such staggering proportions that they will be beyond our capacity to control.[1]

In its essentials, the secretary-general's warning has come true. Although planetary extinction has thus far been averted, the depth and scale of the problems U Thant cited have indeed increased to nearly unmanageable proportions, as I document in the next section. Few government leaders have shared his sense of urgency; most have acknowledged one or another aspect of a global crisis, but have not considered that the problems are symptomatic of a contagious and potentially fatal disease. Life, and politics, go on as before.

It is indeed strange that at one and the same time, monumental leaps of scientific creativity occur for the benefit of humankind while political leaders stick to tired formulas and outdated rituals in pursuit of self-interest. The practice of politics has not kept pace either with scientific advances or with global ecological, economic, military, and social changes. U Thant appealed for a "global partnership" because he believed the future of the human species itself was imperiled. But the governments he addressed were not (and clearly still are not) ready to integrate global changes into narrowly national perspectives. And therein lies a crisis of our times that is equally as burdensome as any U Thant described: a crisis of political will in the nation-state system.

The emphasis throughout this book is on information, explanation, and argument. This chapter begins with some basic facts about the global crisis and what they tell us about the changed shape of world politics—in a word, its *interdependence*. I introduce the two schools of thought that dominate writing and thinking about world politics—Realism and Corporate Globalism—along with a third school—Global Humanism—the values and analytical method of which I use throughout the present study. In Chapter 2, Realism and Corporate Globalism are critically examined. An extended discussion of the contemporary world economy and a case study of how it was shaped after World War II enable us to see the ways Realism and Corporate Globalism both compete and collaborate in their real-world application. Chapter 3 elaborates on Global Humanism as an alternative perspective with specific relevance to global human needs. The Third World's oppressed are given special attention here, for they constitute the global majority. This discussion sets the stage for a more specific investigation of insecurity from a human-interest point of view, in the Third World (Chapter 4), the First World (Chapter 5), and the Second World (Chapter 6)—in each case buttressed by brief studies of particular countries. The concluding chapter is policy oriented: It lays out an agenda for changes addressed to the main features of the global crisis.

A BRIEF REPORT ON THE STATE OF THE PLANET

The scope of the global crisis becomes apparent from the following figures:

- Over 2 billion people in the Third World (including four of five persons living in rural areas) do not have access to clean water. A rough estimate by the World Bank and UNESCO is that about half of them (a billion people) are chronically malnourished.[2]
- Despite advances in world literacy, there remain thirty-four countries with over 80 percent illiteracy.[3]
- About 300 million people in the Third World were unemployed or underemployed in the late 1970s, as were about 22 million people in the industrialized capitalist countries. By 2000, it is estimated that well over 1 billion people will be seeking employment in the Third World alone.[4]
- Somewhere around 800 million people live in absolute poverty in the Third World, with incomes below $200 a year; more than 2 billion people have incomes below $400 a year. Their societies have the world's largest and fastest-growing populations.[5]
- By the year 2000, 79 percent of the world's population will live in the Third World. And by then there are expected to be 50 percent more people in the world than at present.[6]
- At current rates of depletion, by the year 2000 the Third World's forests, especially in tropical zones, will be reduced by one-half (thus intensifying an already serious shortage of firewood for fuel). Up to 1 million plant and animal species out of a total of 5 million may become extinct. One-third less topsoil will be available for food production. Already, world food reserves have shrunk to only a 40 days' supply, from over 100 days in 1960.[7]
- The developed-world states (those in the First and Second Worlds) currently account for four-fifths of the world's income but only one-fourth of its population. (The United States, with about 6 percent of the world's population, consumes over 30 percent of its total product.) By contrast, the underdeveloped states account for three-fourths of the world's population but only one-fifth of its income.

- Arms expenditures worldwide have roughly doubled in twenty years, reaching $940 billion in 1985—well over $2 billion a day. Over 80 percent of that amount is spent by the two superpowers, which together possess nuclear destructive power equivalent to about 5,000 World War IIs. In all, about 20 percent of the world's scientists are involved in military research and development.[8]
- Third World governments, especially those under military rule, are the primary customers for arms sold by the United States, the Soviet Union, and various European suppliers. They buy three-quarters of all marketed weapons. They are paying for the arms with their own scarce resources and with money borrowed from the banks and governments of the developed countries, to which the Third World owed close to $1.1 trillion by the end of 1987.[9]
- Alternative uses of tiny fractions of the world's military spending could produce meaningful change in education, health care, and nutrition. For example, the cost of one new nuclear submarine (about $1.5 billion) could educate 160 million school children in twenty-three developing countries. About $3 billion is estimated to be enough to enable the poorest countries to begin moving toward food self-sufficiency. Similar small amounts could probably prevent the deaths each year of about 15 million children from malnutrition, dehydration, and other easily curable conditions.[10]

Statistics of these magnitudes may be difficult to absorb at one sitting. But they give an immediate sense of what a global perspective on world politics does: It highlights the multidimensional and transnational character of a common crisis. And that is why we turn next to the phenomenon of interdependence.

INTERDEPENDENCE

U.S. citizens demonstrate in Washington, D.C., and across college campuses for human rights in South Africa. The Japanese prime minister asks his people to buy foreign products, while U.S. labor unions debate how to respond to Japanese automobile plants being built in the United States. Two hundred million Russians watch a televised conference of U.S. and Soviet doctors discussing the medical consequences of nuclear war. The Indian government briefly arrests the chair of the board of Union Carbide, then sues the company in a U.S. court, after a catastrophic gas leak from the company's branch plant in Bhopal kills over 2,000 people. The government and people of New Zealand express outrage and incredulity when French agents bomb and sink an antinuclear organization's ship in Auckland harbor in order to prevent it from witnessing French nuclear tests. A worldwide emergency food relief effort begins in Ethiopia and Sudan after a BBC broadcast dramatizes the fact that several million people are starving to death. An Islamic terrorist group proclaims: "Let them know that sooner or later we shall reach the heart of the White House, the Kremlin, the Elysée, 10 Downing Street."

These events of the 1980s have one thing in common: They reflect the increasingly complex and transnational character of world politics. The line that once so neatly divided domestic from foreign affairs and foreign from global affairs is now much harder to find. Issues that once were the exclusive prerogative of governments, such as air and water pollution, now are matters of international diplomacy. Other issues that used to be dealt with exclusively by diplomats, such as nuclear weapons, are now subjects of intense popular concern and sometimes massive demonstrations. And both these sets of issues are all the more compelling because of their global, as opposed to merely binational or regional, character. Large numbers of ordinary people are being affected by them as never before—and advances in global information technology are helping create awareness of that fact.

Even the older patterns of *inter-* and *intra*national relations, in which conflict is the dominant feature, have new meaning today. Whether we are talking about wars between states, such as Iran and Iraq; or power plays by major governments, such as the U.S. intervention in Central America and the Soviet Union's pressure on East Germany to resist closer economic ties with West Germany; or nationalist and separatist struggles in Sri Lanka, Spain, and Ireland; or territorial disputes, such as the war between Great Britain and Argentina over the Falkland Islands—the consequences of such conflicts carry well beyond their effects on the contestants. They crisscross national boundaries to involve not only other governments, but also other economies, ways of life (consumer prices, cultures, food supplies, civil liberties, jobs), even natural environments.

The global agenda has therefore become larger, more diverse, and more ominous. We need additional tools to analyze it. International affairs is still politics, of course; but political science is no longer sufficient for the study of international affairs. Economics is equally important, specifically international political economy, the study of the social consequences of national and international economic developments. In addition, biology (studying, for example, acid rain), anthropology (the demise of native cultures in the face of "modernization"), sociology (the international division of labor), feminist studies (women on the global assembly line of transnational corporations), even sports (from U.S.–China ping-pong diplomacy to terrorism and fraternalism at the Munich and Los Angeles Olympic Games)—all have a place in the study of world politics. The transnational phenomenon requires an interdisciplinary approach to do justice to world politics.

And that is the approach of this book. I use the tools and insights of many disciplines in order to explore world politics in its fullest, global sense: across national boundaries, inside as well as outside societies, at many different levels of social activity (governing elites, races, ecological systems, economic classes, and bureaucracies, for example). Since the United States, despite all its vulnerabilities occasioned by global political-economic changes, is still the world's most influential actor, I emphasize its policies and behavior more so than any other state's.

The principal perspective used in the study is referred to as Global Humanism. It combines two approaches. One is a set of *humane values and norms*.[11] These enable us to examine national policies, ideologies, social forces, and institutions everywhere from the particular standpoint of the needs and interests of the planet, considered as a human community and as an ecological system. Global Humanism attempts to provide political and ethical standards that can be applied consistently to evaluating politics in all social systems.

The other approach is *political economy*. As applied to international politics, and as it is used here,[12] political economy focuses on the ways certain systems (such as world capitalism and imperialism) and structures (such as transnational corporations and military-industrial complexes) often decisively influence the distribution of wealth and power within and between nations, and therefore the character of national and international security.

Taken together, these approaches enable us to identify and account for perhaps the most prominent feature of world politics in our time: *inequality*. How the world works to the detriment of the disadvantaged, who benefits from that process, and what such a disequilibrium means for the human condition are central to this study.

"We are stranded . . . between the inadequacy of the nation-state and the emerging imperative of global community," former U.S. Secretary of State Henry Kissinger has said.[13] World politics today might be characterized as proceeding simultaneously along two tracks, with the distance between them getting wider all the time. The first track consists of the traditional statecraft of power politics, of which Kissinger has long been a highly visible exponent. The "engine" that propels movement along this track is commonly known as Realism, a philosophy or paradigm of national interest that we will critically examine shortly. Running along the second track is Globalism, which interprets world politics in terms of transnational forces. Globalism, as we shall see, takes two politically quite distinct forms, one Corporate (reflecting the interests of transnational businesses) and one Humanist (reflecting the human interest within a global community: human rights in the broadest sense). In either form, Globalism contends that politics-as-usual within the framework of competing national interests at the least cannot cope with the kinds of planet-wide problems cited by U Thant. At the most, Globalism argues, Realism risks nuclear holocaust and ecological suicide.

Yet, there is growing agreement between these two perspectives, that world politics is highly interdependent and becoming more so all the time. No event in recent memory brought home this evolving perception more than the Soviet nuclear power plant disaster at Chernobyl, near Kiev, in April 1986. The Soviet leadership had to answer to the world, as well as to its own citizens, for the accident, the worst in the history of nuclear power. Leaders of individual states of course looked to their own interests in commenting on Chernobyl—either out of concern about radioactive fallout or out of a desire to exploit Soviet troubles for their own political benefit. But no one, including Soviet and U.S. leaders, could avoid Chernobyl's global meaning. General Secretary Mikhail Gorbachev said it created the need for international monitoring and reporting of nuclear accidents. President Ronald Reagan said Chernobyl showed that some issues have implications that transcend the national interest. They and other state leaders seemed to accept that, when it comes to species survival, Realist politics is severely handicapped.

"Interdependence" is shorthand for the transnationalization of world politics—not just events, but also ideas, institutions, and decisions. It is a phenomenon that draws societies, and particular groups within societies, closer together, with both positive and negative consequences. As will be discussed later, Realists and Globalists differ about the precise implications of interdependence for the policies that states should pursue. They also differ about whose interests (those of states? of corporations? of particular classes? of persons?) interdependence ought to serve, and about the ways that the various interdependent factors relate to one another. But that interdependence is the central new ingredient in world politics is now widely acknowledged.

Interdependence has a number of connotations that are worth spelling out. Consider the term first in the sense of "mutual dependence." Relationships between states today typically are highly unequal and sometimes dependent. That is the fundamental characteristic of the industrial North in relation to the agrarian South. Yet the dependence is often mutual rather than one-sided. The U.S. economy, for example, is no longer as autonomous and uniquely powerful as it was at the end of World War II, when the dollar, backed by gold, was the only international currency. In 1985 the United States became a debtor nation for the first time since 1914: Its financial obligations to foreigners—from such things as investments and securities holdings—exceeded foreign obligations to the United States. Moreover, U.S. industry has become highly dependent on foreign oil, metals, and minerals; one in every five industrial jobs depends on exports abroad; and one in every three farm acres produces for export. While it has been argued that the United States can nevertheless maintain its economic independence, its leaders have deliberately chosen an interdependent course. Why? Because dependence works both ways, creating benefits for some interest groups (in corporate profits abroad and foreign investments that create jobs here, for instance), while imposing social and economic costs on others.

The arms race provides another example of mutual dependence, for the two superpowers (and, most importantly, their populations) are hostage to each other's nuclear arsenals. They therefore also depend on each other's rationality and sense of security, notwithstanding that both the U.S. and Soviet leaderships constantly refer publicly to the other side's irrationality and take actions that seem designed to create insecurity in the opposing camp. And because each side devotes enormous resources to military buildups for "defense," the two economies are to some extent intertwined as well.

In a related vein, consider interdependence as it describes the world economy as a single integrated unit. No longer are we talking about capitalist versus socialist (or market versus nonmarket) systems. Today, all the major socialist economies, from Eastern Europe to China, are deeply enmeshed in the global capitalist system of trade, investments, and lending. It was Western banks and not the Soviet Union that bailed Poland out of virtual bankruptcy in 1982. Mitsubishi, Pan American, and Occidental Petroleum, not state trading companies, are the key external financiers of China's drive for industrial modernization. Arguments fly back and forth about whether or not a separate socialist community exists any longer as a result of this type of interdependence.

A third way of defining interdependence is in terms of global developments that seem beyond the capacity of nations to control through traditional diplomacy. Terrorism, famine, ecological disasters, nuclear proliferation, and the eradication of whole species of plants and animals are examples. Governments, of course, continue to attempt to come to grips with large-scale issues such as these. But doubts that they can do so have been raised of late even by Realists, some of whom seem prepared to accept the need for new global regimes to perform tasks that require global cooperation. There is a growing consensus, in line with this notion of interdependence, that at least for some purposes we must indeed consider ourselves one species sharing one planet.

Fourth, interdependence may also be thought of as the spillover, typically unintended, of one country's (or region's) problems into another. A "domestic" issue becomes a transnational one. The Chernobyl disaster again comes to mind. Among many other side effects, it angered East and West Europeans alike that the Soviets took so long to report the accident and the radioactive fallout that was moving westward. Chernobyl also raised Soviet requirements for imported food, reduced Soviet food exports, pushed up world oil prices, put a damper on nuclear arms talks, and caused the biggest one-day drop in stock prices Wall Street had ever experienced.

Another example of spillover can be found in the extraordinary numbers of economic and political refugees who have streamed across national borders in search of jobs or safety from war. Still another is acid rain from industrial pollution, which has become a major issue in Scandinavia (an estimated 18,000 of Sweden's 90,000 lakes have been damaged, some permanently, by acid rain from central Europe) and in U.S.–Canada relations. Or consider how inflation in the United States in the 1970s, and recession in the 1980s, were "exported" worldwide through the weak or strong dollar. Of a quite different nature is the deliberate dumping of unsafe chemicals (such as pesticides) and goods (such as contraceptives) by a developed-country's transnational corporation into an underdeveloped country. Here we have a spillover that sometimes spills back, as when pesticide-laced coffee beans are exported back to the country that produced the pesticide.

Yet a fifth way to conceptualize interdependence is as the interrelationship of seemingly disconnected political-economic phenomena. The so-called greenhouse effect is commonly cited to illustrate this type of interdependence. The rapid buildup of carbon dioxide in the earth's atmosphere as the result of unprecedented large-scale use of fossil fuels (coal, petroleum, and natural gas), combined with the destruction of forests due to industrial pollution, may be responsible for a warming of the earth's temperature. Many scientists warn that climatic changes would have serious consequences for food production, world trade, human health, population movement, and even the polar ice cap. A second example is the interdependent linkages among hunger, overpopulation, deforestation, and desertification (the turning of potentially productive land into desert)—all common features of underdeveloped, dependent economies.

Finally, interdependence is manifest in the growing number and political importance of transnational movements and institutions. State-to-state diplomacy remains a fixture in international politics. But it is now supplemented, and in some cases even displaced or upstaged, by the activities of nongovernmental groups (human rights organizations, such as Amnesty International, and various people-to-people assistance programs); by popular movements for social change (such as the antinuclear, ecological, and women's movements that coordinate efforts around the world); by transnational religious and political movements (such as Catholic liberation theology and the Green party in Europe and North America); by powerful transnational corporations, banks, and financial institutions (such as the World Bank and the International Monetary Fund); and occasionally by individuals who act as transnational agents—world citizens, in effect—such as Reverend Jesse Jackson when he traveled to Syria, in the midst of his 1984 Presidential campaign, to negotiate for the release of an American pilot.

Interpreted in Global-Humanist terms, interdependence means that we focus on inequality and human insecurity along many dimensions besides the traditional one of conflict between states. Underdevelopment, the global war economy, deprivations of human rights, and severe pressures on the planet's environment and resources loom even larger in our and our children's futures. The fragility of world security is thus intertwined with the security of nations and persons. Thinking "interdependently," I want to address all three levels of security throughout my study.

CHAPTER TWO

Realism and Corporate Globalism in Theory and Practice

THE REALIST PERSPECTIVE

Throughout the postwar years, Realism has reigned as the dominant way of looking at the world among state leaders and their advisers.[1] Indeed, it might be said that its predominance coincides with the beginning of the nation-state system at Westphalia in 1648. But Corporate Globalism, centered in the United States and the other major industrialized countries that are home to the world's largest corporations, has become a powerful force in its own right in the second half of the twentieth century. Realism speaks to the interests of state power, Corporate Globalism to the market needs of transnational institutions, mainly business and finance.[2] In the next two sections, I want to assess these two perspectives with specific reference to the global crisis and the issues of interdependence they raise. My objective is to show, with the help of a case study of postwar U.S. economic planning, that, notwithstanding important differences of emphasis between Realism and Corporate Globalism, they embrace common values and aims, many of which run counter to the human interest.

For Realists, power is the essential ingredient of politics. It is the instinctive goal of persons (who are considered to be naturally evil-minded and aggressive); and it is the unavoidable objective of nations (since international relations is a jungle). The best leaders seek to maximize their country's power, believing that the "national interest" is thereby served. The standard operating precepts of Realist diplomats are to construct and defend a stable balance of power among rival states; to evaluate the costs and benefits of state actions in strictly national terms; to operate on the basis of what is, not what has been or might be; to disregard expressions of good intentions by other leaders; to trust no one (not even allies) and nothing, other than the justness of one's own national cause; and to rely on military power rather than moral suasion, diplomatic agreements, international law, or an open, democratic decisionmaking process to protect and enforce one's interests.

Chart 2.1 displays what seem to be the principal values that guide the social behavior of Realists, Corporate Globalists, and Global Humanists. While there undoubtedly would be some differences between Realists in different socioeconomic systems—for example, Realists in the West would say they value individualism and liberty, whereas Realists in the East would give priority to collectivism and social conformism—I maintain that in general Realists everywhere share most of the values listed. Clearly, there is an emphasis on accomplishment, decisiveness, competitiveness, and elitism. Transferred to the level of official work ("Institutional"), these values are typically expressed in a determination to defeat the opponent (other bureaucracies and other states) in the "game of nations," and thus to preserve the "national interest." But on closer examination, we find that there is nothing "national" about this interest. In any political system, the "national interest" usually defines the political-economic priorities of an elite— that set of interests which *it* decides national power ought to promote. Realist leaders (as well as Corporate Globalist leaders) do not usually count cooperation, participation, accountability, and social responsibility among the values they apply to national or international politics.

Different values thus help to distinguish the "national interest" from the "human interest." So do different *norms*, or standards of national action (see Chart 2.2). Realism's essence is system-maintaining: It seeks to preserve a status quo favorable to the national interest, but it is amenable to change so long as the underlying structure of power is retained. "Them versus us" is a classic Realist norm;[3] but when outside pressure, for instance from a revolution such as Vietnam's, can no longer be resisted successfully, Realists will yield ground. Like their Corporate Globalist counterparts, Realists concentrate on preserving the "rules of the game" by which the system itself (capitalism, socialism, pan-Arabism) maintains hegemony.

The Brandt Commission Report in 1977 on North-South (developed and underdeveloped countries') issues offers an excellent example of system maintenance through system reform. The report sought to convince Realist leaders in the North that concessions to the underdeveloped South in terms of trade, loans, and aid were a matter of *mutual* advantage—and the report implied that failure to respond to the South's demands for a New International Economic Order (NIEO) might lead to a traumatic global upheaval. By couching its appeal in terms of very modest policy changes in the global economic system, the Brandt Commission clearly hoped to persuade Realist readers of the sensibility of its recommendations.

Chart 2.1: Alternative Values

	Realist	*Corporate Globalist*	*Global Humanist*
Personal	action adaptation aggressiveness ambition amorality competition disingenuousness elitism invulnerability leadership loyalty materialism perseverence power pragmatism progress success toughness	action adaptation aggressiveness ambition amorality competition disingenuousness elitism invulnerablity leadership loyalty materialism perseverence power pragmatism progress success toughness	androgyny appropriateness authenticity community compassion cooperation diversity enoughness equality harmony honesty idealism integrity morality naturalness nonviolence personal power responsibility self-reliance service spirituality spontaneity tradition trust vulnerability

Institutional	bargaining
	competition
	control
	diffused accountability
	flexibility
	gamesmanship
	hierarchy
	influence
	mission
	order
	pluralism
	prestige
	racism
	secrecy
	security
	sexism
	stability
	"standard operating
	  procedures"
	team play
	winning
	worst-case planning
		access
		bigness
		consumption
		control
		diffused accountability
		efficiency
		growth
		hierarchy
		influence
		laissez-faire
		loyalty
		order
		profit
		racism
		secrecy
		sexism
		specialization
		  (division of labor)
		stability
		team play
		technological solutions
			accountability
			appropriate
			  technology
			autonomy
			collectivity
			decentralization
			democratic
			  management
			equal opportunity
			  and rewards
			networking
			openness
			participation
			shared power
			  (empowerment)
			small scale
			voluntary
			  simplicity

Chart 2.2: Alternative Norms and Structures

	Realist	Corporate Globalist	Global Humanist

Norm	alliance system
	bad faith model
	balance of power
	credibility
	crisis management
	hegemony
	independence
	intervention
	national interest
	national mission
	national security
	nationalism
	protectionism
	rules of game
	"them versus us"
	violence
		capitalism
		collective security
		deregulation
		diplomacy
		expansion
		global culture and
		  market
		integration
		interdependence
		  (economic)
		international
		  division of labor
		laissez-faire
		management
		multilateralism
		open door
		peace (but violence-
		  accepting)
		rule of law
		transnationalism
		trickle-down
		  development
			basic needs
			decentralization
			disarmament
			ecopolitics
			human rights
			interdependence
			  (ecological and
			  ethical)
			international law
			international regimes
			NGOs (nongovern-
			  mental organizations)
			nonintervention
			"one world"
			  (global commons)
			peace
			self-determinism
			  world population

Structure	system-maintaining (power blocs)	system-maintaining (liberal order)	system-transforming (world order)

Realism is a paradigm of the philosophy, strategy, and objectives that define the national security state, that complex of institutions, special interests, and powerful bureaucracies which govern all societies. And for the "national security manager" who runs the system, as Richard Barnet observes, "the basic premise . . . is that international politics is a game."[4] A game has stakes, rules, winners, and losers. Peace is threatening to Realists, not because it is undesirable in the abstract, but because it is inherently suspect: Since conflict, not harmony, is believed to characterize the "real world," the national interest is better served by emphasizing positions of strength based on military power rather than diplomacy in resolving disputes. As Henry Kissinger once wrote, "No idea could be more dangerous" than that peace "can be aimed at directly as a goal of policy."[5]

International security in Realist terms is the ability to deter or neutralize threats to national power, rendering them harmless. Hence the Realists' constant emphasis on stability and order, preferably through a balance of power among the major states. Where such a balance cannot be created or sustained, other devices may (and usually have to be) substituted, such as military and economic alliances, containment, spheres of influence, dependent relationships with weak states, or anything else that ensures *hegemony* for the big powers and promotes *manageability* and a measure of *predictability* in the system as a whole.

Should these methods fail, the maintenance of empire requires that Realists be prepared to use force (to "up the ante" and play "hard ball," as they like to say). Destabilization of opponents, who sometimes include friendly governments, comes first, by exerting external and internal pressures such as embargoes, suspension of credits, disinformation campaigns, support of political and military opponents, and diplomatic threats. Next up the ladder are intervention and intimidation using military power to weaken or eliminate those whose actions are believed to undermine a major power's sphere of influence. For example, Soviet forces backed the Communist party coup in Czechoslovakia in 1948 and intervened directly in 1968. Moscow has maintained about 1 million soldiers along the border with China for nearly twenty years. Soviet tanks crushed uprisings in Hungary and Poland in 1956; they lurked in the background when the Solidarity movement of Polish workers threatened to topple communist authority in 1981. U.S. forces landed in Lebanon (1958), the Dominican Republic (1965), Vietnam (1965–1975), and Grenada (1984) to prevent the "dominoes" from falling in those regions. But indirect U.S. pressure proved sufficient to cause changes of government in Guatemala (1954), Chile (1973), and Australia (1975). The Chinese proved they could practice Realist politics, too, when their troops crossed into Vietnam in 1979, in order, their leaders said, to "teach a lesson" to their once close allies.

In every one of these cases, state leaders justified their actions by clothing them in doctrines of national interest. To Realists, principles of sovereignty and self-determination have their limits when national security is believed threatened. But is there really any essential difference between, say, the Brezhnev Doctrine that was used to rationalize Soviet intervention in Czechoslovakia in 1968, on the basis that Czech political liberalization might infect the rest of Eastern Europe, and the U.S.-backed overthrow of Chile's Salvador Allende in 1973, on the basis that (as Secretary of State Henry Kissinger said then) "we [shouldn't] have to stand back and watch a country go Communist because of the irresponsibility of its own people"?[6] Just as the Czechs dared to talk about democracy, the Chilean people had the audacity to elect a socialist president, leading President Richard Nixon to decide that Chile should be "squeezed until it 'screamed.'"[7] "Reasons of state" tend to sound the same everywhere.

Indeed, self-righteous doctrines of the "just war" are among the hallmarks of Realist politics. And herein lies the essential flaw of Realism itself. For, clearly, if all states live by the iron law that might makes right and that success is the only arbiter of action, then international politics is indeed a jungle governed only by survival of the most heavily armed—a self-fulfilling prophecy. Realism thus contributes to perpetuating the disorderly world that justifies itself, in the manner of a doctor who keeps a patient on medication in order to ensure future visits. Little room is left for developing alternatives to power politics and limiting the reach of aggrandizing states. The weak and the oppressed must learn to accommodate the strong—strong elites as well as strong states—or face extinction.

National security thus conflicts directly with *global* security: The search for absolute security that preoccupies Realist leaders intensifies interstate violence, with profoundly adverse consequences for human beings. For the cold-war strategies of states can only divert resources from satisfying people's basic needs: food, employment, housing, security, and sense of self-worth. Operating from Realist premises legitimizes open-ended military spending and buildups, for "enough" is never enough. Inasmuch as "costs and benefits" are weighed in terms of state power, ordinary citizens often are left out of the equation. "In politics the nation and not humanity is the ultimate fact," as Hans Morgenthau, the most-cited Realist, once conceded.[8] As we will see on examining the arms race, Soviet and U.S. citizens pay dearly for their governments' extravagant national-security programs.

Perhaps it is already apparent how difficult it must be for Realists to adapt to an interdependent world system. The more transnational politics becomes, the less relevant (and effective) are policies based on one-sidedly promoting the national interest. While Realists persist in interpreting the world in East-West (cold-war) terms, the key issues are increasingly North-South—those between the highly industrialized and the impoverished parts of the world. And the fates of those parts are mutually intertwined. Yet we can still find Henry Kissinger lecturing a Chilean foreign minister, even before Allende's election, that "nothing important can come from the South. History has never been produced in the South. The axis of history starts in Moscow, goes to Bonn, crosses over to Washington, and then goes to Tokyo."[9] It is as if the strategic balance is the only game in town, and small states can only be bit players in it.

Realists not only choose to *under*estimate the enormous impact that developments in the Third World have on world politics, beginning with revolutionary nationalism (as in Vietnam), economic nationalism (as in Middle East oil), and trade (the emergence of Pacific Rim countries such as South Korea and Taiwan as technological competitors). They also *over*estimate, as in Kissinger's remark above, the ability of big powers to control and manipulate Third World politics. The United States, for example, could no more determine the outcome of Vietnam's, Iran's, or southern Africa's revolutions than the Soviet Union could dictate the course of events in postrevolutionary China, Afghanistan, or the horn of Africa.

Excessive attention to East-West relations has diverted the resources of the major powers (especially the United States and the Soviet Union, as Chapter 5 shows) from other areas besides armaments that affect national security and international influence. The arms race reduces available spending for modernizing industry, maintaining social services, and improving soil quality and productivity. Nor can any military investment in security stave off environmental pollution, trade imbalances, energy shortages, and indebtedness; in fact, it may exacerbate these problems. National power is no longer measurable in purely or even primarily military terms. Today, power is also food, information, energy, capital, skills—commodities that are often more easily moved and manipulated globally by transnational corporations than by governments.

The purpose of statecraft is to ensure a society's security against potential external enemies. But in an interdependent world, that task entails far more than the diplomacy of war and peace. Famine, unemployment and job flight, toxic waste dumping, and massive refugee flows may threaten societies from without and within simultaneously.

Realism's response, however, often takes the form of crisis management. What really amount to *global* problems are treated episodically, as narrow political problems between governments, problems to be contained, often until the next eruption. Thus we had the energy and inflation crises in the 1970s, the recession and unemployment crises in the early 1980s, the food and debt crises in the mid-1980s. Perception of the global crisis in terms of separate, time-bound, national mini-crises, however, can only make the response to crisis inadequate, like putting Band-Aids on gaping wounds.

One reason Realists prefer to treat the symptoms of global disorder rather than search for basic cures is that they recognize and fear the revolutionary potential of deeper structural change. Aid programs, arms sales, food relief, and repression of unrest are more appealing as political tools than are programs that address fundamental inequities in landholding, political power, law, and income. Henry Kissinger recognized the underlying issue when he said, with reference to human rights: "Making [human rights] a vocal objective of our foreign policy involves great dangers: You run the risk of either showing your impotence or producing revolutions in friendly countries—or both."[10] Better to contribute to *state* security at the top than to attempt to ensure the security of billions of people at the bottom. This approach to "solving" problems is a familiar one in any system wrenched by convulsive, sometimes violent, and always unpredictable change. But if we accept that states exist to serve human communities, such an approach is politically and morally irresponsible. Centralized, elite-managed, efficiency-minded, technical mechanisms seem quite inappropriate considering the size and depth of humanity's global crisis.

Until the outbreak of World War I, Realist state leaders could usually count on balance-of-power politics to keep the lid on unwanted violence. But the post-Vietnam era shows imbalance, disunity, and fragility in relationships among allies. Clashes of national interest, usually on economic and security grounds, are the rule. The U.S.–Japan relationship, for instance, seeks to overcome an enormous U.S. trade deficit ($56 billion in 1986) that has led to vigorous protectionist sentiment on the U.S. side. Unity within the North Atlantic Treaty Organization (NATO) has been weakened by the independent nuclear and economic policies of France, disagreements by socialist Greece with U.S. military policies, commercial ties between Western and Eastern Europe, and strong antinuclear movements in nearly all of the member nations. On the Soviet side, the Warsaw Pact has been weakened by the Solidarity resistance in Poland, Eastern Europe's substantial financial and technical dependence on Western banks and trading firms (leading Hungary and Poland to sign up with the International Monetary Fund

[IMF]), and the Soviets' own poor administrative and economic performance. Other alliances have either been reduced to insignificance (the Southeast Asia Treaty Organization [SEATO] and the Central Treaty Organization [CENTO], both pieced together by the United States in the 1950s) or, as in the case of ANZUS (Australia, New Zealand, and the United States), they have been perhaps fatally damaged as a result of New Zealand's antinuclear stance in the mid-1980s. Old allies have gotten bolder in criticism of their senior partners over the years, too. Witness Mexico and Canada in their protests to the United States over energy, investments, trade, undocumented workers, Central American policy, and acid rain.

Two lessons emerge from these discordancies. One is that superpowers cannot give orders and expect to have them followed as they once were. Realist self-interest is no longer their exclusive property, it seems. For another, as the newest students of interdependence, the Chinese, have observed, the superpowers' ability to control events and manipulate their power has been greatly constrained. One Chinese analyst puts the matter this way:

> The strength of the superpowers has been contained and worn down in the course of their confrontation and rivalry, amidst the conflicts inside their own blocs and by the regional wars outside their blocs. As a result, an odd phenomenon has occurred in international relations in that the war capabilities of the superpowers have been augmented to an extent never seen before, while their freedom to use such capabilities to manipulate world affairs and control their own spheres of influence has been unprecedentedly restricted.[11]

CORPORATE GLOBALISM AND THE WORLD ECONOMY

"All freedom is dependent on freedom of enterprise," said President Truman. "The whole world should adopt the American system. . . . The American system can survive in America only if it becomes a world system."[12] The globalization of U.S. capitalism has surely exceeded Truman's hopes: the stock value of direct investments abroad by U.S.-based corporations has climbed from about $12 billion in the late 1940s to well over $200 billion today, and these companies have accumulated profits of $231 billion in that period.[13] What began as a very tentative postwar corporate expansion now is a global movement of capital, technology, labor, information, and culture in which U.S. transnational corporations play the leading, but no longer unchallenged, part.

Planning for overseas expansion, as becomes clear in the next section, had its start before World War II ended. Investments abroad then were considered highly risky, and foreign trade from domestic industries was the preferred route. Now, foreign investment is considered a business necessity. The corporation lives or dies by expansion in the global marketplace; banks depend on making overseas loans. Besides, the profit margin on investments and interest on loans are considerably larger abroad than at home. The risks of loss are lower, too, and the tax rates and general conditions of operation (especially in times of recession at home) are superior. No wonder, then, that the top ten U.S. banks had 169 percent of their equity (about $44 billion) tied up in loans to the Third World in the early 1980s.[14] Much higher interest and service fees could be earned from, say, Mexico, than from U.S. borrowers.

The key to success for Corporate Globalists is the free flow of goods and services around the world. Only then, they maintain, can optimum conditions for expansion be assured. Competition without hindrance from governments is, as Chart 2.2 suggests, an essential norm of Corporate Globalism. To promote it calls for organization, and in 1972 David Rockefeller, chair of the board of Chase-Manhattan Bank, initiated formation of the best-known and most influential Corporate-Globalist organization, the Trilateral Commission.[15]

Composed of representatives from business, media, politics, and labor in the United States, Western Europe, and Japan, the Trilateral Commission gained attention during the administration of President Carter, when a sizable number of its members (including Carter himself, Vice President Walter Mondale, Special Assistant for National Security Zbigniew Brzezinski, and Secretary of the Treasury Michael Blumenthal) took office. No conspiracy here, but merely a concentration of Corporate Globalists in one administration. (Under Ronald Reagan, Trilateralists were many fewer, but included Vice President George Bush, Defense Secretary Caspar Weinberger, and Secretary of State George Shultz, showing that Corporate Globalism spans the political spectrum.) The Trilateralists' objective: to promote intercapitalist cooperation through the removal of barriers to trade and investment among the three major regions represented in the organization and in the socialist and underdeveloped countries as well. Reflecting the essence of Corporate-Globalist thinking, Rockefeller reportedly said he wanted to "make the world safe for interdependence."[16]

For Corporate Globalists, however, interdependence has a particular meaning: augmenting the power of the global corporations and, if necessary, decreasing that of governments. Not accidentally, the Trilateral Commission was founded soon after President Nixon shocked the corporate community in 1971, when he announced a number of steps to halt and reverse the U.S. trade deficit, including taking the dollar off the gold standard and imposing a surtax on imports. To Corporate Globalists, such protectionist steps are poison; they compromise the free flow of currency and trade. When, as happened in 1974 to 1975 and in the early 1980s, recessions and protectionism contracted world trade, Corporate Globalists responded by taking their money out of their home countries and lending it or investing abroad—especially in more profitable competitor TNCs. Thus, for example, Chrysler and General Motors invested in Mitsubishi, Honda, and Isuzu in Japan; and joint enterprises were formed, such as between GM and Toyota and between U.S. Steel and Korea's Pohang Steel. U.S. labor unions complained, but were basically powerless to prevent corporate (and job) flight. Maneuverability is the name of the transnational corporate game; and with well over a half-trillion dollars in assets, the TNCs of the Trilateral states have considerable financial clout to be constantly on the move.

Rapid growth in transnational business has had the most striking results for the U.S. economy. It has literally internationalized industry, cutting deeply into the once-dominant role of the United States in world trade. While the shares of world trade of Western Europe and Japan have risen sharply (to about 39 percent and 7 percent respectively in the mid-1970s), that of the United States has declined just as sharply (from nearly 17 percent of world exports in 1950 to just under 10 percent in 1982). The resulting loss of trade earnings has created a seemingly permanent balance-of-trade deficit: a whopping $156 billion in 1986. But the earnings on investments abroad by U.S. TNCs made up for the lost revenue. Their branch plants overseas, which today handle about a third of all U.S. exports simply in goods traded among them, mean the ability to leapfrog over tariff walls and other national impediments to U.S. exports. By the early 1970s, U.S. government income from the returned profits of TNC branch plants began to exceed income from exports by domestic companies.[17] Just how significantly TNCs depend on overseas operations is shown in Chart 2.3: In 1980, sixteen of the top fifty U.S. TNCs earned half or more of their profits abroad. The foreign earnings of U.S. transnational banks (TNBs) have also increased rapidly, with the top seven banks averaging 55 percent of their total profits in 1981 (over $1.3 billion) from their overseas branches.[18] Profits that are repatriated to the United States by the TNCs and TNBs are very important contributions to the plus side of the balance-of-payments ledger. But they mask serious weaknesses in the U.S. economy that will be discussed in Chapter 5.

The prominence of global corporations in world politics can be further gauged by noting their market dominance and size. About 500 TNCs (of over 10,000 worldwide) account for about 80 percent of total

Chart 2.3: Foreign Sales and Profits of the 50 Largest U.S. Transnationals (1979/80)

Company	Foreign Sales (in billions)	Foreign Sales as Percentage of Total Sales	Foreign Profit or Income (in billions)
1. Exxon	$57.0	72.1	$3.3
2. Mobil	27.4	60.3	1.4
3. Texaco	26.0	67.9	1.1
4. Ford Motor	19.1	43.9	1.4
5. Standard Oil of California	17.5	58.4	1.0
6. General Motors	16.8	25.3	.591
7. IBM	12.2	53.6	1.4
8. IT&T	11.6	52.6	.905
9. Gulf Oil	11.1	46.4	.590
10. Engelhard Minerals	9.8	54.1	.453
11. Citicorp	7.3	66.8	.352
12. General Electric	5.0	21.1	.293
13. Bank America	4.7	50.0	.226
14. Conoco	4.7	36.1	.372
15. Dow Chemical	4.7	50.5	.649
16. Occidental Petroleum	4.6	47.4	1.4
17. Chase Manhattan	3.8	62.3	.146
18. Standard Oil of Indiana	3.7	19.7	.719
19. E. I. du Pont de Nemours	3.4	26.7	.393
20. Xerox	3.3	47.2	.262
21. Eastman Kodak	3.2	40.4	.242
22. Goodyear	3.2	38.5	.242
23. Sun Co.	3.1	29.1	.179
24. Safeway Stores	3.0	21.5	.108
25. Union Carbide	2.8	30.3	.318
26. Procter & Gamble	2.8	29.7	.115
27. Colgate-Palmolive	2.7	60.2	.262
28. Chrysler	2.6	22.0	−.025
29. Tenneco	2.5	22.7	.259
30. F. W. Woolworth	2.4	35.6	.184
31. CPC International	2.4	65.2	.234
32. Coca-Cola	2.3	46.3	.523
33. International Harvester	2.3	27.3	.272
34. Pan Am World Airways	2.3	91.8	.118
35. Union Oil of California	2.2	29.1	.106
36. J. P. Morgan	2.2	61.3	.150
37. General Tel. & Elec.	2.2	22.0	.057
38. 3M	2.1	39.3	.430
39. United Technologies	2.1	23.2	.218
40. Manufacturers Hanover	2.1	53.8	.103
41. Atlantic Richfield	2.0	12.2	.078
42. Phillips Petroleum	2.0	20.7	1.26
43. Monsanto	2.0	31.6	−.024
44. Johnson & Johnson	1.8	43.7	.328
45. Kraft	1.8	28.3	.100
46. American Brands	1.8	48.2	.158
47. Firestone	1.7	33.1	.061
48. R. J. Reynolds Industries	1.7	24.3	.107
49. Caterpillar Tractor	1.6	21.4	.078
50. Sperry	1.6	39.0	.237

Source: *Forbes*, 7 July 1980, pp. 102–106.

world production.[19] A mere fifteen of them, and in most cases only three to six, control world trade in all basic commodities, from food to minerals.[20] When their total output is matched against that of states, TNCs (led by Exxon and General Motors) occupy forty-one of the top 100 places.[21] Their total direct investments worldwide were valued at about $512 billion in 1980, with U.S.-based TNCs investing at a rate of $20–30 billion a year. This figure on total investments represents phenomenal growth: an 89 percent increase over 1975, 400 percent over 1967, and 800 percent over 1960.[22]

Overwhelmingly, the home base of TNCs is in the developed countries—primarily the United States (42 percent), the United Kingdom (14.5 percent), Netherlands (7.8 percent), West Germany (7.4 percent), and Japan (7.3 percent).[23] U.S. predominance is clear, especially in terms of corporate assets and output (Exxon, GM, ITT, IBM, and NCR are among the familiar names); but the European and Japanese challenges are also apparent. Of the 100 largest transnational industrial firms, for instance, 67 were U.S.-based in 1963, 58 in 1971, and 47 in 1979. In banking, U.S.-based transnationals, led by Citicorp, Bank of America, and Chase Manhattan, held 44 of the top 100 positions (and 53 percent of all bank deposits) in 1956. By 1978, however, the U.S. position had slipped to 15 of the top 100 positions and 15 percent of deposits.[24] Socialist state trading companies and nationally owned companies in Europe, Asia, and Latin America have also emerged to compete with U.S. firms, although these together claim less than 5 percent of all direct investment abroad.

Intimately related to the growth of TNCs has been the expanded influence of multilateral financial institutions, notably the IMF and the World Bank. Commanding multibillion dollar budgets (the Bank made $13 billion in loans to seventy-six countries in 1981, while the IMF had $27 billion in outstanding loans in 1983), they are the key institutional links between the Trilateral states on the one side and borrowing countries on the other.[25] The Bank's functions include low-interest loans and assistance on economic development projects proposed by underdeveloped countries. Frequently, these tasks are performed in conjunction with the largest banks of the member states, primarily U.S. banks; these had about $100 billion in loans to indebted governments in 1983. The IMF, whose initial responsibilities were to help countries keep their international payments in balance and their exchange rates stable, has gained notoriety in the present era of global indebtedness by making its loans conditional on major changes in social and economic policies by the recipient government.

Since the mid-1960s, direct aid by the industrialized states to the underdeveloped countries has declined from 55 percent to only about

20 percent of worldwide economic assistance. The contributions of the multilateral agencies (including various regional banks such as the Asian Development Bank and the Inter-American Development Bank) and their commercial bank partners have thus become critical in keeping Third World economies afloat. The former group accounts for about 8 percent of total aid, and the latter for about 61 percent.[26] Politics is inescapable in such circumstances.

The IMF and the World Bank consider themselves independent of the governments which provide their operating budgets. They also claim to make loans on strictly economic criteria. But these claims do not stand up to the evidence.[27] Among other things, consider the preponderant U.S. role in these institutions. As the largest contributor to the IMF and the Bank, and therefore the controlling factor in their votes on proposed projects (the U.S. government has about 19.5 percent of the vote in each body), U.S. preference is almost invariably followed. The inner circles of international finance may have their clubs of the most powerful national or individual members (such as the Group of Eleven in the IMF and the Paris Club of bankers), but U.S. citizens are the chairs of the board.[28]

Like the transnational corporations and banks, the IMF and the World Bank prize stable, orderly growth and open-market economies. They, too, prefer safe climates for investment, which typically means a "disciplined" (i.e., nonunion) labor force, no strikes, authoritarian government committed to law and order, low health and safety standards, tax advantages, and aid to projects that will be run by the wealthiest local entrepreneurs. Since the governments these TNCs and multilateral institutions deal with usually are running balance-of-payments deficits and are deeply in debt, the recommended policy (if they want a loan) is to sharply cut back on social welfare spending and step up exports to earn foreign exchange. For now, we can limit ourselves to the observation that such a recommendation from the IMF or the Bank directly serves the interests of TNCs, which dominate the exporting industries, and commercial banks, which make foreign loans only because the discipline the IMF imposes on lenders affords a hedge against their default.[29]

In the upper reaches of big capital, however, what others might regard as self-serving is justified as promoting global well-being. Corporate Globalists see interdependence as an opportunity not only for profit-making but also for economic development in the Third World. They have traditionally labeled TNCs "engines of development" that transfer technology, skills, and capital to industrialize agrarian societies, fuel growth, universalize information, and extract raw materials for export. Corporate Globalists see it as a good deal for both home and host countries, and as a contribution to world peace as well. In criticism of protectionist sentiment, one TNC executive has said:

> Retreating to fortress America isn't the answer. If we erect walls, we invite a battle. And there is enough tension in the world today without instigating trade wars. World peace, and its economic handmaiden—international trade and development—are far better served by an open and free flow of investment.[30]

The concern among Corporate Globalists about threats to "orderly growth" is genuine, and not just in terms of trade wars. Like their Realist counterparts, these Globalists fear nationalism when it assumes revolutionary form, as in China, Cuba, Algeria, and Nicaragua. Opportunities to invest and trade may be limited or foreclosed altogether. Some Corporate Globalists have therefore responded sympathetically to calls (or demands) from Third World leaders since the mid-1970s for a "new international economic order." They see NIEO as a last opportunity for reforming the global system without restructuring it. Mahbub ul Haq, a Pakistani director of the World Bank, said to his colleagues:

> What is really at issue is a sharing of economic and political power, within nations as well as internationally. It will prove extremely disruptive if existing power has to be changed only through the organization of countervailing power or through unilateral national or collective actions. There is a historical opportunity for all of you to engineer an orderly change, and to minimize the costs of transition.[31]

Here was a warning to the Trilateralist community that unless some of the agenda of NIEO were adopted—improved terms of trade and TNC investments, for example, or ways to reduce outstanding Third World debt and *in fact* transfer skills and technology—global underdevelopment would lead to more revolutionaries rather than more customers.

Keeping an open door to the world market (a concept now preached by Chinese and other socialists and no longer only by U.S., European, and Japanese capitalists) leads to another Corporate-Globalist norm. TNCs are "transmission belts" of global values and culture: competition, growth, materialism, freedom of enterprise, efficiency, management. In their pathbreaking book on TNCs and their "global managers," Richard Barnet and Ronald Müller quote these words of an IBM executive:

> For business purposes, the boundaries that separate one nation from another are no more real than the equator. They are merely convenient demarcations of ethnic, linguistic, and cultural entities. They do not define business requirements or consumer trends. Once management understands and accepts this world economy, its view of the

marketplace—and its planning—necessarily expand. The world outside the home country is no longer viewed as a series of disconnected
customers and prospects for its products, but as an extension of a single market.[32]

We see here the kind of thinking that created the industrial revolution
in the previous century: centralization of large-scale operations, ration-
alization of market strategy and labor, the subordination of the objectives of state managers to those of business managers. As Barnet and
Müller say, the Corporate Globalists' power comes not from a gun but
"from control of the means of creating wealth on a worldwide scale."[33]

Further tying together the world market is control of information.
Ever since the days of colonial empires, information—financial, legal,
marketing, advertising, labor, natural resources—has been central to
the acquisition of wealth on a worldwide scale.[34] Today, the advent of
microprocessors has greatly accelerated the pace of information gath-
ering and centralization of its control in the major global corporations.
IBM, Texas Instruments, AT&T, and McGraw-Hill dominate in computers, data processing, and telecommunications.[35] Western news
agencies (Associated Press in the United States, Reuters in Britain, and
Agence France-Presse in France) supply 90 percent of all the foreign
news in the media of the nonsocialist world.[36] A handful of Western
(overwhelmingly U.S.) book publishers, film companies, advertising
agencies, and radio and television corporations dominate their respec-
tive markets abroad as they do at home.[37] Satellites for broadcasting,
data transmission, and remote sensing of geophysical changes within
countries are mainly under the control of the richest economies.

Such concentrated control of information means power: the reten-
tion, for sale or manipulation, of market data; and the export of ho-
mogenized Western cultural values. It is the kind of power that serves
Realist and Corporate-Globalist interests equally well, enhancing a large
state's leverage against the consumer state and building profits and
market control for a giant corporation. To Third World and many Second World countries, however, it smacks of cultural imperialism, another form of dependence, in this case on (mainly U.S.) entertainment,
news equipment and reports, sales techniques, and editorial training—
all of which are infused with the perspectives and biases of their country of origin. The new cry from the Third World is therefore for a New
International *Information* Order (NIIO). At issue here, as with the
NIEO, is the presumed right of TNCs and their governments to search
for and transmit data across national frontiers (the "free flow of information"), as against the proclaimed right of Third and Second World
states to protect their sovereignty and identity, to make data-gathering

accountable to some authority, and to share in the fruits of the information explosion.

RIVALS OR PARTNERS?

One thing the conflict over trade, investment, and information dependence shows is that Globalists understand the politics of interdependence much better than Realists. They know that people, as customers, can be brought into line far more efficiently by changing their tastes, habits, and ways of thinking than they can if treated as potential revolutionaries who have to be forcibly suppressed. Coca-Cola, powdered milk, Levi's, and television's "Dallas" make more sense than a machine gun if one wants to get people willingly to adopt a particular way of life. Gunboat diplomacy represents old-style international politics; domination of information, advertising, entertainment, and philanthropy is the new style.

This sizable difference in approach has special relevance when it comes to capitalist relations with the socialist countries. Corporate Globalists see commercial opportunities where Realists see only problems of containing radicalism. When the U.S. government makes decisions on whether or not to sell computers, gas pipeline technology, and aircraft to the USSR, China, and other socialist governments, or approve loans to them, we see the Corporate Globalist–Realist conflict expressed at two levels: between private (TNC) and government (state) leaders, and between government bureaucracies (such as the Commerce Department, which wants to promote trade and lower the balance-of-payments deficit, and the State Department, which quails at the thought of "helping the enemy"). Corporate interests have often run afoul of Realist national and bureaucratic interests concerning specific business transactions—and sometimes TNCs have ignored government directives rather than lose a deal.[38]

Divergent positions such as these help explain why Corporate Globalists frequently discount the utility and adaptability of nation-states. They argue that governments by definition cannot operate on a global basis as effectively as TNCs, which have greater financial as well as political mobility. Partisans of the transnational banks, for instance, contend that multilateral lenders such as the World Bank should be given increased U.S. funding that is instead going to military aid programs. Third World "development" can better be directed toward U.S. objectives that way. Furthermore, TNCs can go where governments fear, or are not permitted, to tread, such as to the socialist bloc. "Who knows which political system works?" said an international banker during Poland's debt crisis. "The only test we care about is: Can they pay their bills?"[39]

Moreover, rapid advances in information technology and, since 1977, the resurfacing of protectionism worldwide, are said by Corporate Globalists to demand the kinds of decentralized, branch-plant activities and centralized, home-office operations that only the TNCs can provide. When governments (like that of the United States) cannot properly manage their budgets and run high interest rates that send up the value of their currency, making exports dear and imports cheap, TNCs can move operations to more profitable locations (such as outside the United States), where tariff, tax, labor, and other conditions are optimal. Management, not national security, is the governing ideology.

Governments become the Corporate Globalists' enemy when they interfere with transnational management, such as by imposing tariffs and surcharges on imports, subsidizing home industries, forcing their own TNCs to make investments on "national security" grounds that dollars and cents do not justify, placing embargoes on trade with particular countries, enacting controls against capital and job flight, nationalizing foreign businesses, threatening to repudiate external debts, and forming cartel-like organizations (such as the Organization of Petroleum Exporting Countries, or OPEC) to recapture control of precious resources. To some Corporate Globalists, these interferences by home and host countries undermine the national interest and international security just as surely as a popular uprising strikes fear in the hearts of Realists.

Confronted with these assessments, Realists retort that TNCs are often the culprits when the smooth functioning of the global system is upset. They export jobs and capital abroad instead of investing at home. They use tax havens and other tricks of the transnational trade to avoid making their full contribution to national treasuries. They increase a nation's dependence on strategic minerals by going abroad to find them rather than searching for them at home. They fail to appreciate that the domestic political setting in which Realist state managers operate sometimes requires a positive response to demands for protection of home industry and jobs. They get in the way of traditional diplomacy, and they even compromise national security by investing in and trading with enemy states.

All of this carping may give the false impression that Corporate Globalists and Realists are deadly adversaries. Indeed, there is a school of thought which suggests that TNCs are essentially "on their own" in world politics—powerful, autonomous forces that (Realist) governments ought to leash before they get any more out of control than is already the case. To the contrary, I argue that the two parties cannot do without one another despite occasional clashes over particular issues. To be sure, states and TNCs perform different missions in domestic and international politics that inevitably bring them into contention. Each jealously guards its sovereignty and resents interference in its domain. But these conflicts should not obscure their overall symbiotic relationship.

To begin with, at the level of values (Chart 2.1) there is little to distinguish Realists and Corporate Globalists. For whether serving the state or the corporation, successful Realists and Corporate Globalists tend to be fascinated with power, highly individualistic, loyal, elitist, competitive, security-minded, and anxious to exercise control. Both groups set high store on order and stability, although for different reasons: for Realists, to maintain state security against dissidents; for Corporate Globalists, to ensure an open market. Finally, the values that both groups cultivate and reward, at both the personal and bureaucratic levels, are the same: a "can-do" pragmatism, firm resolve, macho toughness, secretiveness, a disdain for democracy,[40] and sometimes racial and sexual biases.

Even though, as has been shown, differences between Realists and Corporate Globalists emerge when we refer to global norms (Chart 2.2), these tend to obscure the important ways in which mutually supportive ties have formed between the two groups in order for each to achieve its own ends. "Live and let live" seems to be their common credo. And why not? As numerous studies have pointed out, governments benefit from TNC operations in many ways, such as by:

- TNC remittances of their overseas profits, which help to balance a government's international payments
- the ability to reward, punish, and thus control small states that major governments acquire by virtue of TNC, IMF, and World Bank loans and investments (the kind of leverage the United States has long exercised in Latin America)
- the access and control TNCs provide governments over the extraction and marketing of strategic resources, such as oil
- the political influence that one-sided economic linkages can create (such as in East–West, U.S.–Canadian, and U.S.–China trade and investments)
- the bonds forged by Corporate Globalist officials with political and military elites abroad (sometimes by bribery), which create opportunities for their governments to acquire intelligence, strengthen friendships, and neutralize enemies

- the transmission through these corporate bodies of political and cultural norms, for example, the "American (Soviet, French) way of life "

In short, corporate transnationalism, whether of the capitalist (case in point: TNC investments in South Africa)[41] or socialist kind (consider the contributions Chinese banks in Hong Kong make to the PRC's economy, for instance), complements Realism's quest for national security by providing opportunities and services that the modern global power cannot do without.[42]

The deal cuts both ways: Realist practices also make vital contributions to the corporate way of life, promoting and protecting TNC investments. The "safe" environment for investment that Corporate Globalists often speak of includes the military backing they sometimes call upon or like to have near at hand. It may also refer to economic retaliation governments can use or threaten against countries that do not fairly treat "their" TNCs or that seek to weaken a TNC's investment position relative to that of local firms. (Henry Kissinger's protest, in his memoirs, that "national security" considerations, not U.S. investments in Chile, prompted the U.S. decision to help overthrow Allende is beside the point. Both U.S. state and corporate interests benefited, even though each felt threatened by Chilean socialism in a different way.)

Moreover, the major governments, such as the United States, often create market opportunities for their TNCs. For instance, their "aid" to food-poor countries may be tied to the purchase of TNC machinery, processing equipment, and seeds. Promoting its own nationals' trade, private investment, and loans is part of a foreign embassy's business. Governments also facilitate overseas investment through favorable tax policies (such as the U.S. foreign tax credit and deferred tax on repatriated profits); insurance against nationalization of foreign assets (as in the U.S. Overseas Private Investment Corporation); legislation to deny bilateral and multilateral aid to a government that nationalizes private investments (the Hickenlooper and Gonzalez amendments of the U.S. Congress); antitrust relief (which enabled the major U.S. oil companies to become dominant in the Middle East); direct subsidies (such as of the nuclear and oil industries in the United States and most other industrialized countries); deregulation and nonregulation of production and commerce (oil in the first case; the "dumping" of unsafe and unproven products abroad in the second case); and noninterference in those corporate practices (such as transfer pricing and Eurodollar market borrowing) that cost national treasuries and taxpayers huge sums of money.

One does not find corporations complaining about these benefits. Nor about domestic law that is typically enforced loosely to permit multibillion-dollar mergers and acquisitions among the largest corporations; interlocking directorates among the biggest banks, insurance companies, energy corporations, and related institutions; and personnel movements between the private and public sectors that (as in the case of U.S. military officers who move from the Pentagon to military industries) smack of conflicts of interest.

Nor, finally, do TNCs say much about direct government interventions in their behalf, as when the West German government came to the rescue of its industrial giant, AEG Telefunken, or when Washington decided to bail out Lockheed Aircraft, Chrysler Corporation, and Continental-Illinois National Bank when they declared bankruptcy; or when President Carter froze and then permitted Chase-Manhattan Bank to seize $6 billion in Iranian assets during the 1979 hostage crisis; or when President Reagan, despite his opposition to the Polish government's crushing of Solidarity, floated an agricultural loan to Warsaw rather than see it default on its $27 billion debt to U.S. and other banks; or when the U.S. government in 1984 aided the transnational banks with an $8.4 billion increase in its commitment to the IMF, enabling several Latin governments to make payments to the banks and thus (in the strange world of international finance) qualify for additional loans and a rescheduling of old ones.

As if this were not enough, domestic political processes in home and host countries also operate to the advantage of investors and traders. In the United States, for example, the process includes corporate campaign contributions, lobbying, and research costs (nearly all tax-deductible); the provision of research information by corporations to the government; and participation by former and present corporate officers in key government advisory and decisionmaking groups that formulate policy in their areas of interest, such as oil, energy, and arms sales. Abroad, as already mentioned, TNCs and government officials traditionally cultivate close ties with political and economic elites who, out of self-interest, welcome foreign aid and investment and the arms to protect them (and themselves). Thanks to these elites, special foreign-trade zones offering labor, tax, and tariff concessions are available to TNCs in major ports (such as Masan, Korea; Kaohsiung, Taiwan; and Shenzhen, China) for product assembly and export.

Sensitivity in these societies to foreign penetration does on occasion lead to expressions of economic nationalism.[43] But most Corporate Globalists have decided to resist concessions that might undercut profits. They have confidently asserted—and the evidence supports them—that, on balance, these elites can be "co-opted into senior decision-making roles in the management structure of the international economy." "For the most part," this writer, a U.S. State Department official, candidly admits, "Third World elites are even less committed to human equality as a general condition of humanity than we are. They are talking about greater equality between states."[44] So long as Corporate Globalists and Realists can keep the dialogue over global problems at the level of governments and the elites who run them, and away from people's needs, they believe they have a lockhold on the future.

I have discussed some of the common values, norms, objectives, and practices of Corporate-Globalist and Realist leaders. These have spawned several major criticisms (listed below) of Corporate Globalism. But they are also criticisms of Realism, for without the involvement of their home governments, or their government's willingness to turn a blind eye, TNCs would probably have been reluctant to act in the way they are accused. Some of the case studies in Chapters 5 and 6 show that these criticisms, for the most part, hold true.

Briefly, then, transnational commercial institutions (businesses, banks, and multilateral aid agencies) are said to have:

- drawn Third World governments into a debt crisis, from which the only permanent escape is a total overhauling of the global credit structure
- put profit ahead of meeting the human development needs of the societies they have assisted or invested in—often with the result of promoting social and economic inequalities, environmental destruction, and dependent national development
- likewise, with respect to the home countries of TNCs, ignored the human consequences of taking jobs, capital (including taxpayers' money), and technology abroad
- served instead the strategic and economic interests of elite groups in the developed countries, the United States in particular, by attaching conditions to loans that go beyond normal business prudence to incorporate political considerations detrimental to social underclasses
- taken out of the host countries (in the case of TNCs) far more than they have contributed to their betterment, as seen in the technology transfers, the impact on employment and local business, or the actual beneficiaries of profits and products
- in the process of creating a global market and culture, contributed to the undermining of people's identities (whether with nation, tribe, or some other community), and to the intensifying of global conflict (for example, by promoting landlessness, poverty, hunger, and refugee flight)
- incorrectly perceived the global crisis of underdevelopment as a matter of "lifting" Third World countries out of debt and their

peoples out of poverty, when in fact what is needed is not more welfare ("aid") through external intervention but more empowerment of people to be self-reliant—not more "growth" from above but more equity from below

• refused, finally, to confront the implication of these failings for global political-economy as a whole: that system reforms of the kind Corporate Globalists (and Realists, too) typically propose cannot touch the deep structural roots of the crisis, which begin with gross inequities of power and consumption in the industrially advanced countries and extend to privileged elites in the underdeveloped countries

This last is the point of departure for the discussion of Global Humanism in Chapter 3.

A CASE STUDY: POSTWAR PLANNING
FOR THE "AMERICAN CENTURY"

By all accounts, postwar United States represented the most extraordinary concentration of national power in history. World War II had claimed the lives of some 15 million soldiers and 65 million civilians, over 3 percent of the world's population. Europe and Asia were in ruins. But the United States, Pearl Harbor and many casualties aside, had not been touched by the war. In fact, its economy had benefited in several ways, including the start of systematic government-business cooperation on military production, the large-scale entry of women into the workforce, and an unrivaled degree of productivity and production. Two years after the war, in 1947, the United States accounted for half of total world output; it also held nearly 65 percent of the world's gold currency, making the dollar central to all economic transactions. Finally, the United States had a nuclear monopoly: the "secret" (or so its leaders thought) of the atomic bomb and, obviously, the willingness to use it. Henry Luce, magnate of *Time* magazine, had every reason to argue that the rest of the twentieth century should belong to the United States.

The dollar and the bomb were considered the foundation of the "American Century" by the policy planners who, well before the end of the war, met to outline the future.[45] Each element represented an essential tool for remaking the postwar world. For Corporate Globalists, the dollar meant free trade and export-led growth, the integration of world markets, the primacy of Europe (including a revived Germany) as a market for U.S. goods, hostility to national socialist experiments in

Western Europe, and, within the United States, big business and small government. For U.S. Realists, the bomb represented the ability to contain Moscow, rebuild Europe's defenses (NATO, in 1948), and centralize military-scientific-industrial cooperation at home. Heavily influenced by Roosevelt's New Deal, however, the Realist camp leaned toward big government, antitrust actions to undermine big business, and priority to U.S. capitalist goals (such as full employment) over foreign economic expansion.

The working-out of a compromise agenda that could incorporate both Realist and Corporate-Globalist priorities took place roughly between 1944 and 1947. Both the Marshall Plan for European recovery and President Truman's aid program to Greece and Turkey to contain international communism symbolized a historic synthesis. Multilateralism and anticommunism, as Alan Wolfe has observed, made for a new and enduring political consensus:

> Once anticommunism was grafted onto the multilateralism program, the political logjam in the United States was broken. Free trade, an inherently elitist notion, transformed itself into an ideology with mass appeal when it adopted anticommunism as its rationale. Every one of the limitations of the free-trade position could be overcome by an emphasis on the threat that the Soviet Union posed to the United States.[46]

In emphasizing that the shaping of the postwar world was equally the handiwork of Realists and Corporate Globalists, I should further note the different but compatible lessons each "side" brought to its task. For Realists, the main lessons of two world wars were that there is no appeasement of aggression and that military preparedness prevents war. Their key untouchable item was (and remains) the military budget, and their central accomplishment in the years prior to the Korean War was National Security Council document NSC-68, which called for a major U.S. rearmament program to deter the presumed and exaggerated Soviet threat. For the Corporate Globalists, on the other hand, the world wars had taught that closed national markets led directly to the Great Depression. Only open economies in an open world market could prevent a repeat of that experience and the rise of fascism in Europe that followed it. Their greatest achievement was the 1944 Bretton Woods (New Hampshire) Conference, at which the major capitalist allies agreed to create a new international financial system to ensure currency and trade stability. The plan was U.S.-made by government and business leaders who had earlier carved out a "Grand Area" strategy of global trade. The strategy called for creating two new institutions, the World Bank and the IMF, in each of which the United States would have more than a third of the votes.

How was it possible for Corporate Globalists to accept anticommunism and rearmament—"military Keynesianism" (government pump-priming through heavy spending on arms), as Fred Block has called it? Or for the Realists to swallow world economic integration? After all, each agenda would be expensive and would orient the U.S. government toward a different set of priorities, one international and one national.

The brief answer is that liberal (or "cold-war") internationalism, as Wolfe's above-quoted remark indicates, satisfied the main constituencies of both groups. Within the U.S. Congress, for instance, European recovery promised new markets and jobs based on expanded U.S. exports. The Marshall Plan would not be a giveaway program. For the emerging breed of cold warriors, in Congress and in the administration, the Plan meant a tough but also cost-effective stance against the Russians. In the country's higher circles, the combination of the Marshall Plan and containment had additional significance: European dependence on American military equipment for their defense; undermining of powerful communist-backed labor movements and of national socialism; the sealing off of Western Europe from Soviet penetration; and the first step toward European economic (Common Market) and military (NATO) integration. It was the kind of "growth coalition" that liberals and conservatives could get behind. And once the country was hit by the "Red scare" tactics of the far Right—the attacks on the U.S. Foreign Service for "losing" China; charges of atomic spying for the Russians; and Senator Joseph McCarthy's allegations of a pro-Soviet conspiracy in high places—the era of isolationism was over.

A quick look at the key individual actors and what they said in these pivotal years is instructive. The guiding principle of the open door was succinctly stated by Secretary of State James F. Byrnes in August 1945: "In the field of international relations we have joined in a cooperative endeavor to construct an expanding world economy based on the liberal principles of private enterprise, nondiscrimination, and reduced barriers to trade."[47] After George C. Marshall became secretary, he argued (in his address of June 5, 1947, to inaugurate the Marshall Plan) that it was "logical that the United States would do whatever it is able to do to assist in the return of normal economic health in the world, without which there can be no political stability and no assured peace." This made perfect sense to the international corporate community which, in the words of one leading bank executive, was "extremely troubled about the future of free enterprise" in noncommunist Europe. To him the Marshall Plan to provide $17 billion in economic aid was "a smart gamble" because it would enable those who might otherwise take the socialist path "to play the game under the rules we adhere to."[48]

But sending money abroad did not make nearly as good sense to Realists as did tough talk about the Russians. It was one thing for Truman to wax euphoric about the mission of U.S. capitalism and quite another, politically, to say: "Unless Russia is faced with an iron fist and strong language another war is in the making. Only one language do they understand—'how many divisions have you?'"[49] One of his key advisers, Clark Clifford (a later secretary of defense), had given him the consensus of opinion in Truman's inner circle that "the language of military power is the only language which disciples of power politics understand." Clifford advised that the United States, with its military superiority, "should entertain no proposal for disarmament or limitation of armament as long as the possibility of Soviet aggression exists."[50] Here was a prescription for rearmament—not merely the $13 billion military budget of 1950 but, as one of the chief architects of NSC-68, Paul Nitze, was even then urging, a $50 billion budget (which was adopted three years later).

By early 1947 a general agreement had been reached within the U.S. elite that both elements of liberal internationalism—multilateralism and anticommunism—would be needed to ensure a "peaceful" future. On the eve of Truman's containment address to Congress, his secretary of defense, James Forrestal, told him that since "the Russians would not respond to anything except power—a bow to Realism—the only option was to bring government and big business—the Corporate Globalists—together in a single team," deterring the Russians and uplifting the Europeans in one coordinated effort.[51]

This neat division of labor was not cemented, however, until the onset of war in Korea. The U.S. economy went into a recession late in 1948, and there was resistance to increasing imports of European goods. Congress was in no mood to refinance the Marshall Plan. The administration unveiled a new rationale for sending more money to Europe: to provide a defensive umbrella, in NATO, for the reconstruction of Europe. This approach also did not have lasting effectiveness; economic problems at home and abroad continued. The Korean War, and NSC-68, finally bailed out the Marshall Plan and gave liberal internationalism clear sailing. For the war demonstrated the document's wisdom in urging a rapid U.S. military buildup as part of an overall political and economic offensive to counter the Soviet peril. NSC-68 argued that "the integrity and vitality of our system is in greater jeopardy than ever before in our history." A "total struggle" would be necessary—both for economic reasons, to develop "a successfully functioning [trade and aid] system among the free nations"; and for military reasons, to restore world order, lest the United States be "overcome" by the forces of totalitarianism.[52]

The postwar partnership of Realism and Corporate Globalism in the United States has had profound consequences, some of which have already been hinted at and others which are explored in later chapters. Most fundamentally, the partnership gave birth to the *national-security state*—a joining of military-industrial interests with a nationalistic, expansionist great-power ideology. Protecting and promoting national security became the rallying cry. This structural phenomenon, which can be found in many other political-economic systems, spurred ever-higher U.S. military spending on behalf of allies and led to a number of direct and indirect U.S. interventions against "communism." But the economic costs of these activities—in reduced productivity, inflation, the flight of gold-backed dollars abroad, and the military's absorption of scientific know-how—quickly began to erode the U.S. competitive advantage in foreign trade. Western Europe and Japan caught up with and then surpassed the United States as societies on the leading edge of technology and skills. Before the first Eisenhower administration was over, it was clear that national security would have to mean not merely arms buildups and interventionism but also the expansion of private enterprise abroad. A business-government alliance representing both parties was crafted under Eisenhower to develop a "world economy" strategy specifically oriented to fighting communism with transnational capitalism.[53]

Eisenhower premised pursuit of national security on his awareness of how interdependent the U.S. economy had become with the world economy. Twenty years later, in the Carter administration, Andrew Young, ambassador to the United Nations, marked the profound impact that Corporate Globalism was having on Realism when he said that the "rightful role [of the United States is] as the senior partner in a worldwide corporation."[54] But the war in Vietnam lay in the background. With its enormous costs in blood and treasure, the Vietnam War challenged the Realist–Corporate Globalist assumption that the United States could indefinitely finance both "guns" (anticommunist crusades abroad) and "butter" (domestic well-being within an ever-growing global market). Since Vietnam, the "senior partner" has been hard-pressed by forces of interdependence it finds difficult to control. And therein lies one of the main reasons for the emergence of Global Humanism as an alternative paradigm of world politics—alternative to the politics both of empire and of unbridled growth.

CHAPTER THREE

World Politics in Global-Humanist Perspective

*Injustice anywhere is a threat to justice everywhere. We are caught in an ines-
capable network of mutuality, tied in a single garment of destiny. . . . Whatever
affects one directly affects all indirectly.*
— Martin Luther King, Jr.

*I refuse to express myself with [political people's] words, their labels, their slo-
gans, left and right, socialism and communism, capitalism and Luxemburgism.
I express myself with my words: good, bad, better, and worse. And I say: If it
serves the people, it is good. If it doesn't serve the people, it is bad.*
— Lech Walesa, leader of Solidarity

THE SEARCH FOR A THIRD WAY

The Chinese word for "crisis" consists of two characters, the first (*wei*)
meaning danger, the second (*ji*) opportunity. The contemporary global
crisis, as we have seen, holds within it many seeds of danger, including
the undeniable potential for species destruction. But from another an-
gle, every danger can also be an opportunity to transcend and transform the crisis. If Global Humanism can be remembered for just one
thing, it is this *dialectical* understanding of the global crisis in terms of
its two opposing elements. The Global-Humanist outlook accepts neither the unalterable "givens" of Realism nor the inequitable one-world
future of Corporate Globalism. Rather, it persists in the conviction that
doomsday is a real possibility that humanity can yet overcome.

A number of Realists and Corporate Globalists have lately begun to
acknowledge the need of new concepts and values to deal effectively
with global problems. "Something beyond nationalism is slowly taking
root in the world," a former senior U.S. official and foundation president wrote in 1977; "the signs of a developing sense of common human destiny are present."[1] A World Bank director says that "what the
world badly needs today is a new vision for this ailing planet."[2] *North-
South*, the report of the Brandt Commission, agrees. Generations of

41

people are needed, says the report, who will be "more concerned with human values than with bureaucratic regulations and technocratic constraints."[3] Clearly, thinking about international politics is evolving.

But whether such movement will be fast enough to head off one or another kind of global catastrophe is very much in doubt. We are reminded of how far our thinking still must go, and how thin is the margin of survival, every time hostages are seized by political groups for exchange upon satisfaction of certain demands. In 1979 and 1985, for example, large groups of U.S. citizens were taken hostage for prolonged periods—in the first instance, for 444 days, by Iranian students loyal to the new revolutionary Islamic government of the Ayatollah Khomeini; in the second, for seventeen days by a Shiite Moslem faction in Lebanon's civil war. In each case traditional power politics proved useless: Neither naked threats nor ordinary diplomacy could get the hostages back. Power and impotence were transformed; many innocent lives hung in the balance. In the absence of a common ethical code, agreement on when and how political change should occur, and impartial mediation to which all sides in the conflict could resort, incidents such as these became international crises that locked the participants into unbridgeable positions.

On those two occasions, there was no threat of a *global* catastrophe. But the stakes might be different the next time. For what will happen when a political group threatens to set off a nuclear bomb in a major city, or poison its water supply, unless its demands are met? Or when entire countries, regions, and even the planet itself are at the mercy of a few people at the heads of state and corporate bureaucracies? After all, armed minorities are not the only protagonists. Do not the leaders of the United States and the Soviet Union in effect hold the world's people hostage to the 50,000 nuclear weapons under their control?

The central question for Global Humanists is, Who speaks for the planet? "Could we," as the late Professor Roy Preiswerk inquired, "study international relations as if people mattered?"[4] Interdependence, at its most fundamental level, means that, increasingly, millions of lives and fortunes are simultaneously at stake when vast, usually unaccountable bureaucracies make decisions. That is why the core element of Global-Humanist analysis is *the primacy of the human interest above any other—state, ideological, economic, or bureaucratic.*

The human interest frames the main issues in world politics that Global Humanism studies. Professor Yoshikazu Sakamoto has defined them in terms of four interrelated world crises of our times: human rights, participation (democracy), conflict, and underdevelopment (including destruction of the environment).[5] These crises shape the priorities of the global agenda: investigating and seeking to change conditions of oppression and repression; defining the inequalities among states, classes, and persons; critically assessing policies justified by "national security"; and weighing the human and environmental consequences of economic growth. By devoting considerable space later in the chapter to the personal experiences of various political figures, it is hoped that these crises will come alive for the reader.

To speak of priorities is to draw attention to their underlying values and norms. In contrast with Realism and Corporate Globalism, which claim to be merely frameworks for understanding the international system, Global Humanism openly acknowledges the principal values and norms that determine its orientation. The task of defining core or preferred values has not been an easy one[6]: It has required coming to grips with cultural and class biases that reinforce one's awareness of how differently blacks and whites, intellectuals and workers, Third World and industrialized world, socialists and capitalists interpret the world. Nevertheless, initial efforts have been made (see Charts 2.1 and 2.2 for one such effort). We can now explore how these values and norms enable us to analyze crisis and change in global politics.

VALUES, METHODS, MEASUREMENTS, OBJECTIVES

In this section I explore Global Humanism's distinguishing characteristics, which might be divided according to eight main beliefs and approaches:

(1) Certain values are primary: *peace* (meaning the minimization of violence and the institutionalization of nonviolent ways to resolve conflict); *social and economic justice* (movement toward equity in reward and opportunity for all without the imposition of arbitrary distinctions); *political justice* (civil liberties guaranteed in law and fact); *ecological balance* (including resource conservation and environmental protection); and *humane governance* (popular participation in, and the accountability of, government).[7]

Although these "preferred values" grew out of a multinational forum called the World Order Models Project in the late 1960s, they are more than the handiwork of intellectuals. A number of international documents to which most of the world's states adhere enshrine these values, such as the Nuremberg Principles derived from the Nazi war crimes trials (1945), the Universal Declaration of Human Rights (1948), the Convention on the Prevention and Punishment of the Crime of Genocide (1948), the International Convention on the Elimination of

All Forms of Racial Discrimination (1965), the International Covenant on Economic, Social, and Cultural Rights (1966), and the International Covenant on Civil and Political Rights (1966).[8]

(2) These values carry with them a set of *positive assumptions about the nature of humankind* and optimism about the prospects for humane change. Although it is tempting to explain Global-Humanist optimism with reference to the Idealism of the 1920s and after (see below), there is more substantial philosophical bulk to it. Among its diverse sources are humanist psychology (e.g., the works of Sigmund Freud, Erich Fromm, Abraham Maslow, Rollo May, and Carl Rogers); Eastern philosophy and spirituality, as well as Western syntheses of them (e.g., Zen Buddhism, Taoism, mysticism, Gandhian *satyagraha* or "truth force," and the writings of J. N. Krishnamurti, Carl Jung, and Alan Watts); early and more recent feminist writings (from Rosa Luxemburg to Kate Millett); the physical and social sciences (e.g., the works of Margaret Mead, Ashley Montagu, Rene Dubos, Fritjof Capra, E. F. Schumacher, Carl Sagan, and Kenneth Boulding); and political philosophers and economists across the spectrum, from Karl Marx's "Economic and Philosophical Manuscripts" and Mao Zedong's writings on voluntarism to Thomas Jefferson's community democracy and John Stuart Mill's essay "On Liberty."

From this eclectic (and sometimes contradictory) collection comes a positive conception of humanity, conviction in the human potential for cooperative living, and an understanding of politics that integrates spiritual and material development. Global Humanism, in direct contrast to Realism, assumes that human beings are by nature good-hearted, peaceful, sharing, and infinitely creative; that lawful, equitable, cooperative societies that live in harmony are realizable, and, in fact, have already been created[9]; that belief in permanent enemies, intractable conflicts, and competition for power is the product of social conditioning that can be redirected into trusting behavior patterns[10]; that the differentness of peoples and cultures should be celebrated as one of the most enriching features of human existence; that our *personal* insecurities in large measure account for our fear of differentness, our defensiveness, and our reluctance to trust others ("We have met the enemy and they is us," in the comic character Pogo's classic formulation); and, therefore, that the struggle for power and profit that goes on at the international level is very much a struggle within each person to determine just what it is that makes us feel secure.

(3) Global Humanism has an *explicitly normative approach* to politics: "It seeks to shape and inspire a world movement for systemic change, and is not content with understanding how the present system operates."[11] With Karl Marx, Global Humanists contend that "the phi-

losophers have only *interpreted* the world in various ways; the point, however, is to *change* it." *System transformation*, not simply reform, is the Global Humanists' ambition. The nation-state is the key world political structure to be transformed, although whether its authority should devolve to smaller political units, be supplanted by international regimes or even a world government, or coexist with a new global structure is a matter of ongoing debate among Global-Humanist theorists.

(4) Global Humanism is prompted by both *idealism* and a hard-headed political-economic concern about *structural violence*. Idealism as a school of political philosophy exerted its greatest influence between the two world wars. It was an effort to direct moral outrage and political reforms at those national institutions that were believed responsible for war-making. To combat state rivalries and aggression, Idealism emphasized the development of a system of international collective security and the realization of national self-determination. The Kellogg-Briand Pact of 1928 outlawing war as an instrument of national policy, the League of Nations, and, after World War II, the United Nations and the Universal Declaration of Human Rights were all products of Idealism's search for the conditions of peace.

Global Humanism retains Idealism's moral content, its optimism about human nature, and its suspicions of balance-of-power, state-centric politics. It also shares Idealism's preeminent concern about peace. But Global Humanism takes these concerns several steps further. Peace is not merely the absence of war. Even if the nearly forty conflicts currently going on around the world were miraculously to cease tomorrow, violence would still be the order of the day for most of the world's people. Global problems such as poverty, hunger, environmental destruction, terrorism, and the arms race point to additional, equally prevalent and malevolent forms of violence—and to the need for analyzing their structural roots, without regard to the political or economic character of states.

Why a *structural* approach? Because the most common explanations of inequity, oppression (both visible and "invisible"[12]), and violence within and between societies—in terms of personal, bureaucratic, or social and cultural practices—while useful, are often superficial. They do not probe deeply enough into the mechanisms and institutions that tend to perpetuate conditions of inequality. Glaring and widening gaps exist worldwide between the wealthy and the impoverished, the well-fed and the malnourished, the heavily armed and the physically weak—all *despite* overall increases in production, income, and knowledge. Understanding how poverty, the arms race, or authoritarian rule is structured into social systems can significantly advance analysis of problems and the search for their solution.

(5) Precisely because oppression is so universal while the means of attaining personal and group security are so inequitably distributed, Global Humanism takes a critical look at the *policies for national security* of state leaderships. What it finds is that as their objective power increases, states, regardless of their social systems, will embrace increasingly expansive conceptions of their national-security "needs." Ultimately, as with the United States and the Soviet Union, the entire globe must be secured in order for national leaders to feel confident about domestic security.

When state leaders globalize their quest for security, however, real planetary and national security suffers. At home, the economic and social costs of maintaining a world order favorable to constant "growth" (of consumption, output, and profit, for example) become increasingly difficult to justify politically, even in the most closed societies. Abroad, interventions, arms sales, dependent economic and military relationships, the export of inappropriate development models, and the extraction of food and other critical resources by the industrialized countries add to the impoverishment and instability of the underdeveloped world.

Global Humanism offers an alternative approach to national and international security. It rejects the inevitability of war, permanent enemies, and permanent crisis. It seeks to bring the "needs" of national security into line with the needs of the global community, in particular the Third World's powerless and marginalized. Seeking to inject realism into its idealism, Global Humanism looks for points of identity and mutual interest between different communities—between nation-states and international regimes, between workers at home and workers abroad, between capitalist and socialist systems. The objective is to *make the world safe for diversity* in the process of transforming it along equitable lines.

(6) Global-Humanist analysis seeks to go beyond left and right, us-versus-them dichotomies. Capitalism and socialism, when practiced for self-serving ends by state leaders, are seen as increasingly irrelevant tools for accurately explaining, much less resolving, global crises of human rights.[13] To be sure, each has made major contributions to human security: liberalism's emphasis on intellectual freedom, the rule of law, and the rights of the individual, for example; and socialism's emphasis on collective rights, the redistribution of the social product, and the creation (as in Cuba and China) of a "new person" motivated by service to the community. But in the name of free enterprise and liberal political goals, we find regimes on the right commonly downgrad-

ing or dispensing with social and economic justice, exploiting the environment on behalf of powerful local and foreign interests, and promoting crass commercialism that numbs people's awareness of their basic spiritual, cultural, and economic needs. Likewise, on the left, collective welfare typically becomes a vehicle of state tyranny, extra-constitutional oppression of "the masses," and enforced conformity to rigid, unassailable bureaucracies. Economics serves politics, often resulting in great inefficiencies, unmotivated and poorly rewarded workers, and a sharp gap in privileges between elites and everyone else.

Alongside these contradictions between theory and practice are several disturbing similarities between capitalist and socialist systems. Both accept the widespread alienation of working persons and discriminate against women, ethnic minorities, and homosexuals. Both overcentralize control of technology and resources, resist the devolution of power to community levels, waste precious resources, and have increasingly remote and inefficient forms of governance. Leaderships in both these systems are materialist and rationalist: "The contemporary apostles of abundance through mastery of nature are as likely to be found at the chamber of commerce as at the Central Committee of the Soviet Communist party," writes Richard Barnet.[14] The promise of satisfying people's basic needs, which are usually defined in strictly material terms, often becomes a smokescreen behind which elite politics goes on as usual. Meanwhile, both systems cling to concepts of national security that ensure perpetuation of the war system and global underdevelopment. As Johan Galtung has observed, capitalism and socialism are equally capable of pursuing imperialist policies, that is, maintaining the core country's *dominance* over its partners in the periphery through unequal and dependent ties.[15]

Beyond left and right may lie both a new political synthesis and a new realism. The synthesis would mean adapting socialist and capitalist thought: hence, the values of social and economic justice (from socialism) and political justice (from capitalist liberalism); the preference (under capitalism) for adjudicated, nonviolent change, but the acceptance (under socialism) of violent alternatives when oppression reaches unbearable proportions; the upholding of individual rights (as under capitalism), but the use of class analysis (as under socialism) to discern how individualism can become a weapon of mass exploitation; the enormous potential of capital and technological movement worldwide to uplift societies (capitalist), and their equal propensity for manipulation to create scarcity, destroy ecosystems, and "develop" some societies at the expense of others. Thus, at every step of humanist political analysis, we pause to ask "who benefits?" and "who loses?" as the result of this or that social condition and change.

The new realism would lie in "thinking globally" (or interdependently) from an ethical foundation. Mass impoverishment, nuclear terror, and the widespread deprivation of universally recognized human rights cannot be effectively dealt with as discrete social science "problems" that are best left to national decisionmakers to work out. These are interconnected global phenomena that demand a global response, both out of self-interest—in the sense suggested by Martin Luther King, Jr., that "whatever affects one directly affects all indirectly"—and out of profound moral concern about the responsibilities of the more fortunate for the less fortunate. As the National Conference of Catholic Bishops declared in their second draft letter on nuclear war:

> An interdependent world requires an understanding that key policy questions today involve mutuality of interest. . . . The moral challenge of interdependence is to shape the relationships and rules of practice which will support our common needs for security, welfare and safety. The challenge tests our ideas of human community, our policy analysis and our political will.[16]

(7) Thus, Global-Humanist realism is *activist*: "not to conform with what is happening, but to be able to see what our present options mean, what could result from them, and what changes we have to envisage, drastic as they may be."[17] Popular national and transnational movements for social change, such as the Green party in West Germany, the antinuclear movement, the women's movement, and alternative energy groups, are considered part of an important trend in world politics. At their best, these organizations are generally characterized by political diversity, commitment to humane change, and decentralized organizational structure. They are prompted by a vision of greater self-reliance and local control of resources and decisions. They hold out the promise of a global future that remains interdependent but is less tightly linked economically, much less militarized, and more attuned to the necessary balance of human and natural forces.

Fulfilling that promise is another matter. Those who promote social change must overcome a problem that has bedeviled social activists everywhere: the tendency to replicate precisely those rigidities of leadership, such as fear of opposition, dogmatic thinking, sexism, and elitism, that they fought to overthrow. Any "new" system is not new if it replaces the old guard with political structures and institutions that are just as oppressive, as the revolution of Ayatollah Khomeini is demonstrating in Iran. The Brazilian educator of the poor, Paulo Friere, is eloquent on this point, warning us about manipulative leaders who use revolutions to postpone genuine social transformation:

> In the revolutionary process, the leaders cannot utilize the banking method [of education—i.e., telling people what they should know] as

an interim measure, justified on grounds of expediency, with the intention of *later* behaving in a genuinely revolutionary fashion. They must be revolutionary—that is to say, dialogical—from the outset.[18]

Friere is really talking about democracy: a system's openness to change, respect for diversity of cultures and opinions, and receptivity of leaders to people's involvement in their own destiny (self-determination). This is also the view of Global Humanism, which rejects authoritarianism of all stripes and supports a high level of political participation by citizens. Global Humanism therefore also resists recent Realist and Corporate-Globalist interest in limited democracy—the idea, put forward with equal vehemence by industrialized and Third World state leaderships, both capitalist and socialist, that too much popular participation is a dangerous thing. Such thinking invariably creates pretexts for expanding central authority, police power, and limits on press freedom and party competition, all in the name of "stability" and "law and order."

(8) How should we *measure* human progress? The indicators consulted by Global-Humanist analysts differ markedly from those used by Realists and Corporate Globalists. The former look for signs of qualitative advances in well-being for popular majorities and in the environment. The latter prefer gross measurements of state or corporate achievement. No wonder that the two groups cannot have a constructive dialogue about political and social trends; they are like two ships passing in the night. Making use again of our four global crises (human rights, democracy, conflict, and underdevelopment), we can illustrate the wide disparity in measurements that inform these opposing views of planetary developments.

The gulf in interpreting progress in *human rights* was most clearly revealed in the late 1970s, when President Jimmy Carter announced that human rights achievement would be a cardinal element of his foreign policy. Carter's policy had the great merit of putting human rights on the global agenda. But it was riddled with contradictions. One was that the traditional U.S. emphasis on individual civil liberties clashed with the Third World's and the socialist countries' insistence that collective economic "rights" should take precedence. A second glaring contradiction lay in U.S. policy itself: When it came to choosing between human rights and "national security," such as on the question of whether or not to sell arms to a repressive but economically and strategically important government, "national security" invariably won out. And, the U.S. record on human rights, several governments charged, was hardly exemplary.

What emerged out of that period was the not surprising discovery that "human rights" is interpreted by governments in self-serving ways—to promote their own domestic and international interests while undermining the interests of adversaries, whether ideological foes abroad or ethnic minorities at home. *No* government spoke for the human majority or planetary resources, let alone for its own diverse citizenry. *Every* government invoked "human rights" but in fact spoke mainly for itself, as the sole source and arbiter of "rights." Each government's list of acceptable rights was not only very partial—liberty, social justice, a multiparty system, a new international economic order, disarmament—but seemed *designed* to respond to any other government's list.[19] The whole process was a classic example of Realist self-righteousness garbed in humanitarian verbiage.

There is not, and probably cannot be, a definitive, universally acceptable list of human rights. As was mentioned earlier, a number of declarations broadly defining the scope of human rights have been widely endorsed by governments. Needless to say, endorsement and implementation are two entirely different matters. One of the deficiencies of these declarations is, in fact, that they rely on governments rather than independent bodies to initiate action and ensure compliance. National experiences are too diverse, moreover, to expect agreement among state leaders on which rights have priority. (Is it more important to end hunger or arbitrary arrests?) Nevertheless, a few guidelines concerning human-rights priorities can be suggested.

To be as nearly globally applicable as possible, human rights would seem to require having certain characteristics in common. First, they should be rights fundamental to all political systems, that is, divorced from a particular ideological preference. Second, they should have universal appeal and not be specific to a culture. Third, they should take account of the different levels at which human rights are threatened—global, state, and individual. Fourth, they should include nonmaterial as well as material human needs. Finally, they should be specific enough to point to political action that will realize them.

With these guidelines in mind, Fouad Ajami[20] and Richard Falk[21] have proposed somewhat different lists of "core" human rights. Ajami's are:

1. The right to survive; hence the concern with the war system and with nuclear weaponry
2. The right not to be subjected to torture
3. The condemnation of apartheid
4. The right to food

Falk's list comprises five categories of rights:

1. Basic human needs ("food, housing, health, and education")

2. Basic decencies (including freedom from "genocide, torture, arbitrary arrest, detention, and execution, or their threat")
3. Participatory rights ("including choice of political leadership, of job, of place of residence, of cultural activity and orientation")
4. Security (the right to "minimal physical well-being and survival," including "ecological security")
5. Humane governance ("the rights of individuals and groups to live in societies and a world that realizes the rights depicted in 1–4")

Except for the absence of nonmaterial (spiritual, emotional) needs from Ajami's list, and the unimplementable nature of Falk's fifth item, it would seem that both listings satisfy the five criteria laid out above. They flow clearly out of the writers' common commitment to Global-Humanist values. Perhaps most importantly, the rights they propose neither draw from nor depend for their implementation upon government or party sanction. They rest instead upon an interpretation of the human interest, the most profound of which, given the nature of the global crisis, is *security.*

The crisis of *democracy,* or *participation,* should likewise be measured with due regard for ideological and cultural biases. Should we talk only about parliamentary democratic norms and exclude social and economic democracy? Global Humanists think not. It is important, using the Western tradition, to measure democratic progress in terms of political competition, press freedom, constitutional rights and duties, and the manner and extent of representation. It is equally important to identify signs of participation and accountability elsewhere than in the formal institutions of government. Grassroots democracy in the workplace and the community is vital too, and in some societies is more meaningful to people's livelihoods than elections and constitutions. Access to public services, such as health care; people's involvement in local decisionmaking groups, such as educational boards; and unofficial but influential channels of communication between people and their leaders—these, too, should count as democratic practices, as the Chinese system (discussed in Chapter 4) suggests.

Finally, we should take account of when appearances of democracy are a cover for an undemocratic reality—a phenomenon even more pervasive than either the carefully controlled, one-party systems of the Soviet Union and Eastern Europe, or the pretense of free elections, such as those held by U.S.-supported regimes in (formerly) South Vietnam, the Dominican Republic, and, most recently, Pakistan and El Salvador.[22] It is what Eqbal Ahmad calls the "neo-fascist state," which one finds throughout the Third World—a state in which terror and repression, backed by foreign powers, are critical elements for enforcing the authority of a highly concentrated elite. *Preventing* political association, not merely punishing it, is among the neofascist state's central purposes.[23] Examples are Argentina under military rule in the 1970s, Iran under the Shah Reza Pahlevi and under Khomeini, Greece after the generals' coup in 1967, Kampuchea (Cambodia) under Pol Pot (since 1975), post-Allende Chile, South Africa yesterday and today, Haiti under the Duvaliers (1957–1986), Paraguay under Alfredo Stroessner (since 1954), and Soviet-occupied Afghanistan. In all these states, democracy was or is still fervently preached by their leaders even as their internal security forces commit unspeakable horrors. Regimes of this type are commended by their foreign allies, who typically excuse certain "excesses" in repression by arguing that "stability" must be the first order of business in a "young democracy" beset by ("communist" or "capitalist") "terrorists."[24]

The Global-Humanist approach measures *conflict*, the third global crisis, in the manner of a doctor holistically examining a patient. Armed disputes and structural violence are symptoms of a planetwide disease whose consequences extend well beyond the usual toll of human casualties, territory gained or lost, incidences of war and terrorist acts, effects on the balance of power, and weapons in national arsenals. It is appropriate to speak, rather, of the *epidemiology* of global violence—the full psychological, social, ecological, and other human costs of conflict and preparation for conflict.[25] What the Physicians for Social Responsibility, an international group founded in the United States, has been saying about nuclear conflict applies more generally to all forms of international violence: It is the world's number one public health problem, for it threatens the survival of life as we know it.

Listed here are some of the consequences of conflict that an epidemiological approach calls for us to consider:

• *First*, the *trade-offs* of global militarization: What could the money spent on weapons buy in nonmilitary goods, productive potential, and the prevention of malnutrition and disease? Developing an answer would have to contend with facts such as these: Military spending in the Third World on average is almost as high as public spending on health and education, and per capita is rising nearly as fast as Gross National Product (GNP) per capita.[26] In the developed countries, capitalist and socialist, military spending rose by more than $400 billion between 1960 and 1982, but their foreign economic aid only increased by $25 billion.[27] High military spending, not surprisingly, correlates closely with declining social and economic performance.[28] The money spent on a single jet fighter plane could supply an entire Third World country with vaccines.[29] Underdeveloped countries with high indebtedness are also major arms importers, with about 20 percent of their debt increases in recent years being accounted for by such imports.[30] Military establishments are voracious consumers of nonrenewable energy and raw materials.[31]

• *Second*, the high *social costs* of arming, fighting, and selling weapons: The United States and the USSR lead the way in the arms race at enormous social cost in, for instance, domestic inflation, economic (including trade) decline, indebtedness, lost job opportunities and productivity, and wasted human and material resources.

• *Third*, the number of persons *trapped in the war machine*—as *combatants* in any of the thirty-six conflicts now taking place in forty-one countries; by virtue of direct or indirect *employment* (roughly 25 million people are currently under arms worldwide, and another 25 million are involved in paramilitary forces and military research, production, and administration);[32] by living under *military governments*, as approximately 1 billion people do;[33] as *refugees* fleeing war, dictatorship, and other forms of oppression (conservatively estimated at 8 million persons in 1983);[34] and as *potential victims*: the tiny (by today's standards) atomic weapons dropped on Hiroshima and Nagasaki in August 1945 killed about 210,000 people, whereas the current global nuclear stockpile of about 20 billion tons of TNT, roughly equivalent to a *million* Hiroshimas, theoretically could kill 224 *billion* people, or fifty-one times the present world population.[35]

• *Fourth*, the *psychological and ecological damage* that has been, and might be, done as the result of mass violence: Nuclear anxiety has emerged as the latest psychological manifestation of the war crisis. Like cancer, which is also directly linked to nuclear weapons and research, it is overwhelmingly a First- and Second-World illness. Studies have already found a high incidence of dread about nuclear war that extends to school-age children, in the Soviet Union as much as in the United States.[36] More research on the traumatic effects of conventional warfare, terrorism, and enforced uprooting to escape war needs to be done. We know a good deal, for example, about the Vietnam War's devastating psychological consequences for U.S. GIs. But one wonders about the war's effects on the minds of the Vietnamese, particularly those who withstood U.S. bombing that was "the equivalent of one Nagasaki bomb per week for seven and a half years."[37]

The same ferocious bombing also made Vietnam an ecological catastrophe. Its dimensions have been captured by some U.S. scientists in a study appropriately entitled "The Cratering of Vietnam."[38] Only recently have governments and scientists begun to pay attention to how warfare affects plant and animal life, the land's productivity, water quality, and incidences of disease. Chemical warfare, although banned by international agreements, is nevertheless being prepared for in a number of countries. It was used by the United States (as Agent Orange) in Vietnam as a defoliant, probably has been used by the Iraqis in their war with Iran in the 1980s, and may have been used (in the form of mycotoxins, or yellow rain) by Soviet-supported forces in Kampuchea and Afghanistan.[39]

And there is more: The ecology of war should also take into account the much-discussed phenomenon of "nuclear winter" (the potentially catastrophic environmental effects of a multimegaton nuclear exchange),[40] experimentation by some major powers with manipulation of the environment for military purposes, and the public health effects of highly toxic wastes from the production of nuclear and other weapons in military reactors.[41]

The last of our four global crises, *underdevelopment*, may provide the clearest case of how differently Realists and Corporate Globalists, on one hand, and Global Humanists, on the other, perceive and evaluate a central issue in world politics. For the former, development and underdevelopment can everywhere be measured in terms of *gross* production and *average* distribution, using indicators such as Gross National Product, gross profit, per capita income, total exports and imports, and, in the socialist economies, targets under five-year or other central plans. Such indicators can be useful general guides to economic performance; but they have been roundly criticized for many years. Among other things, they distort the real-world picture of losers and beneficiaries from economic growth. Gross and average measurements typically draw attention from the mass of impoverished people to whom economic benefits rarely trickle down. They discount the ecological consequences of economic growth. Furthermore, an increase in a gross measure such as GNP may not be the most desirable kind of growth in a society filled with malnourished, unhealthy, uneducated people. The question should concern production and consumption: for whom and of what?

Overall, Global Humanists seek to inject equity, social justice, and environmental considerations into their calculations of development. Foremost is that "development" be bottom-up rather than top-down, that it focus on meeting basic human needs and not on further enriching the privileged few. They want to know whether or not a national budget serves basic needs: what percentage for public services, military programs, interest on external debts? How are people taxed, and who might be subsidizing whom? They will take a close look at exports and imports: Are food and other commòdities capable of being produced at home being imported or exported despite a local need? Do local or foreign entrepreneurs control foreign trade, and which sectors of it? To what extent is export promotion serving human development needs such as employment as opposed to elite needs?

Global Humanists are also concerned about social-group differences: What is the gap in income, protein consumption, health and educational benefits, and life expectancy between the richest and the poorest segments of the population, between men and women, between urban and rural dwellers, and between majority and minority ethnic groups? They also want to know about the quality of goods produced, how they are distributed internally, how profits are shared, what the cost of waste is, what real purchasing power (after inflation) is, how the type of production affects employment (is it capital- or labor-intensive?), how much energy is consumed by particular kinds of production, to what extent social justice is reflected in company management and job retraining, and what the social costs of production are in terms of pollution, resource extraction (such as valuable timberland), and workplace health and safety. Where transnational corporations are involved, Global Humanists also will inquire into their impact on employment and small business, the extent of technology sharing with the host country, the amount of profit reinvested and repatriated, and the relevance of the goods or services produced to the needs of an underdeveloped economy.

The environmental costs of development, and the simultaneous underdevelopment of both economies and environment, deserve special mention. Whether one is speaking of ecological destruction in the Third World (documented, for instance, by the Chilean political economist Osvaldo Sunkel)[42] or in the First and Second Worlds, the costs are high and quickly mounting. In the Third World, taking our cue from Sunkel, we need to explore problems such as

> a great intensification and large shifts in the exploitation of natural resources, both renewable and nonrenewable, as well as intensive technological change; a considerable spatial redistribution of human activities and in particular massive urbanization and industrial concentration; and a new, vastly expanded, and highly concentrated process of generation of industrial, agricultural and urban wastes, pollution, and contamination.[43]

Africa in particular has been an ecological nightmare of expanding deserts, contracting rain forests, eroding soil, reduced rainfall, and shifting climate zones. The extent to which misguided aid programs and agricultural development models imported from the outside, as well as traditional African farming practices, are responsible for this devastation is urgent to explore.

Transnational corporations contribute to the ecological devastation of Third World countries by encouraging farming for export and by setting up factories there that pollute the environment or become dumping grounds for pesticides.[44] Industries whose output of wastes goes beyond permissible levels in their home countries find safe havens abroad, encouraged by local authorities eager for foreign investment and perhaps open to a bribe. The pesticide leak at the Union Carbide plant in Bhopal, India, in December 1984 seems to be one such instance of a pollution-dumping tragedy. But the explosion in Mexico City only weeks earlier of liquefied gas tanks owned by the government oil corporation, Pemex, which killed about 450 slum-dwellers, shows that the poor can be as easily victimized by national as by transnational companies. In the industrialized countries, meanwhile, we likewise find ecological nightmares and near-disasters. The names of Three Mile Island, Love Canal, and Stringfellow in the United States; of Chelyabinsk and Chernobyl in the Soviet Union, sites of nuclear disasters in 1957 and 1986; of Seveso, Italy, scene of a major dioxin spill in 1976; of Germany's treasured forests, where one in three trees has now been damaged by acid rain—these evidently represent only the tip of an ecocidal iceberg.[45]

Ecopolitics is a perspective and field of study that has emerged in response to the enormous destructive potential, within and among countries, of uncontrolled exploitation of the environment in defiance of natural system balance. As defined by the West German Green party, ecopolitics

> understand[s] human beings and our environment as being part of nature. Human life, too, is embedded in the life cycles of the ecosystems; we interfere with our actions and this, in turn, acts back on us. We must not destroy the stability of the ecosystems. In particular, ecological politics presents an all-encompassing rejection of an economy of exploitation and plundering of natural resources and raw materials.[46]

Measuring the extent of environmental damage and catastrophes-in-the-making in national and transnational terms becomes an important task in the overall assessment of development and underdevelopment.

Finally, Global-Humanist analysis of underdevelopment considers the costs and benefits, from a human-interest standpoint, of alternative production, consumption, and investment patterns. In what ways can more self-reliant, autonomous development take place? How might a better balance between economic growth and environmental protection be achieved? What needs to happen politically, as well as economically, in order for people's basic needs to be met? How can foreign trade and aid be altered so that they serve, rather than are merely served by, the working population? These kinds of questions will probably only be asked by analysts who accept the necessity of political transformation. Until now, the dominant models of modernization employed in the West and adopted in much of the Third World reflected Western capitalism's own development, stressing the virtues of the private sector, bigness, and stable, steady-state politics. And there is undoubtedly merit to the argument[47] that such models have been directly encouraged in the United States and elsewhere by government and foundation research support.

This review of the Global-Humanist methodology has emphasized the special importance of human-centered values, norms, and assumptions to the definition, not to mention the analysis and potential solution, of global political problems. The methodology has emerged alongside and has been shaped significantly by the global crisis. The consequences of that evolution are both positive and negative. It has shown the need—indeed, the urgency—to break down intellectual barriers to cross-disciplinary research and to science with ethical content. It has helped to redirect political inquiry to human beings while raising critical questions about prevailing categories of political-economic analysis, including models of development, definitions of national security and human rights, and left-right ideological distinctions. It has infused the notion of "interdependence" with new meaning— not simply "interconnectedness" or "multilateralism," but shared insecurities about life on a planet facing simultaneous threats from rampant expansionism. Finally, Global Humanism reflects an optimism about the human prospect that may point to entirely different ways of providing for human security, concrete and potential examples of which are mentioned in the last chapter.

On the negative side, Global Humanism must take account of several important criticisms. Realists take aim at its excessive idealism and unwarranted de-emphasis of interstate power politics. They remind us that as much as world politics has become infused with greater complexity, its dominant actors remain states locked in competition with one another. From Corporate Globalists comes the charge that Global Humanism is anticapitalist and disregards the many positive contributions transnational corporations make to both national and international well-being. The global corporation *can* be a positive force for material progress and global exchange. The radical left, on the other hand, often considers Global Humanism too "soft" on capitalism, reformist rather than revolutionary, and (in agreement with the Realists) unjustifiably idealistic about the prospects for humane change. All three groups of critics take Global Humanism to task—rightly, in my view—for failing thus far to propose a specific world or national policy agenda to effect the transition "from here to there," that is, from global crisis to global balance.

Criticism of Global Humanism has also come from the Third World. Some groups committed to a new international economic order see the basic-needs approach as yet another foreign (Western) intervention in Third World affairs, or at least as a diversion from the central task (as they see it) of rectifying inequitable trade and investment relations between underdeveloped and industrialized states. Others in the Third World express misgivings about Global Humanism's equal emphasis on social-economic and political justice (and its concern about human rights generally), seeing that, too, as an ill-informed intervention. And there is hostility to any implication that the Third World, having already sacrificed its development to the industrialized world's, should now cut its economic growth in order to contribute to reversing global ecological problems such as pollution, toxic waste, and resource scarcity.

How well Global Humanism, in theory and practice, responds to these criticisms may be judged in the remaining chapters. But no picture of the global crisis, and no debate about its acute dimensions, would be complete without hearing the voices of the oppressed. Exploitation, the Brazilian scholar Fernando Henrique Cardoso tells us, has precipitated a worldwide struggle for equity and security that reflects a "crisis of values." That crisis must be resolved if there is ever to be "another development."[48]

THE OPPRESSED

They come from everywhere, these voices. From the slums of São Paulo, the streets of Prague, the Indian reservations and black ghettos of the United States, the far provinces and major cities of China, the underground of Moscow, the torture chambers of Argentina and Paraguay and El Salvador. They speak as one across time, ideologies, and academic theories. For oppression has become transnationalized: "We are caught in an inescapable network of mutuality," as Martin Luther King, Jr., once said. So that, as Gandhi constantly reminded his followers, not only is the inhuman treatment of one person an injustice to all; the manner of response to injustice is also a message to the world.[49]

The significance of these messages reaches far beyond the individuals who speak or write them. We cite the personal statements because they are authentic: They come from direct experience. In global perspective, however, they are anything but personal: They speak for the oppressed everywhere, in all three "worlds." Each individual story is different; only for the sake of analytical convenience are the voices grouped together. The power of the testimony dramatizes why Global

Humanism regards human security as the essence of the global crisis. Here, then, are the oppressed.

Poverty

Estimates of the number of people living in absolute poverty range from 750 million to 1 billion people, depending on the income floor chosen.[50] Until the Chinese Revolution triumphed in 1949, absolute poverty had been the lot of ordinary Chinese for millennia. Said Mao Zedong in 1958, on the eve of China's "great leap forward" experiment with large-scale communes:

> The outstanding thing about China's 600 million people is that they are "poor and blank." This may seem a bad thing, but in reality it is a good thing. Poverty gives rise to the desire for change, the desire for action and the desire for revolution. On a blank sheet of paper free from any mark, the freshest and most beautiful characters can be written.[51]

Mao understood the revolutionary potential of poverty from personal experience. Although born into a relatively well-off peasant family, he described (in his only autobiographical account) how he came to question the right of people who did not work the land to own it and make the peasants work for them. Then, "an incident occurred in Hunan [his home province] which influenced my whole life":

> There had been a severe famine that year, and in Changsha thousands were without food. The starving sent a delegation to the civil governor, to beg for relief, but he replied to them haughtily, "Why haven't you food? There is plenty in the city. I always have enough." When the people were told the governor's reply, they became very angry. They held mass meetings and organized a demonstration. They attacked the Manchu yamen, cut down the flagpole, the symbol of office, and drove out the governor. [A subsequent promise of change was not fulfilled.] . . . A new governor arrived, and at once ordered the arrest of the leaders of the uprising. Many of them were beheaded and their heads displayed on poles as a warning to future "rebels."
>   This incident was discussed in my school for many days. It made a deep impression on me. . . . I never forgot it. I felt that there with the rebels were ordinary people like my own family and I deeply resented the injustice of the treatment given to them.[52]

In Portuguese-controlled Guinea in the 1960s, on the other hand, another revolutionary leader, Amilcar Cabral, found that among the impoverished, the urban workers had the greatest revolutionary potential. He wrote:

As far as Guinea is concerned, the idea of the national liberation struggle was born not abroad but in our own country, in a milieu where people were subjected to close and incessant exploitation. Many people say that it is the peasants who carry the burden of exploitation: this may be true, but . . . it is easier to convince the workers and the people employed in the town who earn, say, 10 escudos a day for a job in which the European earns between 30 and 50 that they are being subjected to massive exploitation and injustice, because they can see.[53]

V. S. Naipaul has achieved worldwide renown as a novelist. Born in Trinidad of Hindu parents, he went to India to find that the country's great human resources were being absorbed by the past, especially poverty. His is a chronicle of despair:

In the village [in Bihar] I went to, only one family out of four had land; only one child out of four went to school; only one man out of four had work. For a wage calculated to keep him only in food for the day he worked, the employed man, hardly exercising a skill, using the simplest tools and sometimes no tools at all, did the simplest agricultural labor. Child's work; and children, being cheaper than men, were preferred; so that, suicidally, in the midst of an overpopulation which no one recognized . . . , children were a source of wealth, available for hire after their eighth year for, if times were good, fifteen rupees, a dollar fifty (U.S.), a month.[54]

Elsewhere, a model village: "There was little more that they needed, and I began to see my own ideas of village improvement as fantasies. Nothing beyond food—and survival—had as yet become an object of ambition."[55] "The poverty of the land is reflected in the poverty of the mind," Naipaul sadly concluded.[56]

Racism

Few societies in the world are like Japan's: racially or ethnically homogeneous. Virtually none, including Japan's, is without racial or ethnic bias that presents a major social problem. (In Japan's case, it is the presence of large numbers of Koreans and children of mixed marriages with *gaishin*, foreigners.) Following are two accounts of racism, the first by the Black Muslim activist preacher in the United States, Malcolm X, and the second by the black student activist in South Africa, Steve Biko. Both were murdered—Malcolm X in his pulpit in 1964, Biko by prison guards in 1977. First, Malcolm X:

The white people I had known marched before my mind's eye. From the start of my life. The [Michigan] white people always in our house after the other whites I didn't know had killed my father . . . the white people who kept calling my mother "crazy" to her face and before me and my brothers and sisters, until she finally was taken off by white people to the Kalamazoo asylum . . . the white judge and others who had split up the children . . . white youngsters I was in school with, and the teachers—the one who told me in the eighth grade to "be the carpenter" because thinking of being a lawyer was foolish for a Negro . . . the whites who piled into the Negro speakeasies for a taste of Negro *soul* . . . the social workers . . . the Middlesex County Court people . . . the judge who gave me ten years.[57]

Next, Biko:

It is not surprising, therefore, that in South Africa, after generations of exploitation, white people on the whole have come to believe in the inferiority of the black man, so much so that while the race problem started as an offshoot of the economic greed exhibited by white people, it has now become a serious problem on its own. White people now despise black people, not because they need to reinforce their attitude and so justify their position of privilege but simply because they actually believe that black is inferior and bad. This is the basis upon which whites are working in South Africa, and it is what makes South African society racist. . . . Black Consciousness defines the situation differently. . . . We must seek to restore to the black man the great importance we used to give to human relations, the high regard for people and their property and for life in general; to reduce the triumph of technology over man and the materialistic element that is slowly creeping into our society. These are essential features of our black culture to which we cling. Black culture above all implies freedom on our part to innovate without recourse to white values.[58]

Patriarchy

Chinese women, Mao reported in 1927, were shackled not only by the "three systems of authority" that dominated men: political, clan, and religious. They were "also dominated by the men (the authority of the husband)"; altogether, "four thick ropes binding the Chinese people." But Mao saw, earlier than most, that the disintegration of the rural economy would undermine male domination; women's participation in labor, he believed, would shake "the whole feudal-patriarchal ideology" to its foundations.[59] To an extent it did; but even in China, one of the few countries in which women have made major gains in social and economic standing, sex-based discrimination is still widespread.

The reality for women is that neither "liberation" into the work force nor worldwide adoption of the principle of female equality (in the UN Charter) has eliminated patriarchy. In the most recent comprehensive survey of the status of women worldwide, Ruth Leger Sivard concluded: "Whether in the economy, education, health, or government, there is no major field of activity and no country in which women have attained equality with men."[60] In both developed and underdeveloped countries, socialist and capitalist, women generally earn far less than men, eat less, are less well educated (and more likely to be illiterate), advance professionally less often than men, are politically far less represented in legislatures and decisionmaking bodies, are less healthy, have shorter life spans, and enjoy many fewer legal rights in marriage, property relations, and the workplace. About the only area in which women generally have more than men is their total daily work load.

Still, Mao's point about the importance of the work process as the basis both of women's oppression and their potential liberation has merit. It emerges in this account by Domitila, the wife of a Bolivian tin-mine worker:

> We women, the compañeras of the men, work with them in the job that they're involved in. We women were raised from the cradle with the ideas that women were made only to cook and take care of the kids, that we are incapable of assuming important tasks, and that we shouldn't be allowed to get involved in politics. But necessity made us change our lives. Fifteen years ago, in a period of tremendous problems for the working class [in the mines], a group of seventy women organized to win freedom for their compañeros who were leaders and had been imprisoned for demanding higher wages. The women got everything they asked for, after a ten-day hunger strike. And from then on they decided to organize in a group which they called "Housewives' Committee of Siglo XX."[61]

But such activism is far from the norm. In *Women in the Global Factory*, Annette Fuentes and Barbara Ehrenreich describe the exploitation of cheap, abundant, docile female labor by transnational corporations. These women, usually young, single, and willing to do repetitive assembly-line work, make ideal employees. "Young male workers are too restless and impatient to be doing monotonous work with no career value," a personnel manager in Taiwan is quoted as saying. "If displeased they sabotage the machines and even threaten the foreman. But girls, at most they cry a little."[62] Women workers can be relied on not to protest unsafe, unhealthy work conditions; and when, as commonly happens, they contract a work-related illness—such as, in South Korean factories, conjunctivitis and other eye diseases caused by working with microchips—they are easily replaced.[63] Hence they feel trapped, like the Taiwanese factory worker who said:

> I've sold five years of my youth to the company. I need a rest from this brainnumbing work for two or three weeks. But there is no way I can leave without quitting or taking a big loss. There are so many regulations you feel you are tied up with ropes till you can't budge an inch. And I've given them five years of my life![64]

The women's movement has been one of the major political forces for change in recent years, notably in the United States and Western Europe. Petra Kelly personifies modern-day feminism as one of the spokespersons of the Green party:

> Women must change their consciousness, break from the patriarchal circle and free themselves from such ill-suited ideas as those of the masculine, patriarchal and nuclear society. All too long we have been told that to gain equal chances and equal opportunities, we must accept the equal rights and equal duties of men. But it cannot be emancipation, to stand beside men in the various national armies and learn to shoot and learn to kill. It cannot be emancipation to learn how to operate a nuclear reactor or to be able to sit in a nuclear silo and control the control board.[65]

Underdevelopment: Colonialism, Imperialism, and Neocolonialism

Some of the people we have quoted, such as Mao, Cabral, and Domitila, linked their experiences of oppression to a broader, systemic phenomenon: the underdevelopment of their countries by colonialism, neocolonialism, or imperialism. (There are also persons who explicitly refused to do so, such as Steve Biko.) India's first prime minister, Jawaharlal Nehru, wrote at length about British colonial domination of his country. His description of how British rule evolved into a "new imperialism," in which local landlords and officials became tied into the authority and class structure of England, applies today in a number of noncolonial situations:

> We find that the British, the most advanced people in Europe at the time, ally themselves in India with the most backward and conservative classes. They bolster up a dying feudal class; they create landlords; they support the hundreds of dependent Indian rulers in their semi-feudal states. . . . And they tried to make India a purely agricultural country producing raw materials for their industries. To prevent factories growing up in India they actually put a duty on machinery entering India. . . . The object of this was to help British cotton goods from Lancashire to compete with Indian textiles.
>
> In this way modern industry grew slowly in India. The richer classes in India cried out more and more for industrial development. . . . [After World I] this growth of industrial conditions created a class of industrial workers who worked in the city factories.
>
> The workers in the factories soon found that the slightly higher wage did not go very far. Everything cost more in the cities; altogether the cost of living was much higher. The places where they had to live were wretched hovels, filthy, damp and dark and insanitary. Their working conditions were also bad. . . . Sometimes, in very despair, they had a strike—that is, they stopped work. But they were

weak and feeble, and could easily be crushed by their wealthy employers, backed often by the [colonial] government.[66]

Equally powerful is the portrait of the psychology of colonialism by Frantz Fanon, a black psychologist who gained fame for his work in French and postindependence (1958) Algeria. In testimony that, again, echoes in many other Third World accounts, Fanon wrote:

> The well-known principle that all men are equal will be illustrated in the colonies from the moment that the native claims that he is the equal of the settler. One step more, and he is ready to fight to be more than the settler. . . . [T]he native discovers that his life, his breath, his beating heart are the same as those of the settler. He finds out that the settler's skin is not of any more value than a native's skin; and it must be said that this discovery shakes the world in a very necessary manner. All the new, revolutionary assurance of the native stems from it. For if, in fact, my life is worth as much as the settler's, his glance no longer shrivels me up nor freezes me, and his voice no longer turns me into stone. I am no longer on tenterhooks in his presence; in fact, I don't give a damn for him. . . . The total result looked for by colonial domination was indeed to convince the natives that colonialism came to lighten their darkness. The effect consciously sought by colonialism was to drive into the natives' heads the idea that if the settlers were to leave, they would at once fall back into barbarism, degradation, and bestiality.[67]

For India, for Algeria, for over 50 countries after World War II, independence was the great quest of nationalist leaders. Some of them, like Ho Chi Minh in Vietnam, were inspired by earlier anticolonial struggles in the West. On September 2, 1945, the day the world war officially ended in Asia, Ho and his colleagues issued a declaration of Vietnamese independence that began with the words of the American Declaration of Independence and the French Declaration of the Rights of Man. "Nevertheless," the Vietnamese document continues:

> for more than eighty years, the French imperialists, abusing the stand of Liberty, Equality, and Fraternity, have violated our Fatherland and oppressed our fellow citizens. They have acted contrary to the ideals of humanity and justice. In the field of politics, they have deprived our people of every democratic liberty. They have enforced inhuman laws; they have set up three distinct political regimes in the North, Center, and the South of Viet-Nam in order to wreck our national unity and prevent our people from being united. They have built more prisons than schools. They have mercilessly slain our patriots; they have drowned our uprisings in rivers of blood.[68]

Nationalism as antiforeignism has been a frequent rallying cry across the Third World: "India shall be a nation! No foreigners of any sort! Hindu and Moslem and Sikh and all shall be one! Hurrah! Hurrah for India! Hurrah! Hurrah!"[69] But it has happened all too often that independence from foreign rule has merely substituted internal for external exploitation: domestic instead of (or in addition to) foreign capital, local police and bureaucratic tyrants instead of foreign-trained ones, a home-grown dictator in place of a colonial regent. And the oppression continues: old wine in new bottles. Fouad Ajami has written:

> An earlier generation of Third World nationalists came to learn the traumatic lesson that the liberal values of the West were not for export and that those who valued nationalism for themselves denied it to others. Now the same lesson has to be learned about Marxism. Marxist internationalism is a thin construct: behind the ideological masks can be seen the age-old desire of powerful men and societies to hoard and to dominate.[70]

No one has captured this *neo*colonialism more grippingly than the Kenya writer, Ngugi wa Thiong'o, in his novel *Petals of Blood*—so much so that Ngugi was thrown in jail shortly after the book's publication in 1977. His novel is a tale of great hopes for independent Kenya betrayed by greed, blind ambition, and the persistence of a colonialist mentality among the powerful. A black lawyer sums up for Ngugi the case against the new masters:

> I look back on the wasted chances, on the missed opportunities: on the hour, the day, the period, when, at the crossroads, we took the wrong turning. . . . We could have done anything, then, because our people were behind us. But we, the leaders, chose to flirt with the molten god, a blind, deaf monster who has plagued us for hundreds of years. We reasoned: what's wrong is the skin-colour of the people who ministered to this god. . . . So we go on building the monster and it grows and waits for more, and now we are all slaves to it. At its shrine we kneel and pray and hope. Now see the outcome . . . dwellers in Blue Hills [Nairobi's elite suburbs], those who have taken on themselves the priesthood of the ministry to the blind god . . . a thousand acres of land . . . a million acres in the two hands of a priest, while the congregation moans for an acre! and they are told: it is only a collection from your sweat. . . . Meanwhile, the god grows big and fat and shines even brighter and whets the appetites of his priests, for the monster has, through the priesthood, decreed only one ethical code: Greed and accumulation. I ask myself: is it fair, is it fair, our children?[71]

The betrayal of independence does not require a colonial past, as with Kenya and India. Neocolonialism is typically associated with an influx of foreign capital and the creation, as in Brazil, of close political, military, and economic ties between local and foreign elites. The consequence of this dependence is, again, underdevelopment. It is depicted here by a Brazilian labor leader, Luis Inacio Da Silva, popularly known as Lula:

We know that the economic situation of the country is bad. We know that there is widespread hunger and starvation among our people. We do not plant beans anymore; we do not plant rice anymore; we do not produce food anymore. We are building armaments, nuclear plants, missiles. Behind this is not the will to develop Brazil. The objective is to satisfy the polluted minds of the military which rules this country [until late 1984]. They say they want to make Brazil a world power. A country is not powerful by the quantity of arms and bombs it produces. A country is not developed by the amount of tanks and machine guns it possesses. A country is powerful and developed when its people are healthy, educated, are proud of their multiracial ethnicity. When the people have a full stomach, housing, and health, then the country is developed.[72]

Religion

Persecution of people for their religious beliefs is one of the oldest forms of oppression. It has taken a new twist in Latin America today: As the Catholic Church has increasingly aligned itself with the poor, the apparatus of state repression has turned on the priests. But to many in the Third World, organized religion has more commonly been a tool of oppression, forming what Ngugi wa Thiong'o refers to as the "Holy Trinity": "Christianity, Commerce, Civilization: the Bible, the Coin, the Gun."[73] I will cite from both kinds of experiences, beginning with Ali Shariati, an opponent (and victim) of the Shah's Iran, and one of contemporary Iran's greatest spiritual-political philosophers:

> From Palestine to Iran, from Egypt to China and throughout all parts of the earth where there was civilization, we had to carry the loads of stones to construct temples, palaces, and graves. Again in the name of charity, the representatives of the "gods" and the successors of the prophets began to loot us. Again, in the name of holy war, we were pushed into the battlefields. We had to sacrifice our innocent children for the "gods," temples, and idols!
>
> My friend, for thousands of years, our destiny became worse than yours. Three-fifths of the wealth in Iran went to the *Mobedans* [clergy] in the name of the gods. We became their servants and slaves. Four-fifths of the wealth in France was taken from us by the clergymen of God. The Pharoah clergymen and spiritual teachers of religions have always been successful. . . .
>
> I do not know where to go! Where should I go? Should I go to the *Mobedans*? How could I return to those temples which were built to enslave me? Should I join those who claim to be examples of our national freedom but in essence are attempting to gain their inhuman privileges of the past? The mosques are no better than those temples![74]

Shariati found sanctity in Islam; but one can imagine his continuing agitation had he lived to see the oppressive form Islam has taken under Khomeini, whose anti-Shah struggle Shariati supported.

A religious revolution of a different sort began in Latin America in 1968 at an extraordinary conclave of bishops.[75] These meetings in Medellin, Colombia, inaugurated by Pope Paul, set in motion what has now become known as liberation theology: an historic reversal of the Catholic Church's role in Latin America, from firm supporter of established political-economic authority to proclaimed ally of the destitute. The price of this profound shift may be seen in Argentina, Brazil, Bolivia, and Ecuador. Their governments were particularly notorious in the 1960s and 1970s for their arrests, tortures, kidnappings, and murders of Christian ecclesastic and lay leaders. The official charge, predictably, has been that those priests who support land reform and peasant organization are communists. (Through its support of these governments and of right-wing elements in the church, the U.S. Central Intelligence Agency was deeply involved in the repression.)

In recent years, the center of antichurch activity has been El Salvador. The murder in 1980 of Archbishop Oscar Romero of San Salvador is the central event in a veritable reign of terror against the church. There is little doubt that Romero was murdered by a right-wing death squad; other murders and kidnappings of church people have been linked to official Salvadoran security forces. A Peruvian liberation theologian said of Romero's death: "Before Romero the Church tended to say: these Christians died for political not religious reasons. He was killed not because he defended the rights of the Church, but because he defended the rights of the poor."[76]

Yet within the church itself, the issue of how far and in what ways priests should be "political" remains controversial. Father Leonardo Boff, a Brazilian, has clashed repeatedly with the Vatican because of his radical interpretation and practice of church doctrine. He has gone so far as to charge that the church hierarchy has itself violated human rights. In one of his books, Boff presented a radical-humanist agenda for liberation theology that has resonated throughout Latin America:

> The long-range Christian strategy is to achieve a liberation that guarantees a self-sustained development that meets the real needs of the people, and not the consumerist needs of rich countries and groups associated with those countries. . . . [We should] recognize the privileged status of the poor as the new and emerging historical subject which will carry on the Christian project in the world. The poor, here, are not understood simply as those in need; they are in need but they are also the group with a historical strength, a capacity for change, and a potential for evangelization. The Church reaches out to them directly, not through the state or the ruling classes. Thus, we are no longer speaking of a Church *for* the poor but rather a Church *of* and *with* the poor. From this option for and insertion among the poor the Church begins to define its relationship with all other social classes.

It does not lose its catholicity; its catholicity becomes real and not merely a matter of rhetoric.[77]

State Terror

Jacobo Timerman is a Jew who for a number of years published one of the major newspapers in Buenos Aires, Argentina. In the mid-1970s he was imprisoned for nearly two years. This was a dark chapter in Argentina's history, during which successive military juntas authorized the abduction, torture, and "disappearance" of at least 9,000 and possibly as many as 30,000 persons. (A number of these military leaders were tried and sentenced after a democratically elected government took office in December 1983.) Timerman's testimony speaks directly to the evils of the neofascist state:

> The members of the Argentine military claim impunity in the unleashing of brutality, insisting that the war against [communist] terrorism was imposed upon them, in which case methods matter less than destiny. . . . In Nazi Germany, the Jews were guilty through birth, the liberals through weakness and corruption, the Communists through ideology. The same equation of guilt proved suitable for the enemy of the Argentine military. . . .
>
> How can a nation reproduce in every detail, though employing other forms, in every argument, though employing other words, the same monstrous crimes [of the Nazis] explicitly condemned and clearly expounded so many years before? That is the Argentine mystery.[78]

Terror is a daily reality in El Salvador, too. A rough estimate is that 45,000 people have died in the civil war there since 1979, the overwhelming majority at the hands of death squads and official government forces. In Manlio Argueta's compelling novel of El Salvador, *One Day of Life*, we experience the immediacy of this terror as we live, at close range, with a peasant family. Not only do we become familiar with their fears, outrage, and ultimate courage; we also see the repression from the perpetrator's standpoint, that of a pure fascist out to pacify the opposition at any cost, just as his gringo instructors taught him. In the sequence cited below, two soldiers confront a peasant woman with the barely living body of her husband, whose "crime" is that he was a member of a peasant association. She denies knowing him to protect her granddaughter:

> "I don't know what my granddaughter has been up to. I only know that she is a child who has other ambitions because we old people are half dead; we have allowed you to kill us slowly. But we've come to our senses while it's not too late. My granddaughter is alive and you are not going to kill her slowly. . . . She lives for all of us, she breathes

for us, she is being born while we are in our death throes; it is also possible that she will save us."

I don't know how I uttered these words. . . . I have to close my eyes to be able to speak. So as not to see you, Jose, so your inspiration can reach me better.

Private Martinez: "We want you to look in this mirror. That's how you're going to end up, all of you who don't love the rich, because the enemies of democracy have poisoned your hearts . . . so you'll hate the rich people."

Adolfina: "If you don't have anything else to do, if you have enjoyed giving all of this abuse, you may go eat the gentleman you have hanging there."

The buck private: "Sir, don't let them be so disrespectful. If you want, I'll take care of this bitch."

Private Martinez: "Don't butt into what's none of your business. The girl is right."[79]

There is no truly accurate figure on the number of victims of official terrorism. Considering the many ways in which a person can be victimized—from apprehension to murder—it is difficult to imagine how high the figures might be. What can be reported is that in forty-eight Third World countries, torture and other forms of official violence are *systematically* practiced.[80]

Denial of Political Freedoms

The government of Czechoslovakia is a signatory of the international covenant on civil and political rights; the governments of China and South Korea are not. But a number of basic individual freedoms are denied in both societies, as they are in much of the world. Following are protests of such restrictions in those countries. The first is by Charter 77, a group of broad participation formed in 1977 "to work individually and collectively for respect for human and civil rights in Czechoslovakia and the world." The second was written by the Alliance for Human Rights in China, which was founded in 1979. It was part of a very short-lived human-rights movement that featured the common Chinese practice of putting up big-character posters, in this case on "Democracy Wall" in the center of Beijing (Peking). The testimony of South Korea's leading human-rights spokesperson, Kim Dae Jung, is the last selection.

The Czech statement reads in part:

[Publication of the international human-rights covenants], however, is at the same time an urgent reminder of the many fundamental human rights that, regrettably, exist in our country only on paper. The right of free expression . . . , for example, is quite illusory. Tens of thousands of citizens have been prevented from working in their professions for the sole reason that their views differ from the official ones. They have been the frequent targets of various forms of discrimination and chicanery on the part of the authorities or social organizations; they have been denied any opportunity to defend themselves and are practically the victims of apartheid. . . .

Freedom of speech is suppressed by the government's management of all mass media, including the publishing and cultural institutions. No political, philosophical, scientific, or artistic work that deviates in the slightest from the narrow framework of official ideology or esthetics is permitted to be produced. Public criticism of social conditions is prohibited. Public defense against false and defamatory charges by official propaganda organs is impossible. . . . False accusations cannot be refuted, and it is futile to attempt rectification or to seek legal redress. Open discussion of intellectual and cultural matters is out of the question. . . .

Religious freedom . . . is systematically curbed with a despotic arbitrariness: Limits are imposed on activities of priests, who are constantly threatened with the revocation of government permission to perform their function; persons who manifest their religious faith either by word or action lose their jobs or are made to suffer other repressions; religious instruction in schools is suppressed, et cetera.[81]

The Chinese statement declares:

1. The citizens demand freedom of thought and speech. We call for the release of those who have been imprisoned all over the country because of the opinions they hold. It is part of one and the same absurdity that a single person's thoughts (Mao's) are referred to in the Constitution which, together with the Party Statutes, also appoints his successor. This is a violation of the principle of freedom of thought and speech. . . .
2. The nation demands that effective guarantees be written into the Constitution whereby we have the right to criticise and judge the leaders of the Party and the State. . . .
3. The national minorities must be granted a real measure of autonomy. China has not only a variety of ethnic minorities but also a variety of parties, and we must take them all into account in order to develop socialism. . . .
4. We demand universal suffrage in elections for the State leadership, and local leadership, at all levels. . . .
11. We call for the utter rejection of the system whereby people are allocated to work units for life. We call for the freedom to choose our jobs, to move from place to place, and to be able to dress according to our own taste.[82]

Kim Dae Jung has been the leading critic of authoritarian politics in South Korea (see the case study in Chapter 4) for about fifteen years. In the last direct election for president there in 1971, he placed a close second. Since then he has survived government surveillance, arrest, torture, a sedition conviction, exile in the United States, and house arrest on his return home in 1985. Kim's political career, including his decision to return from exile, bears remarkable parallels to that of Benigno Aquino in the Philippines—except that Aquino was assassinated at the airport on his return to lead the Filipino opposition to the dictatorship of Fernando Marcos. Following are excerpts from an interview Kim gave in early 1985, before leaving for Seoul. What he had to say is all the more interesting in light of the massive student-led protests that engulfed Korea during the spring of 1987, leading to a remarkable turnabout in official policy.

> We can expect national security only when there is democracy. We need something to secure. Without democracy we can never expect real security in South Korea. Our experience has demonstrated my assertion. . . . In Korea, thirty years ago, in wartime, we demonstrated that we can defend our country. It was because of enjoyment of democracy that we succeeded in defending our country. If there is democracy we can become another West Germany. We know how West Germany is confident of its ability to deal with East Germany. A democratic government will be supported by our people fully and voluntarily. Then there will be sovereignty and security. Then we can force North Korea to give up its long-time ambition to communize South Korea; North Korea cannot help but do so.[83]

Ecocide

No group has been more deeply affected by environmental degradation than the North American Indian. The Indian's way of life, spiritually and materially, is inseparable from Nature. That way has been subjected to relentless assault by white "civilization," from pollution of ancient waters and lands to uranium poisoning and strip mining. Like African, Southeast Asian, and Latin American tribes, the North American Indians are forced to fight a rearguard action to defend their homelands. Now many non-Indian communities are coming to recognize that the global issue of ecological suicide—ecocide—is not exclusively tribal; it can be as close as their own backyards.

Following are two Indian appeals: the first was written by Hopi leaders to President Nixon protesting stripmining on Indian lands by a transnational corporation subsidiary; the second is the "Haudenosaunee Statement to the World—May 1979," passed in the Six Nations Council of the Iroquois.

> Today the sacred lands where the Hopi live are being desecrated by men who seek coal and water from our soil that they may create more power for the white man's cities. This must not be allowed to continue for if it does, Mother Nature will react in such a way that almost all men will suffer the end of life as they now know it. The Great Spirit said not to allow this to happen even as it was prophecied to our

ancestors. . . . Your government has almost destroyed our basic religion which actually is a way of life for all our people in this land of the Great Spirit.[84]

And from the Iroquois:

> Brothers and Sisters: Our ancient homeland is spotted today with an array of chemical dumps. Along the Niagara River dioxin, a particularly deadly substance, threatens the remaining life there and in the waters which flow from there. . . . The fish of the Great Lakes are laced with mercury from industrial plants, and fluoride from aluminum plants poisons the land and the people. Sewage from the population centers is mixed with PCBs and PBs in the watersheds of the Great Lakes and the Finger Lakes, and the waters are virtually nowhere safe for any living creature. . . . Only a people whose minds are twisted beyond an ability to perceive truth could act in ways which will threaten the future generations of humanity. . . . In our territories, we continue to carry out our function as spiritual caretakers of the land. In this role as caretakers, we cannot, and will not, stand idly by while the future of the coming generations is being systematically destroyed.[85]

These many voices of the oppressed speak eloquently for themselves. In Global-Humanist perspective, they take on added significance. They originate in heartfelt concern, not political doctrine. In some cases, ideology systematized this concern, but it did not replace it. Fundamentally, these are protests of greed, injustice, indecency, intolerance, and narrow vision, human and systemic weaknesses that are universal. They reinforce the importance of values. They also reinforce the importance of understanding *structures* of inequality at different social levels, including patriarchy, class, and the capitalist and socialist state. Finally, these explanations, appeals, protests—anguished voices all—help to clarify why *resistance* of one kind or another remains such a fixture of contemporary world politics. And in understanding why, we become able to respond to the call for action of Alexander Solzhenitsyn, perhaps contemporary Russia's most prominent dissident:

> We have to condemn publicly the very idea that some people have the right to repress others. In keeping silent about evil, in burying it so deep within us that no sign of it appears on the surface, we are implanting it, and it will rise up a thousandfold in the future. When we neither punish nor reproach evildoers, we are not simply protecting their trivial old age, we are thereby ripping the foundations of justice from beneath new generations.[86]

CHAPTER FOUR

The Third World:
Human Rights and
Underdevelopment

Multinational executives who have been watching one Latin American country after another pull back from the radicalism of the early 1970s today consider the region to be one of the world's major investment opportunities. . . . "It is all there—protein, minerals, forests, water" [says one executive].
—*Business Week*, August 9, 1976

Our nations must learn from the developed countries to avoid stumbling into the same pitfalls as they. It is absolutely essential that our creative endeavour should be directed towards the formulation of genuinely Latin American solutions. Hence there is no point in persisting in a race for development that takes no account of the values inherent in developed society.
—Gustavo Lagos

DEFINING THE "THIRD WORLD"

Anyone who has visited an underdeveloped country knows the scene: the sharp contrasts between rich and poor. At first sight, the modern capital city, with its international airport, skyscrapers, traffic jams, business men, high-walled private homes, neon signs advertising luxury goods from every continent—and beggars, pollution, and shantytowns just beyond view of downtown. And then there is the rest of the country: unrelieved squalor, too many people for too little land, children with distended bellies, the most primitive technology, thatched-roof dwellings, a closeness to death. Destiny or politics? Merely two societies, one modern and advancing, the other backward and decaying; or a structurally unequal system, the smaller part feeding off the larger?

The purpose of this chapter is to use the Global-Humanist approach in political economy to examine the crisis of human insecurity at closer range. I want to bring to life my previous generalizations about global problems, connecting them with the voices of the oppressed by presenting case studies of underdevelopment and human rights in five countries: China, South Africa, Nicaragua, the Philippines, and South Korea. The first task, however, is to clarify this "Third World" I have been generalizing about.

Conventional definitions divide the roughly 100 countries of the Third World according to a national average GNP per person, yielding high-, low-, and middle-income categories. The merit of this division is that it enables us to distinguish (as the World Bank does) the 22 upper-middle-income newly industrializing countries (NICs) (among them, South Korea, Singapore, Yugoslavia, and Brazil) and the 5 high-income oil exporters (including Saudi Arabia and Libya) from the 34 most impoverished and unindustrialized countries (such as Bangladesh, Ethiopia, and Haiti) and the lower-middle-income group of 38 countries (such as Egypt, Thailand, and Nicaragua). Nevertheless, an average-income classification such as this falls short from a human-interest point of view. While it evidently is useful for international lending agencies and transnational corporations, since it assists them in making decisions about loans and investments, the classification says nothing about the *quality of life* and the *distribution of social benefits* within societies. The significance of these omissions becomes clear in the country studies at the end of the chapter.

A second way to define the Third World is quintessentially Realist: It consists of the "developing" economies *in relation to* the "developed" ones, as measured by the value of their resources, markets, and strategic situation. Third World countries are then defined as either threats to or opportunities for furtherance of one developed country's or region's national interests. Consider, for example, the official U.S. view of recent years.[1] The Third World is threatening insofar as it has been fertile ground for revolutions, has been the setting of many East-West confrontations (Vietnam, Cuba, Lebanon), and may deny the United States access to investment markets and "vital" resources such as oil. As opportunity, the Third World's importance to standard U.S. interests goes far beyond the traditional geopolitical concern about allies and overseas bases. Third World countries purchase 40 percent of U.S. exports; account for one of every twenty manufacturing jobs and one of every five acres of farm production; host about one-quarter of all U.S. foreign investment and return one of every three dollars of overseas corporate profits; supply over 40 percent of all U.S. imports, including many valuable minerals (such as bauxite, tin, and cobalt) and cash crops (coffee, rubber, cocoa); and offer TNCs cheap labor that allegedly reduces consumer costs for Americans.

Here again, the human interest, except insofar as the U.S. lifestyle is concerned, is not taken into account. Who in the Third World benefits from all this trade and investment? What human price, at home as well as abroad, is paid to preserve strategic and economic interests? This official version of the "Third World" is typically offered to justify economic and military aid programs before Congressional and public audiences, and not in order to shape a consensus on behalf of the global poor.

Then there is the Third World's own version of the "Third World." It emerges whenever leaders of the underdeveloped countries gather to make their case for NIEO, or for nonalignment on global political and military issues. About 120 countries now belong to what had originally been the Group of 77 UN members that gathered to discuss trade and development issues in 1964.[2] Such meetings are opportunities to make a united case against the inequities of the global (capitalist) system: for instance, the declining Third World share of world production (about 21 percent) matched against its increasing proportion of world population (about 75 percent)[3]; the widening gap in average personal income (comparing India and the United States, for example, an increase of the gap from $5,000 to nearly $8,000 between 1955 and 1980)[4]; ongoing difficulties in marketing primary products because of fluctuating prices and rising protectionism in the industralized world; overall economic growth rates which, while increasing, cannot keep pace with either population growth or with what is economically necessary to narrow the income gap with the industrialized world [5]; and the devastating costs of indebtedness.

This shared sense of weakness is compounded by the widespread conviction in the Third World that advanced communications technology is further exploiting it. On one side come demands from the developed world's governments and TNCs for unimpeded access to Third World societies for advertising, television and radio programming, banking and financial services, data-gathering (including news) and dissemination, and satellite-resource mapping. From another side, the major Western news agencies typically convey an image of the Third World that stresses disaster and violence. *Their* "Third World" consists of coups, mass starvation, the stereotypic restless natives whose cultures and dignities have long been buried. Calls from across the Third World for a New International Information Order (NIIO) have been made in response to this two-pronged assault.

But there is more here than meets the eye. However justified demands for NIEO and NIIO may be, they are meant only to bring about equity *between* states. Equity *within* states is another matter: Many of the same state leaders who make eloquent calls for a new *international* order are last in line when it comes to building new *domestic* orders that emphasize human rights, such as self-determination for minorities and freedom of speech and press.[6] Third World leaders in fact tend to use the same standards of equity, such as average income and GNP, and the same arguments in favor of state power that are employed in the industrialized world. NIIO, which might legitimately be raised by Third World leaders as a defense against invasions of sovereignty, has also become a device for muzzling the press and minimizing political opposition. Likewise with NIEO: In some cases, Andre Gunder Frank asserts, NIEO has been merely a cover for mass repression. And since those who call for it represent a nation's dominant social and economic interests, any benefits from NIEO would go first to them, leaving the satisfaction of basic needs just where it now is—in the very distant future.[7] "The state that once loomed as salvation and for which men and women fought and continue to do so has too often become an instrument of terror and a means to self-enrichment," Fouad Ajami concluded of Third World nonalignment so far.[8]

The NIEO version of the Third World is further weakened by important economic and political differences within the underdeveloped community. Some countries, notably the OPEC members, are not shackled with debts or plagued by a population explosion. They have accumulated multibillion-dollar surpluses, have substantial investments in the United States and Europe, and import labor from Asia and elsewhere. Others, like the Pacific Rim states (from South Korea to Singapore), have become exporters of cars, steel, and advanced electronics. These countries have large export surpluses and high per capita average incomes—hardly the usual in the Third World. Politically, meanwhile, Third World unity remains largely a fiction. All may decry the arms race and uphold nonalignment. But some Third World states vigorously pursue a nuclear option (including hostile neighbors such as India and Pakistan, Iran and Iraq), take sides on international disputes involving the superpowers (such as the Arab-Israeli conflict and Afghanistan), welcome the military aid or bases of the major powers, produce and export arms (Brazil, Israel, China, South Korea), and (as in Central America and the Middle East today) interfere in one another's internal conflicts.

To talk of these contradictions in the NIEO and nonaligned movements is not meant to diminish the justifiability of their demands and aspirations. As already observed above (and further discussed below) even the most economically well-off Third World states are militarily vulnerable and dependent. Those with oil, gas, cheap, labor-intensive consumer goods, and other commodities desired by the advanced economies must always remember that the larger economies determine currency values and can quickly erect tariff and other barriers to imports. Some Third World governments have gained controlling interest over production and extraction of their resources. But a handful of transnational corporations dominate the marketing and distribution of food, oil, and most other goods,[9] not to mention information and international credit. In this study the point remains, however, that such international inequities should not blind us to the internal inequities that turn state leaderships from victims to victimizers.

Rather than define the Third World in terms of state interests, developed or underdeveloped, I choose a planetary perspective that embraces *human* interests and *structural* problems. From that perspective, the "Third World" consists of that three-quarters of humanity—and especially that 80 percent and more of the three-quarters—whose basic survival needs, cultural and spiritual identities, and quite possibly personal self-esteem have been badly eroded by forces largely beyond their control. These forces, both internal and external to their communities and countries, have prospered at their expense. They form part of a comprehensive national, regional, and ultimately global *system* of production, distribution, and control whose purpose is to maintain and expand upon a fundamental inequality. Regardless of how one characterizes this system—imperialism, dependence, unequal exchange, a single (world capitalist) mode of production, corporate transnationalism—it amounts to basically the same end result: The world works to benefit the few at the expense of the many.

How that thesis gets played out in the real Third World requires investigation, not mere assertion. Those who seek to use the system to their advantage are frequently in conflict with one another; and those who seek to avoid the system's consequences, or overturn it, are equally a part of the total picture. In any country, both change and the status quo threaten vested and human-development interests. Still, important generalizations can and should be made. An abundance of evidence and experience from throughout the Third World can be synthesized to create a profile of a typical country's internal and external settings. Here and in the country studies that follow we can see how and why the global crisis continues.

A THIRD WORLD COUNTRY PROFILE

• *First, this typical Third World country has a clear class structure.* It is reflected in a huge income gap between the highest 10 to 20 percent and the lowest 40 percent of the population, and in the concentration of land ownership, the main source of wealth. Each of these features deserves additional comment.

Income distribution sheds light on both North-South and intra-North, intra-South inequalities. For example, Gustavo Lagos compared income distribution in the United States and Latin America in 1971. *Within* each there were (and are) striking income inequalities: the top 20 percent of the U.S. population owned nearly 45.5 percent of the wealth, and in Latin America, the same group owned nearly 63 percent. *Between* the United States and Latin America, income differences were even more striking: "The 5 percent group in the highest income bracket in the U.S. receives more in monetary terms than all the groups in Latin America put together; in other words, 10 million privileged inhabitants of the U.S. receive more than the entire Latin American population."[10]

Brazil offers an astonishing illustration of inequality in the midst of great material abundance. Half the national income is earned by 10 percent of the households, while the bottom 40 percent of households earns only 7 percent. The gap has been steadily widening for over twenty years.[11] Yet Brazil is often touted for its high rate of growth and per capita income, and for the size of its modern industrial sector, which exports iron ore, steel, and autos, and now produces its own computers. Or take El Salvador, which is far more underdeveloped. There, average annual per capita income is roughly $650. But (according to a human-rights report in 1982) "the wealthiest 5 percent of families receive 38 percent of the income, and the wealthiest 20 percent receive 67 percent, while the bottom 40 percent of families receive only 7.5 percent." Wealth means land control: Perhaps 2,000 families (.002 percent of the population) own 40 percent of the land, and 10 percent of the landowners own 78 percent of the arable land.[12]

What is happening in the Americas is happening globally: the rich are getting richer, the poor poorer, and the middle class is backing into poverty.[13] Development fails to trickle down as promised. The phenomenon is particularly noticeable in a number of industrializing Third World countries, where heavy indebtedness and enforced austerity (by the IMF) have resulted in riots to protest price increases on food and other staples. (In the 1980s these riots, usually leading to police repression, occurred in Mexico, Brazil, Turkey, Egypt, and Peru, among others.) At such times, working people become aroused to income gaps of the kind Lagos discusses, for it is the bottom 40 percent (or more) of wage earners who bear the brunt of recessions and austerity programs, which are often imposed by external debt agencies such as the IMF.

Income gaps are widening even as the total "national product" and average per capita income are increasing. In fact, the faster a Third World economy grows, the *wider* the income gap (measured in per capita GNP) seems to become. In 1979 the difference in income between developed and underdeveloped countries averaged about $5,500 per person. One writer has shown that this difference would narrow to

Chart 4.1: Income Distribution in the Third World

Percent Share of Household Income, by Percentile of Household Groups

	Lowest 40%	Middle 40%	Next 10%	Highest 10%
Bangladesh	18.2	39.6	14.8	27.4
Tanzania	16.0	33.6	14.8	35.6
Thailand	15.2	35.0	15.7	34.1
Turkey	11.5	32.0	15.8	40.7
Costa Rica	12.0	32.2	15.3	39.5
Malaysia	11.2	32.7	16.3	39.8
Israel	18.0	42.1	17.3	32.6
Mexico	9.9	32.4	17.1	40.6
Japan	21.9	40.6	15.6	21.2
Sweden	20.0	42.8	16.0	21.2

Source: World Bank, *World Development Report 1984*, Table 28, pp. 272–273.

just over $3,000 a person if the overall rate of growth were zero, but would widen to over $44,000 a person if the growth rate jumped to 10 percent.[14] Chart 4.1 shows the skewed distribution of income in the 1970s for ten representative countries. The pattern of inequality is unmistakable. And from what we have just said, it is equally unmistakable that increases in GNP do not necessarily ameliorate, and may in fact worsen, the inequality.

• *Second, this Third World country has high unemployment and underemployment in both the rural and urban areas.* Income distribution figures do not adequately reflect these people—some 300 million in the 1970s—who constitute the core (but far from the whole) of the Third World's most destitute.[15] These are people who lose their land to powerful landlords, the onset of rural technology and a money economy, the transformation from growing food to exporting it, and drought. Peasants in these circumstances *may* have a choice to stay on in serfdom or as landless tenants, as in El Salvador and the impoverished northeast of Brazil.[16] Or, as in South Korea, they will drift to the cities in hopes of employment, usually to end up as squatters.[17]

In urban centers, technology also dispossesses. While many TNCs have shifted operations to the Third World precisely in order to take advantage of cheap labor, the largest of them find automation to be even more cost-effective. Yet a study of Kenya suggests to one scholar that the main reason for the preference of capital-intensive production over labor-intensive methods is political: A Third World government would rather have a large, powerless underclass struggling for its daily bread than have the rich, whose support is essential to regime survival, pay for its education, health care, and low-priced staples.[18]

• *Third, the status of women is deplorably low.* Women, as the Brandt Commission noted, suffer most in conditions of rural underdevelopment. They work in the home and in the fields, often putting in longer hours than the males, but at a fraction of men's pay and without education, training, health and safety protection, child care, or access to credit. Women are far more likely than men to be displaced by technology, to work for subsistence rather than cash, to be illiterate, and to suffer from malnutrition.[19] As is discussed below, women also bear the brunt of dangerous methods of population control. The status of women is therefore a sure indicator of how humane "development" really is.

Law (as in the Arab states), culture (such as Latin American machismo), and tradition (as in Africa) have prevented women from deepening their political involvement. Here we must talk about global trends and not only conditions in the Third World. With respect to the vote, only in New Zealand was women's suffrage achieved before early in the twentieth century. A survey by Susan J. Pharr has found that at the next level of political activity—participation in voluntary political work—women have gained marginal acceptability in very few countries (the United States, the USSR, Scandinavia, and Britain). When it comes to holding high office, women have made exceedingly few inroads—less than 10 percent of all elective or appointive offices—anywhere in the world (and particularly in the Second and Third Worlds).[20]

Perhaps most disturbing is that even when women do gain entry to political office, they tend to represent the same elite and class interests as their male counterparts. What has been written of Mexican women in politics may be generally true: "While women elites in Mexico deserve more political offices to represent their sex, they are no more representative of Mexican women than are male leaders of Mexican men."[21] This leads to the further conclusion that the *values* of such women are not representative of rural, low-income, working class female populations but instead are the same traditional ones held by male politicians. Women in politics evidently must play by the same rules as the men.

• *Fourth*, because the quest for "growth" typically takes the form of top-down production and distribution, *the political system favors those already in positions of authority*. Preserving the political-economic status quo has priority over strategies for change, such as land reform and labor-intensive production, that would feed and employ many more people. The Green Revolution that gained popularity with many Third World leaderships beginning in the 1960s illustrates this priority. The "revolution" worked insofar as the new seed varieties significantly increased wheat and rice yields. India is a prime illustration of this success. But to succeed required large amounts of water, chemical fertilizer, and of course, seeds—hence also irrigation tubewells, capital, and mechanization. As a substitution of energy and money for land, the Green Revolution worked to the benefit of local powerholders, their political patrons in the capital, and, in some countries, the TNCs that control international trade in fertilizer, seeds, and machinery.[22] The landholding system was preserved and in fact further consolidated, while peasants were forced onto marginal lands or forced to sell out to landlord-moneylenders.

• *Fifth, by every indicator, people's basic needs are very far from being met.* World Bank statistics show how misleading it is to talk about *average* improvements in (for example) Third World income, literacy, and health, particularly since nearly one-half the world's people live in the most impoverished countries (such as China). In those countries the literacy rate in 1980 was about one-third that of the United States, Britain, and Sweden *in 1900.*[23] Life expectancy in the poorest countries had pulled about even with what it had been in these three advanced economies (plus Japan) in 1900; but even that *relative* improvement masks a bitter reality: Whereas in the latter countries today, the rate of infant mortality (deaths of children under one year old) is ten per thousand, it runs anywhere from 78 (China and India) to over 200 (Afghanistan and Kampuchea) per 1,000 in the low-income countries, and is quite high in "wealthier" Third World countries too (for example, 73 in Brazil, 108 in Saudi Arabia, 55 in South Africa).[24] The death rate everywhere falls off dramatically after the child reaches one year; but as a UNICEF report noted, 15 million young children—an amount equal to all the children then alive in the United States—died in the Third World in 1982, mostly from malnutrition and dehydration.[25]

Improvements in education in the Third World can also be deceptive. Over the last twenty years, enrollment in primary schools has increased substantially overall. Most of the NICs have enrollment rates that are equal to those of the major industrial economies. But important qualifications emerge when we examine the individual records of the poorest Third World societies, compare male with female enrollment, and look at enrollment rates in secondary school and higher education.[26] The gains compared with 1960 are impressive in most cases, but the road still untraveled is a long one.

Indicators of personal health are also important to consider.[27] As with education, infant mortality, and literacy, we do not have breakdowns according to income groups within countries. Still, national averages can be revealing here. For instance, in the industrialized countries, the daily per person supply of calories is over 3,300; among the NICs, about 2,850; among lower middle-income countries, about 2,500; and among low-income countries, about 2,200. (Similar differences exist in meat and protein consumption.[28]) Using availability of physicians as another marker, this time including representative countries within each of the above income groups, we find: one physician for every 550 persons in Canada and 570 in Poland; one physician per 1,900 and 1,210 persons, respectively, in Oman (an OPEC member) and Hong Kong (one of the NICs); one per 1,800, and one per 11,530 in the lower-middle income countries of Nicaragua and Indonesia; and a ratio of one doctor to every 3,690 people and one to every 58,490 in India and Ethiopia.

Beyond these figures are even more fundamental (but also less readily available) ones, such as those on access to clean water. Polluted, stagnant water, together with malnutrition, accounts in large part for the high incidence of infant mortality in the Third World and, if the child lives beyond infancy, for abnormal mental development. For adults, contaminated water leads to the transmission of diseases, such as typhoid and dysentery, that exact a heavy toll.[29]

• *Sixth, this Third World country has very high population growth caused mainly by its underdevelopment, one result being more widespread hunger and malnutrition.* It has been well-established that impoverished families, facing high infant mortality, little and marginal-quality land to work, limited (if any) educational opportunity, traditional restrictions on women, and no health care or old-age security, will seek to have many children, particularly males. That way, they perpetuate the family, have more hands to work the soil, and ensure care of the elderly.[30] Hence, poverty is the main factor in the Third World's population explosion, and not the reverse. The poorest Third World countries have the highest birth rates as well as the highest incidences of infant mortality and malnutrition.

Unless development gives prominence to meeting basic needs, even the most affluent Third World country will still have high population growth, centered in its poorest regions. In Brazil, for instance, the population is growing rapidly alongside malnutrition that affects nearly two-thirds of the people. Food production is stagnant; yet Brazil exports soybeans, a major protein source. By the same token, a relatively poor country, such as Cuba, "which has benefited women with improvements in health care and education and has the most equal income distribution in Latin America, has halved its birth rate since the 1959 revolution, a record unmatched" in Latin America.[31]

What these facts tell us is that checking population growth, while important (as in China's one-child-per-family policy), is not the most essential key to preventing mass starvation and malnutrition. The land is capable of sustaining many more than the current world population, provided it is widely distributed and wisely used. But in the absence of adequate land, fertilizer, water, credit, education, and fair prices to producers, additional hands will go on being created to attempt to bring forth the precious rice or wheat. If conditions of human development and agriculture were shaped with the family farmer in mind, the examples of China, Taiwan, Nicaragua, and Cuba show that population growth would begin to slow down and agricultural production would increase dramatically.

Unfortunately, checking population growth has become caught up in politics. In the 1980s the U.S. government, influenced by religious fundamentalists, cut off aid to overseas family planning programs. Yet these programs have also been pushed by the United States and other governments, international agencies, and TNCs whose interests were threatened by land reform. Population *control*—through, for instance, the U.S. aid program in Bangladesh, which has promoted sterilization of women with the enticement of gifts of cloth—is often looked upon as an efficient way to prevent overpopulation from evolving into a revolution of the hungry. And it can be profitable: Health-threatening contraceptive devices such as the Dalkon Shield and Depo-Provera (which are barred from sale in the United States) can be sold by TNC branch plants abroad. These products not only enrich the manufacturers; they satisfy the home government's desire to increase exports, and they make money for the importing country's elite, some of whom have invested in the company.[32]

• *Seventh, this Third World country's economic objective is industrialization and export-led development, often leading to the neglect of agriculture* and, notably in Latin America and Asia, a dominant role for transnational business. We typically see an economy which, if it is especially poor, keeps to the traditional pattern of exporting primary products (usually only one or two) and importing the developed countries' processed and manufactured goods. The trade and investment practices of both capitalist and socialist developed countries reinforce this pattern.[33] If the Third World country is already semi-industrialized, it probably has moved into the export of manufactured goods and begun importing financial services and advanced technology.

In either case, the country's external dependence increases. TNCs move in to dominate in the industrial sector, a process known as denationalization because local firms are bought up or outcompeted in the marketplace. The Brazilian electrical, pharmaceutical, and automobile industries are examples of this external (mostly U.S.) domination.[34] The larger picture is not very different. TNCs accounted for 28 percent of the entire Third World's industrial output, including 47 percent of Latin America's, in 1972. These giant firms are even more critical to Third World manufactured exports, accounting for 37 percent of total exports (and 25 percent of Latin America's) in that year. Food products, chemicals, and transportation equipment are specific sectors in which the transnationals tend to have controlling interests.[35]

The net result for both the poorest and the richest Third World economies is that they become net importers of food and overall growth becomes unbalanced.[36] In the first instance, which characterizes much of Africa, agricultural diversification and productivity have been undermined by political and commercial opportunism, mainly on the part of local urban officials and traditional powerholders.[37] In the second, these same authorities have linked up with transnational business, banks, and their home government—usually meaning the United States—to give industrialization for export first priority. Foreign investors and banks get the red-carpet treatment: tax and other incentives to attract their money, supportive policies from the World Bank and IMF, and official "development" aid—a fair proportion of which winds up in the pockets of local officials or in secret foreign bank accounts—in order to stimulate manufacturing and convert food-producing land to cash crops for export. Agriculture, once productive enough to meet local needs and generate a surplus for export, now must be supplemented by food imports (again, largely an American operation).[38]

Hunger is a predictable result of agricultural neglect combined with rigid class structures. All other things being equal, there should be enough food for everyone; worldwide, there is a large grain surplus. But distribution of food is not equal. Food may be prohibitively expensive (in the poorest countries, two-thirds of a family's income will be spent just on food); farmers are underpaid, making them reluctant to produce; increasingly large quantities of food will be used for non-human purposes, such as to pay for imported oil or exported to fatten a richer country's cattle;[39] and food imports, including aid (notably, the U.S. P.L. 480 program), have a history of winding up on the tables of the urban well-to-do and the military, or on the black market, rather than in the hands of the poor.[40]

• *Eighth, the neglect of agriculture in the movement to export-led development has profoundly adverse ecological effects.* Time and again it has been shown that the small family farmer, in any society, is more likely than an absentee landlord or large agribusiness to take good care of the land. Topsoil erosion, conversion of prime farmland to nonagricultural uses, overuse of pesticides, and escalating land and produce prices (brought on by concentrated land ownership and energy-intensive production methods) are among the consequences of pushing family farmers off the land.[41] In ecopolitical terms these practices seriously erode the quality of land and water, deepening dependence on foreign grain suppliers and worsening hunger. In the process, as seen throughout Central Africa, once fertile land turns to desert.

Deforestation is the companion to desertification. Conversion of farmland to cattle grazing for export, as in Central and South America, is one way that forests are destroyed and soil erosion sets in on marginal lands to which farmers are displaced. In Brazil's Amazon basin, the clearing of land, or its conversion to pasture, accelerates erosion and lowers rainfall, with major adverse consequences not only for that country's food production but also for the entire planet's oxygen supply and species of insects, plants, and birds.[42] Deforestation is also occurring because, in most of the Third World, wood is the main fuel, and because the developed countries have greatly increased their demand for tropical hardwoods. The clearcutting practices of transnational firms have been instrumental in the latter case.[43] Both desertification and deforestation can be seen not merely as ecological problems, but as part and parcel of underdevelopment and the exploitation of resources mainly for profit.

Corporate hands, local as well as transnational, are also deeply involved in another ecological tragedy: pesticide poisonings. The World Health Organization reports that there are about a half-million cases a year in the Third World. Dumping pesticides, many of which are banned for use in the country of origin, is a common corporate practice. The health consequences for the workers who use them, and for the consumers of the products sprayed with them, do not seem to enter the corporate equation.[44]

Placed beside the impact on urban areas of this kind of Third World growth (toxic waste buildups and extensive air pollution, for example), these ecological disasters round out Sunkel's portrait of the "transnational style of development" referred to earlier. Growth without public accountability and austerity programs that favor transnational (export) businesses give short shrift to ecological considerations.[45] Here is one point where we can see clearly the "interdependence" of developmental models, for what Sunkel describes in Latin America has been happening in the industralized world, East and West, for many decades.

• Ninth, *"development" that favors narrow state and elite interests in our hypothetical Third World country means a huge debt burden for all except the oil-exporting countries of OPEC.* Although all of these oil-importing countries *together* bring in less oil than the United

States, they have suffered the most from the oil price hikes of the 1970s. As the 1980s began, these underdeveloped countries were paying 5.3 percent of their GNP just for oil, almost twice what they had paid only two years earlier.[46] The worldwide recession at that time cut still more into these countries' ability to finance imports. As a result, they had to borrow and borrow again in a desperate effort to pay for oil and other vital imports and to make interest payments on existing debts. The big banks were far from helpful: They had encouraged Third World countries to take advantage of cheap money during the high inflation of the late 1970s, at a time when they were awash in OPEC petrodollars. Now, in the 1980s, the banks are faced with numerous big-ticket customers who cannot even make interest payments on their loans, let alone begin repaying the principal.

Many Third World countries, but particularly the poorest of them, which have neither capital nor plentiful indigenous energy resources, have essentially mortgaged their futures to the lending governments and the major banks. In 1982, for example, Mexico owed $50.4 billion (31 percent of GNP); Brazil, $47.6 billion (17 percent of GNP); South Korea, $20.4 billion (28.3 percent of GNP); Argentina, $15.8 billion (29.5 percent of GNP); Turkey, $15.9 billion (29.7 percent of GNP); Egypt, $15.5 billion (52.8 percent of GNP); and Israel, $14.9 billion (64.6 percent of GNP).[47] By 1985 high interest rates and still more bailout loans had upped the ante dramatically. Mexico, for instance, now owed $95 billion and Brazil about $100 billion. But at least these two are large enough, and *owe* enough, to maintain their credit-worthiness, that is, to keep rolling over their loans. Not so most others.

Interest and service payments on external debt take an ever larger share of an underdeveloped country's export earnings (e.g., nearly 30 percent of Mexico's exports, 20 percent of Turkey's, and 25 percent of Argentina's in 1982.)[48] That figure, too, keeps rising: By the mid-1980s, for example, interest and service payments were devouring nearly *60 percent* of Mexico's and Argentina's export earnings. The prospect of repayment is virtually nil even if (as has not been the rule) bank interest charges were to hold steady or decline. And here is where the power of the IMF and the World Bank is felt, for they hold the keys to more credit and therefore, in most cases, the leverage to enforce cutbacks in social-welfare spending as the price of credit. Third World leaders, in Brazil and Mexico for instance, have shown their displeasure with such pressure, but the great majority of them eventually accede—to the delight of the transnational banks and exporters. The big losers are the middle and lower classes, whose cost of living rises while wages and government social spending are cut back sharply;[49]

and small businesses, which suffer in competition with foreign-owned corporations, and are often absorbed by them or go bankrupt.[50]

A common misperception about this cycle of indebtedness is that Third World countries are soaking up huge amounts of capital in loans and other forms of aid and returning virtually nothing to lenders. The truth of the matter is quite different. For one thing, the wealthiest citizens deposit enormous sums in the same foreign banks that made loans to their governments. Mexico is a particularly striking case of such capital flight. For another, World Bank loans to the Third World return a handsome profit: $1.2 billion in fiscal year 1986. Actually, *net* transfers from the World Bank and the IMF to the Third World have been moving toward zero in the 1980s. The reasons? Mainly, that interest payments on loans remain staggeringly high while development aid has been declining.[51]

• *Tenth, repression becomes an indispensable tool of social order.* In circumstances of gross and obvious inequality, in which national sovereignty is (or seems to be) sold out to foreigners, a Third World regime inevitably falls back on police power to maintain itself. It has already alienated peasants, ethnic minorities, and the impoverished; now it starts to lose many traditional supporters of authoritarianism, such as local businesses, the church hierarchy, and sometimes nationalist elements of the military. "Social discipline"—i.e., the national security state, as in Chile under General Augusto Pinochet and El Salvador under Jose Napoleon Duarte—becomes the order of the day: vigilantism in the form of death squads; censorship of the press and radio; disruption and elimination of political opposition and organized labor. Politics is encapsulated within a seemingly permanent state of siege. Foreign support from both the capitalist and the socialist camps (in arms, computers, economic aid, and numerous other means of repression and sustenance) becomes increasingly critical to the regime's survival.[52]

As has already been suggested, there are likely to be severe economic as well as civil-liberties costs from the shift to outright authoritarianism. One careful study concludes that "the economic effects of military expenditure [in the Third World] have been negative. . . . [T]o the extent that military expenditure does produce economic growth, the poorest members of Third World societies are the least likely to benefit from that growth."[53] The negatives include increased indebtedness, reduced capital for other kinds of investment, and the siphoning off of skilled workers by the arms industry.

• *Eleventh, repression goes hand in hand with the further concentration of political power.* The elite's base and its apex narrow. In some cases, it may assume the form of the absolutist state, as in Iran under

the Shah and, evidently, again under Khomeini. In pursuit of despot-
ism, the Shah had tight control over the military, a secret police force
of several thousand agents (the CIA-trained SAVAK) and the flow of
money and political favors. Having enormous oil earnings to work
with, he purchased a huge inventory of the most advanced weapons
from the United States which, had he remained in power, would have
made Iran the fourth largest military force in the world. Yet the Shah
turned a blind eye to corruption, the expansion of the state bureau-
cracy, and declining agricultural production.[54]

Should political order give way to social chaos, the military can be
expected to step in to "save the nation from the politicians and the
communists/capitalists." Military coups have become a trademark of
Third World politics: There were ninety of them (thirty-seven in Africa
alone) from 1960 to 1982, resulting in an average of sixteen years of
military rule.[55] Military governments seem to engage in even more
widespread repression than their civilian counterparts.[56] But whether
directly running the country or exerting influence backstage, the military can usually count on acquiring expensive weapons from abroad
to deal with supposed threats to "national security." Not coinciden-
tally, the most repressive Third World governments have been among
the major arms importers of recent years, and several of them—Argentina (before 1984), South Korea, Taiwan, Ethiopia, and Vietnam—had
significant military influence at the top.

• *Twelfth, underdevelopment and its frequent companions,
repression and civil war, lead to the large-scale flight of people and
their skills*. Those who are not trapped by poverty, famine, and warfare and have the means to flee are likely to do so, to judge from refugee statistics.[57] Over 3 million people have left Afghanistan and over
1.5 million have fled from Indochina. In El Salvador, where the fighting
and inadequate public health have decimated the population, over
350,000 persons have fled their homes.[58] Perhaps 2 million undocumented Mexican workers, peasant farmers who are victims of agricultural "modernization" at home, are estimated to be in the United States.
Such huge numbers of people strain the resources of any host country,
but obviously the poorest most of all.[59] Famine and warfare in Africa
created over a million refugees for the Sudanese government at a time
of severe drought. A quarter-million Cambodian refugees who have set
up shelters along the border area in Thailand are a major problem for
the Thai government, since these camps are periodically attacked by
Vietnamese troops. Many of the refugees who find their way to North
America and Western Europe are professionals. They are very unlikely
to return to their native country—a gain for their adopted land, but a
costly loss in desperately needed skills for their homeland. This famil-

iar "brain drain" adds to the already monumental human and social costs of underdevelopment and war.

CASE STUDIES OF CRISIS AND RENEWAL

China: Revolution and Transformation

In a political fable familiar to every Chinese, Mao Zedong told in 1945 of "The Foolish Old Man Who Removed the Mountains." Defying the skeptics, the old man announced he and later generations would keep digging until the two great mountains that obstructed his way were leveled. Mao's point was that China's underdevelopment could likewise be conquered:

> Today, two big mountains lie like a dead weight on the Chinese people. One is imperialism, the other is feudalism. The Chinese Communist Party has long made up its mind to dig them up. We must persevere and work unceasingly, and we, too, will touch God's heart. Our God is none other than the masses of the Chinese people. If they stand up and dig together with us, why can't these two mountains be cleared away?[60]

The Chinese revolution won out four years later, and the equally difficult struggle began to implement the revolution's objectives: the transformation of the economy, of the people, and of the international order. A good part of the "two big mountains" has now been dug up, and yet the socialist modernization of China, which its leaders have always regarded as being central to the country's domestic and international security, is still only in its initial stages.

To appreciate the extraordinary changes that have occurred in postrevolutionary China, and particularly in the quality of life of its over 1 billion people, we must take account of what China looked like on the eve of the communist victory. Its industry, transportation, and communications were in near-total disrepair. Inflation was rampant; paper money was worthless. "Government" had reverted to the traditional system dominated by clans and landlords and their private military forces. Landlord-class control in rural China meant that, taking the country as a whole, about 10 percent of the rural families owned just over half the land.[61] Poor and still poorer farmers were the mainstay of the population, constantly victimized by the weather, landlord usury, exorbitant rent and land taxes, and extortion—all of which conspired to force the sale of children, female powerlessness, hunger, illiteracy, indebtedness far into the future, and early death. Worst of all, poor peasants assumed these conditions were meant to be and were unalterable.[62]

The first business of the communist movement was to empower peasants to believe in the possibilities of change for the better. Central to that objective was the land question: land ownership, organization, and increased production. For, as one witness wrote, "Without understanding the land question one cannot understand the Revolution in China, and without understanding the Revolution in China one cannot understand the world."[63] Before 1949, the Chinese Communist Party (CCP) carried out a modest land reform and rent reduction program in areas it controlled. The program mainly benefited poor and middle peasants at the expense of the landlord class. Afterwards, in the 1950s, the CCP instituted a radical collectivization of the countryside, where 80 percent of the people still live. People's communes were established that placed both economic and political decisionmaking in large (and eventually unwieldy) clusters of villages. The leaders, with Mao the driving force, formulated an integrated plan of economic development in which agricultural growth would feed into, and be expanded by, heavy and light industry. Self-reliant development was the guideline from 1958 on: Economic growth was based overwhelmingly on Chinese resources; foreign trade was kept small and in balance; and China's debts were paid off by the mid-1960s. State economic planning was highly centralized and inflexible, reflecting Soviet influence; but local initiative, by peasants and factory workers as well as party cadres, was strongly encouraged. Those who exemplified the revolution's ideals of self-reliance, initiative, thrift, and readiness to "serve the people" were held up as models of the "new socialist person."

Converting revolutionary ideals to reality was regarded as a fundamentally political problem and not merely a matter of economic management. The vehicle was class struggle—"continuous revolution"—the most visible form of which was periodic mass movements or campaigns. As Mao conceived of them, their purposes were to sustain revolutionary momentum and prevent "backsliding" by cadres into bad habits, such as bureaucratism, use of coercion and monetary incentives to increase production, careerism, and failure to consult with peasants and workers—what the Chinese called "mass-line democracy." The approach typified Maoist politics, at once authoritarian and participatory. But these movements, notably the last of them (the "Great Proletarian Cultural Revolution," which lasted from 1966 to 1969), also entailed a good deal of chaos and unplanned violence because of official encouragement of "struggle" against real and imagined class enemies. The economy and the educational system were badly disrupted. People's morale flagged under the weight of constant mass campaigns and the disruptions they caused to their lives. The Maoist faction was willing to accept these negative effects as the price of ensuring that future generations of Chinese would be reliable revolutionary successors, and that Chinese socialism would not degenerate into "state bureaucratic capitalism" of the Soviet type. Mao's opponents, notably Deng Xiaoping, disagreed. They are now in charge.

Whereas Mao favored mass-line politics because he was suspicious of intellectuals and organizations (including the CCP), upon his death and the ouster of a competing "ultra-left" faction (the Gang of Four) in October 1976, his successors strove for social unity and economic stability. They relaxed social controls, sharply de-emphasized class struggle, substituted market and material incentives (profits, bonuses, managerial autonomy) for ideological ones, dismantled the communes, upheld individual achievement and specialization in education, the workplace, and management, and announced an "open door" for foreign capital and technology. This new system, firmly in place since the end of 1978, remains socialist in that it is state-directed and therefore still highly centralized and bureaucratized. But it is a distinct alternative to the Maoist era. There is more scope than ever before for individual and corporate initiative, for competence and professionalism, and for personal enrichment.

Considering the vast demographic and geographic problems any Chinese leadership must face—for instance, a very youthful population, 65 percent of which is under thirty; great differences in land and water quality and availability; and some sixty minority groups—it is difficult to exaggerate how much security and dignity the ordinary Chinese has acquired in so short a time. To begin with, there is the system's ability to meet the basic needs of an overwhelming majority of these people.[64] They have land, food, housing, medical care, and old-age insurance at extremely low cost. Health care, built around prevention and paramedical workers (the "barefoot doctors" program, recently terminated) in the rural areas, is widely regarded as one of the world's finest for delivering service where it is most needed. Emphasis on children's health has meant an extremely low infant mortality rate (67 per 1,000). The daily average caloric intake of Chinese (2,526) is one of the highest among lower-income Third World countries. Life expectancy (sixty-five for men, sixty-nine for women) is high and contrasts with the usual Third World pattern for women. Primary-level education is universal; secondary and higher education is extensive compared with other Third World societies. The longstanding emphasis on labor-intensive production and (until recently) state assignment of jobs has meant a low unemployment rate—but also inefficient use of labor and insufficient pay for the most productive workers.

Increased productivity is now being spurred by higher wages for urban workers and higher returns to individual peasant households on their output. The results so far are encouraging: Between 1978 and 1986, per capita income rose 160 percent in rural areas and 30 percent in urban areas (after adjusting for inflation); unemployment dropped from 5.3 to 2 percent; and people's savings increased over ten times.[65] China's agricultural reforms and production compare very favorably with the stagnation of Soviet agriculture, where grain output has declined since 1978, largely due to a lack of incentives to farmers to produce more.[66] Although generalizations about public opinion are especially perilous in the case of China, the observations of numerous visitors and Chinese polls suggest that, on the whole, working people have responded very positively to the new production and consumption opportunities afforded by the post-Mao policies.

Other signs point to how far Chinese society has progressed, whether one compares today's China with prerevolutionary periods or with other Third World countries. Even with greater play now being given to individual rather than collective performance, income distribution falls within a narrow range: about a one-to-four ratio between the top and bottom 20 percent of the population.[67] The Chinese women's liberation movement has resulted in tremendous gains in local-level (but not top-level) leadership, economic opportunities and rewards, education, and family rights. The Marriage Law of 1950, revised in 1981, bestows a number of legal guarantees for women and children not found in many Western societies with respect, for instance, to marriage, divorce, and property disposition.

Population growth, now regarded by the leadership as the main threat to modernization, has been reduced to slightly over 1 percent annually. (The goal is ambitious and probably unachievable: zero growth and a population of 1.2 billion by the year 2000.) A combination of measures has been used: social pressure, the general limitation of one child to a family, and the wide availability of various birth control methods, including free abortions and vasectomies. Environmental protection began early in the PRC's history with nationwide afforestation, massive flood control projects, and pest control. These continue today, augmented by waste recycling and the first serious efforts to deal with urban air and water pollution.

Civil liberties have always been restricted in China. Periods of "letting a hundred flowers bloom," during which intellectual and artistic freedoms were officially encouraged and criticism of the leadership was permitted, have typically been followed by crackdowns on dissenters. But the debate between intellectual freedom and state control is at least being conducted more openly today. Personal movement has also always been subject to state regulations. Yet in 1985 there were about 40,000 Chinese studying abroad in over thirty countries, a development of potentially far-reaching importance for the individuals involved and for China's economy. The role of law may also be changing. Only recently has a legal code been drawn up and a clear judicial structure been established, these in response to past abuses and the absence of clear avenues of appeal. Yet foreign lawyers and jurists who visited China even before these reforms remarked on the virtues of a legal system that emphasized popular involvement and conciliation— "law without lawyers."[68] Nevertheless, such informal processes normally did not (and do not) apply in "political" cases. As indicated by the crackdowns on human-rights protesters in 1978 to 1979, and on party intellectuals who, in 1987, called for Western-style democracy, political dissent is still not dealt with charitably in China. The country has its share of political prisoners.[69]

From an official Chinese point of view, socialism has fulfilled those human rights that count the most: national self-determination and the elimination of an exploitive economic system so that the economy could serve mass needs and China could become strong enough to earn international respect.[70] Civil and political freedoms are regarded as promoting individual interests and elitist, factional politics. Noncommunist and communist Chinese governments alike have typically denounced "Westernization" of that kind as being an obstacle to economic development. Considering China's history of exploitation from within and without, this view of human rights is understandable. It stems from a deep-seated pride that China's achievements in social and economic justice have cemented national sovereignty rather than sold it out as the price of "development." But insofar as that view rationalizes excessive concentration of power in state and party organs, it leaves much to criticize.

China's international position is probably more secure today than ever before in its modern history. It is not deeply in debt (the foreign debt is about $4 billion); foreign investment (just over $20 billion committed by the end of 1986) is a new but still very small factor in China's economy; and military spending, once about 15 percent of the GNP, declined to 7.5 percent in 1985 to permit greater public spending on consumer needs. The island province of Taiwan, although still a long way from becoming part of the mainland system, has been offered terms for reconciliation that would grant it considerable autonomy. These may be hard for Taiwan's anticommunist leadership to resist for many years more, especially now that Britain and Portugal have agreed to the return to China of Hong Kong in 1997 and Macao in 1999.

China's historical dilemma is how to adapt Westernization, preserve the civilization's "essence," and transform weakness into strength. The response of China's post-Mao leadership is a strategy of "socialist modernization" that relies on an open door rather than self-reliance. Whether or not such a strategy can continue to improve the quality of life of China's people is a major issue both for China and for the world, as much now as in 1949.

South Africa: The Apartheid Regime

The Republic of South Africa is the only state in the world whose political legitimacy and economic stability rest on racial domination: the system and ideology of apartheid. A white settler minority of under 5 million (mainly English and Dutch descendants) controls all the instruments of power in a country of over 22 million Africans, 2.5 million persons of mixed race ("coloureds"), and over 800,000 Indians. In the face of mounting, increasingly violent resistance to its rule, the apartheid regime uses every source of leverage at its disposal—from modest social reforms to indiscriminate terror—to maintain its power and a fast-eroding international support.

South Africa has become a pariah in the international community. Pledged to support the UN Charter and Declaration of Human Rights, it has consistently been condemned by the organization for gross violations of their provisions. Blacks are not permitted to vote or hold political office. Until 1986 their movements were restricted by the infamous pass laws, or influx control measures. These required that blacks carry small passport-type identity books at all times, helping to restrict rural-to-urban migration. Persons without a pass book were arrested (on average, about 200,000 such arrests a year). The Group Areas Act, lack of housing, and government "emergency" legislation ensure, however, that, pass laws or no, nonwhites will stay in residential and business areas the government has designated for them. (Under its resettlement program, the government has moved over 4 million nonwhites to new areas, many by force.) The still-larger official plan is to get Africans out of South Africa altogether. Ten bantustans, or "homelands," have thus far been established within South African territory; four have been proclaimed independent states but recognized as such only by South Africa. Africans have been reduced in status to migrant workers, citizens without a country.[71]

Blacks who seek to express their human rights in South Africa run a risk of being imprisoned—South Africa having the highest imprisonment rate in the world—and worse. A variety of "internal security" acts legalize repression. Blacks who, for instance, protest or organize against apartheid or speak out (in or outside the country) for economic sanctions against the government are guilty of subversion. At its discretion, the government may hold such persons without trial, charge, or communication with the outside. (This is precisely what happened in 1986, after the pass laws were abolished to appease international opinion. A state of emergency gave the minister of law and order sweeping and uncontestable powers of arrest, search and seizure, and censorship in "unrest areas." South African sources conservatively estimated that 20,000 people, perhaps one-third of them children, were detained without charge during the year.) Torture and isolation techniques are commonplace; several black leaders (among them, Steve Biko) have died in prison. In some cases, persons and groups critical of the government have been silenced by a form of internal exile known as banning. Rigid censorship laws make it extremely difficult for antiapartheid books to be sold or for those newspapers not intimidated by the government to report police detentions or quote black leaders without themselves being jailed. Arbitrary searches of people's homes by the police occur frequently.

Denial of basic human rights to blacks and others extends to economic and social injustices. They are severely restricted as to where they can do business or own land. The "homelands" to which they are confined comprise about 13 percent of the land; it is the least arable in the country. Black workers could not, until recently, join labor unions; now these are exclusively for blacks and are subject to strict government regulation. Only a few of them have the funds or membership to be politically powerful. Racial segregation continues to exist in education and most public places; the few hotels, restaurants, and theaters that serve blacks need special government permits.

Racial injustice is also reflected in the distribution of economic and social rewards and opportunities. Whites typically earn five times the pay of blacks and hold the top positions in all industries. The average South African white will live thirteen years longer than a black, will eat twice as well, and is over fifty times more likely to have access to a doctor. An African child will on average receive about eight times less money for education and is about twenty times more likely than a white child to die in infancy.

To understand why the white minority leadership clings so tenaciously to apartheid, we must briefly note its origins.[72] Apartheid evolved from colonial exploitation of native labor to the point where racism, like other forms of inhumanity, became deeply structured into the country's way of life. Contrary to both traditional and Marxist concepts of modernization, racial distinctions in South Africa were neither eased nor erased by economic growth. Instead, they intensified as

South Africa "developed." This occurred primarily to accommodate changes in the economy and the emergence of new social classes. But apartheid was also strengthened, as we have heard Biko explain it, because racism took on a life of its own as whites came to "actually believe that black is inferior and bad." In the modern era, apartheid, although fundamentally a cover for exploitive racism, has broadened into a nationalist ideology designed to appeal to all of the country's whites.[73]

The first white settlers came to South Africa in 1652 in the employ of the Dutch East Indian Company. Those who stayed took up farming, gradually penetrated the interior, and ousted the natives from the best lands. In 1806 the British occupied the cape and began to colonize it, pushing the Dutch descendants (the Boers) into African tribal lands, which they seized and proclaimed states. In the 1800s, when diamonds and gold were discovered in these regions, the British invaded. What had once been an agricultural (and largely subsistence) economy based on African labor was dramatically transformed into a mining economy based on foreign capital, urbanization, and a cheap, reliable (therefore controlled) African work force. After South Africa's independence from Britain in 1910, British investors and Boer nationalists set aside their conflicts in a common effort to maintain white authority, exclude Africans from the political process, and ensure an adequate labor supply. All the restrictive race laws mentioned earlier flowed from these objectives.

South Africa's contemporary leadership, based in the National Party, owes its political domination to successful appeals to white purity, nationalism, and anticommunism. As its leader said in 1948, after the party had won the general election and formed the first entirely Afrikaner (Dutch-descended settler) government:

> [Will] the European race in the future be able to maintain its rule, its purity and its civilization, or will it float along until it vanishes for ever, without honour, in the Black sea of South Africa's non-European population? . . . Will the ever encroaching and all destroying communist cancer be checked, or will it be further allowed to undermine our freedom, our religion, our own South African nationhood and our European existence, our honourable traditions and our racial and civil peace?[74]

Such an agenda demands repressive methods for its fulfillment. By the same token, it also invites resistance.

With a logic common to all repressive systems, exploitation in South Africa has been met with increasing resistance, which has set in motion more indiscriminate official violence, more restrictive laws, and better organized resistance. Beginning with a strike of African mine workers in 1946, black resistance has developed principally along two lines. The African National Congress (ANC), founded in 1912 on a policy of noncooperation, has long been fighting a guerrilla war directed from its headquarters in Lusaka, Zambia. It seeks to make South Africa "ungovernable" through armed struggle in white areas and against black collaborators. Nelson Mandela, once its leader, has been in jail since the early 1960s. Black trade unions are a second line of resistance. Representing upwards of 300,000 mine, food processing, and metal workers, the unions focus on strikes and other job actions.[75]

Overarching these two forces is the powerful voice of nonviolent resistance of the black church, represented by the 1984 Nobel Peace Prize winner, Bishop Desmond Tutu. Although Tutu distinguishes his advocacy from Gandhian nonviolence, saying that one cannot turn the other cheek in the face of Hitlerian tactics, he urges "peaceful change" as the only alternative to "Armageddon." Tutu's message has been spurned by the South African leadership, but it has been picked up by other whites who agree that a bloody civil war will engulf the country unless substantial concessions are made to black interests.

There have always been South African whites, even in the parliament, who have protested apartheid; and since 1985 some, major business and political leaders, for the most part, have defied the government by meeting with ANC leaders. The concerns of these whites have evolved with the economy, that is, to an emphasis less on state enforcement of racism than on the assurance of labor stability and continued foreign investment.[76] But their concept of social reforms stops short of challenging the racial order; and it may be a classic case of too little, too late. Unlike Tutu, who insists (like all black political leaders) on the complete dismantlement of apartheid and acceptance of the "one person, one vote" principle, white liberals emphasize economic gains that will eventually trickle down to blacks. Evidently fearing "another Rhodesia"—there, whites lost political privileges when black revolutionaries turned out the ex-colonial regime and proclaimed the new state of Zimbabwe in 1980—these whites argue that only continued "growth" and foreign investment can create a just society.[77] But South Africa's history argues the opposite case: Economic growth has been the basis of ever more "sophisticated" forms of racial domination. And by the mid-1980s, as the violence escalated on all sides, it was hard to see how, even if repression proved temporarily successful again, black leaders could be satisfied with anything short of real political power-sharing.

Just how crucial economic expansion is to the apartheid system becomes plain when we look at the role of foreign capital. The major transnational corporations and banks, principally British and U.S., do business in South Africa for all the usual reasons: a "safe" investment climate; high profitability (higher, in fact, than the worldwide average); cheap labor; and hard, convertible currency.[78] Retaining foreign business confidence is, certainly in the eyes of the white elites, the key to its continued predominance. "Another Rhodesia" to them means not only a black revolution but, perhaps even more, the abandonment of foreign support, just as happened when Washington and London presided over the transfer of power in Zimbabwe. If most foreign, and especially U.S., investments and loans should cease or be withdrawn, the impact would be calamitous for the regime. A major source of investment capital would dry up (meaning over $4 billion in U.S. loans and investments alone); the regime's ability to repay its substantial foreign debt (about $24 billion in 1986) and support very large military and police forces (which absorb roughly 20 percent of the state budget and account for about the same percentage of all Africa's military spending) would be undermined; loans from multilateral sources, such as South Africa has received from the IMF, would be cut off; important markets for South African exports would probably shrink; and critical sources of both advanced technology (in, for example, mining, automobiles, and especially computers, which have internal security applications) and fuel (from the major oil companies) would be lost.[79]

That most U.S. and other corporations and banks have not ceased operations in South Africa, and will do all they can (including promoting modest political and economic reforms) to stay there, is understandable in light of the attractions a "stable" and profitable country offers. But stability not only depends on the maintenance of apartheid in some form, it also requires that governments support their corporations. Once again in South Africa, we see the happy marriage of Corporate Globalism and Realism. Pro-Western governments have consistently supported investments and loans in South Africa for two primary reasons, both rooted in "national security": the strategic minerals that South Africa exports and the white minority regime's anticommunism.

South Africa accounts for significant percentages of world production of a number of precious minerals: antimony (16 percent), chrome (27 percent), diamonds (18 percent), manganese (24 percent), and uranium (15 percent). Equally significant amounts of these and other minerals are imported from South Africa by the United States, such as 55 percent of its chromium (used in making stainless steel), 49 percent of the platinum group of metals (used as catalysts in industry), and 39 percent of manganese (used in steelmaking). Pretoria relies on this dependence for its political leverage to retain U.S. support. The economic dependence of South Africa's landlocked, labor-poor neighbors also helps its cause. But South Africa's best asset is its vigorously anticommunist line, which has always found a receptive audience among U.S. policymakers concerned about black revolutionaries overrunning southern Africa. The overthrow of Portuguese colonialism in Angola and Mozambique and of British colonialism in Rhodesia in the 1970s confirmed to U.S. officials the threat of "Soviet encroachment" on the wings of African nationalism. This fear fits perfectly with the South African regime's activities: its suppression of domestic political opponents (who are invariably labeled "communists" or "terrorists"); its armed intervention in Angola, a socialist neighbor; and its self-described role as a "bulwark" of capitalist stability in Africa.[80]

Various U.S. administrations have therefore subscribed to the call for evolutionary, peaceful change in South Africa made by liberal whites there and by transnational businesses. Clearly, the intersection of business and "national security" interests explains that policy much better than concern about the fate of human rights for the majority population.[81] "Constructive engagement" and "quiet diplomacy," as U.S. policymakers have variously termed their approach, are oriented to preserving U.S. stakes in South Africa—and even expanding them, as in the case of nuclear energy cooperation in the 1980s—while nudging the Pretoria regime to implement reforms sufficient to keep the social pot from boiling over.

Substantial political and social change in South Africa, it is clear in the mid-1980s, will not be inspired by governments or transnational corporations. Full-scale civil war in the country is a distinct possibility. The "invisible hand" that may prevent a massive bloodletting is the transnationalization of the apartheid issue. Concerned citizens in the United States, Britain, and other countries whose TNCs support apartheid with their investments have responded to Bishop Tutu's appeal for help. Through their efforts, a number of U.S. city and state governments, universities, labor unions, and other institutions that own the stocks and bonds of corporations doing business in South Africa have stopped investing in them or have divested altogether. Some corporations have already pulled out of South Africa in the face of such pressure and in the belief a black political victory is only a matter of time. Others have ceased making new investments or have sold their affiliates to local (white) businessmen. Whether South Africa will follow the path of a revolution or of a negotiated settlement among its own citizens is uncertain at this writing. What *is* clear is that sustained global anguish about South Africa has made it impossible for governments and corporations to sweep the human tragedy of apartheid under the rug any longer.

Nicaragua: Human Rights Under Fire

When a revolutionary movement takes power, as the Sandinistas did in Nicaragua on July 19, 1979, they are likely to confront almost immediate opposition from two quarters. Within, they must deal with social forces that were allied with and prospered from the old guard, now overthrown. Without, they can expect to be treated as enemies by the hegemonic power with which the old guard had been closely tied economically and militarily. The Chinese and Vietnamese revolutionaries went through these experiences; in the 1980s it was the Sandinistas' turn. Having eliminated the dictatorship of the Somoza family that had reigned for over forty years, the new government was soon at war again once it set the wheels of a social revolution in motion. And, as had happened on seven previous occasions when the United States had intervened militarily in Nicaragua to preserve its "interests" (the first in 1894, the last between 1927 and 1933), a small country's sovereignty was being disputed by a big power playing (so it believed) for global stakes.[82]

The tragedy of postrevolutionary Nicaragua is that its people had already paid a terrible price in their struggle for self-determination. Fifty thousand Nicaraguans—about 2 percent of the population—lost their lives and some 100,000 were wounded during the twenty-year civil war. Hundreds of millions of dollars were lost in physical damage and capital flight. The Somozas left behind a national debt of about $1.5 billion, putting the government in immediate need of aid to finance debt repayment and necessary imports. At the time of the Sandinistan takeover, the people suffered from high malnutrition, illiteracy of over 50 percent, official unemployment of 22 percent, and extremely high rates of death among infants and children under fourteen.[83]

Added to these deplorable social conditions were the familiar outlines of class domination.[84] Thirty percent of national income was in the hands of five percent of the population, whereas the bottom half of society shared fifteen percent. Over half the farmland was controlled by fewer than 2,000 landholders, who used it mostly for grazing cattle and raising crops for export. Meanwhile, a third of the peasant farmers were landless. The Somoza family had its hands in every major sector of the economy, from coffee to cattle. It owned half of the largest farms and one-fourth of all industry.

Against this background of decay and inequity, the Sandinistas' paramount objective of economic transformation is understandable. They began by planning a mixed economy based on an expanded state sector, a reformed private sector, and a new cooperative sector. All natural resources, foreign trade, and the bankrupt financial system were nationalized. The government took control of the Somoza family's properties. But large private producers were given bigger roles than the state in the agro-industrial and export agricultural sectors. Thus far, in fact, the state and cooperative sectors are a minority of the total economy (less than 30 percent), although that share is scheduled to more than double by 1990. Foreign investments were permitted to remain, although under tighter regulation than ever before. Over three-fourths of arable land was redistributed to farm cooperatives and individual small producers, to whom the government made low-interest loans (triple the number under Somoza).

Immediately after the revolution, the Sandinistas launched a series of mass mobilization campaigns to implement social democracy.[85] Here lies the key to assessing human rights in Nicaragua today. In education, a national literacy crusade was responsible for lowering the illiteracy rate from 50.3 percent to 12 percent in 1980. This volunteers' program, which emphasizes rural school construction, has reversed many decades of state neglect. In health care, government spending likewise shifted to the rural areas. A public health campaign mobilized 80,000 volunteers to carry out vaccinations, environmental sanitation, malaria control, and other preventive programs in the countryside. Volunteers also helped to set up numerous health posts, staffed by nursing aides and physicians. As a result, 70 percent of the population now has regular contact with medical care. Thousands of people have access to water safe for drinking and to latrines and housing for the first time. United Nations agencies and many other international groups have lauded these achievements.

Even more striking has been Nicaraguan progress in growing food for its own consumption and creating a surplus for export. They are reversing the prerevolutionary pattern of malnutrition and export dependence.[86] Under the Somozas, Nicaragua's agriculture had been heavily weighted in favor of the largest landowners. Nearly 70 percent of GNP was invested in agricultural exports, virtually all agricultural credit went for export crops, and basic grains that could have been produced at home were being imported in increasing amounts. It was an economic situation that *required* repression to maintain it, and that is precisely what the U.S.-created National Guard had carried out. The Sandinistas, by contrast, have stressed local production of basic foods, such as corn and beans, and increased output of the traditional exports of cotton, coffee, and sugar. To achieve these goals it has designed a program of incentives for small producers that includes credit, higher prices for crops, increased availability of consumer goods, and the opening up of idle lands to peasants for planting food crops. And by taking control of foreign trade, the government has ensured against the export of needed crops.[87]

These major social strides have taken place in the midst of flagrant U.S. economic and military pressure. What began shortly after the revolution as an effort to deny the Nicaraguans food aid and international credit escalated into direct U.S. support and direction of antigovernment forces known as *contras*, or counterrevolutionaries. These rebel forces operate mainly from Honduras to the north, where they comprise a substantial number of former Somoza national guardsmen. Their support from the United States, although small in dollar terms, has seriously depleted Nicaraguan resources, disrupted its economy, and taken the lives of numerous civilians. The "Iran-Contragate" scandal that rocked the Reagan administration in 1987 brought out the extent of U.S. involvement, which continued even when banned for a time by Congress. It has included CIA intelligence and training of the *contras*, direct military support to the *contras* and to the Honduran and Costa Rican armed forces, millions of dollars in open and secret aid by U.S. allies (such as Saudi Arabia), overflights of Nicaragua, provocative military exercises in neighboring Honduras and off the Nicaraguan coast, the mining of Nicaragua's harbors, and encouragement of private U.S. groups to assist the *contras*. The U.S. objective is officially described as the prevention of Nicaraguan aid to revolutionary groups in nearby El Salvador. But the U.S. State Department has been unable to document any such aid since 1981. The inescapable conclusion is that the U.S. aim is to overthrow the Sandinistas or, if that is militarily impossible, compel them to abandon their social revolution and bargain with the *contras* for political power.

Governments in the midst of civil war frequently restrict political rights. The U.S. civil war is an old example; that of Nicaragua is a recent one. At various times, the Sandinista government has declared a state of emergency and used it to limit opposing views in the press, unions, churches, and political parties. Various individual civil liberties, such as freedom of movement and habeas corpus, have also been denied from time to time. The autonomy of Indian minorities, rarely respected by any Nicaraguan government, has been abused. Yet the revolutionary leadership has hardly been the tyranny Washington has accused it of being. It held popular elections in 1984 that many on-the-scene observers considered fair, pointing out that the Sandinistans received only 67 percent of the vote, that secrecy of the ballot was assured, that 75 percent of those eligible to vote did so even though voting is not legally required, and that the major manipulation of the process came from the U.S. embassy, which tried to persuade the six opposing parties to withdraw from the elections.[88] Political opposition continues, with the three small communist parties being as critical of the Sandinistas as the parties on the right. Religious freedom remains alive amidst vigorous debate within the church between pro- and anti-leftist clergy.

It may well be that the Sandinistas, as some who have left their movement charge, have a limited conception of democratic politics. But the United States, bent on destabilizing Nicaragua as it once destabilized Chile, has shown no interest in giving the new government an opportunity to demonstrate either its independence or its commitment to political pluralism. Washington has instead rejected the World Court's finding (in 1986) that its support of the *contras* violates international law. U.S. officials in fact argue that the World Court lacks jurisdiction in matters affecting Central America. It has also turned aside persistent efforts to negotiate bilateral and regional settlements with Nicaragua under the auspices of the Contadora group (Mexico, Venezuela, Panama, and Colombia). The U.S. government has painted a picture of Nicaragua that serves its domestic political purposes but is wildly distorted—a picture of a brutal dictatorship, subservient to Moscow and Havana and opposed by "freedom fighters" who love democracy. Conveniently ignored is the long history of U.S.-supported authoritarianism in Nicaragua, not to mention the terrorist methods of the *contras*. If the Sandinistas are to complete their agenda of social and economic justice, they will have to do it under the most trying of circumstances—while looking down the barrels of U.S.-made guns.

The Philippines: The Unraveling of a Dictatorship

> Sister Maria has ministered to the rural poor in the Philippines for twenty years. She describes the unrelieved misery of the people—the extreme malnutrition, the sense of powerlessness, the lack of adequate land. And she talks of political decay too: domination of the economy by transnational corporations, of the political system by some eighty families, and of the voting process by corrupt politicians who can buy a vote for a bag of rice. She is particularly distraught by the spiritual impoverishment of her people—their loss of dignity, and their obsequiousness, which she attributes to the Philippines' colonial past. She wants them to stand tall and be able to answer the question, Who am I? Sister Maria is in the United States to visit a sister. She says: "I had to come here to eat a large tomato from my own country."[89]

The Philippines is an archipelago consisting of over 7,000 islands. It has been a colony of Spain, from 1521 to 1898, and of the United States, from 1898 until independence was granted in 1946. Japan occupied the islands during World War II. This history has left deep imprints on every aspect of Filipino life—from the attitudes of its people (their political culture, so to speak) to the educational system (which, with its emphasis on U.S. values and language, is said to have made the Filipino "a foreigner in his own country, speaking a language whose nuances he had not mastered and, at the same time, ignorant of his own cultural heritage").[90] But the most worrisome legacy is the United States' impact on the country's political economy. For in the process of bequeathing a commitment to representative democracy and a market economy, the United States also helped prepare the way for authoritarian rule, machine politics, pervasive official corruption and greed, and widespread inequality.

On February 25, 1986, the twenty-year dictatorship of Ferdinand Marcos abruptly ended. World attention was drawn to his precarious position by the assassination in August 1983 of his leading political opponent, former Senator Benigno Aquino, who was returning from exile in the United States. An official tribunal upheld Marcos's claim that the assassination was the work of a single procommunist agitator, but an overwhelming majority of Filipinos and foreign observers were convinced that Aquino was murdered on orders from the top. His widow, Corazon, carried on, putting together a coalition of disenchanted businesspeople, Catholic church leaders, intellectuals, and ordinary citizens—"people power," as she called it—that dramatically triumphed in a special presidential election. Actually, the Marcos-dominated national assembly declared him the winner. But the election was marked by government fraud and violence on such a huge scale that even Marcos's senior military leaders turned against him. So did the U.S. government, whose representatives were witness to Marcos's grotesque effort to carry on the charade.

Behind the drama of high politics, however, lay a history of social and political problems that Marcos either created or exacerbated, and that will not depart the Philippines with his removal. The country's economy reflects most of the usual dilemmas of outward-oriented development. After declaring martial law in 1972, Marcos gave economic priority to attracting foreign investment to a country with low labor costs, industrial peace, and high profit opportunities. The investments came (those from the United States, the Philippines' major economic and military partner, total about $5 billion) but the results have been disastrous. Agricultural exports, mainly sugar, are subject to sharp price fluctuations and heavy competition for markets. In the 1980s the sugar economy was in serious trouble, pushing many farm families to the brink of survival. Foreign control of key industries, such as sugar and banking, is extensive. Economic mismanagement and corruption (see below) add to this dependence. One set of consequences has been the failure of numerous local businesses, the flight of capital abroad ("about $2 million a day since mid-1982"),[91] a sharp decline in GNP and employment, a very low rate of worker productivity compared to other Southeast Asian countries, and inflation of around 40 percent. Another consequence is indebtedness: The foreign debt, which was about $2 billion in 1970, reached $29 billion in 1984.[92] Marcos's regime by then had become a virtual stepchild of the World Bank and the IMF, constantly readjusting the economy to their dictates in order to stave off a day of reckoning. As of 1986 the Philippines was the sixth largest recipient of World Bank funds.

The central role of the Marcos regime in economic management also accounts for the crumbling of his authority. Economic power was increasingly concentrated in the government's hands and was used to reward a privileged few in and around the official family. Two of Marcos's friends, for example, held near-monopoly control of coconuts and sugar.[93] His wife, the mayor of Manila and a political power in her own right, had millions of dollars invested at home—and probably abroad. When the government was dealing with the U.S. Export-Import Bank on the financing of a controversial (and now-completed) purchase of a nuclear reactor, a Marcos cousin-in-law and close friend acted as go-between. He reportedly received a multimillion-dollar bribe and subcontracted the insurance and construction work to firms which he controlled.[94] Marcos's confidantes controlled the country's banks and its major newspapers. Public spending on projects such as the nuclear plant, office complexes, and other showcase structures was not only terribly wasteful, it enriched the political and military elite at the expense of an impoverished majority.

The real Philippines lies just behind the corporate and government offices:

> A 1971 University of Philippines study reports that 69 percent of the rural people live below the poverty line. In 1975 that proportion rose to 71.3 percent. Malnutrition plagues 70 percent of the population and, according to the Food and Nutrition Research Institute, malnutrition causes fully 40 percent of the mortality. . . . In Metro-Manila, 1.5 million people live in slums. In the countryside there are 4 million landless squatters.[95]

Predictably, it is precisely in the areas of greatest poverty that a leftist guerrilla movement, the New People's Army, has had its major successes. Numbering perhaps 15,000 soldiers, by 1985 the NPA was operating in nearly all of the Philippines' seventy-three provinces. It probably cannot score a military victory over the professional army, which has been well-armed by the United States but is riddled with corruption and nepotism. But the NPA's rapidly increasing strength attests to deteriorating conditions in the countryside.

Political rights also suffered under Marcos. Martial-law government paved the way for the widespread repression of opposition politicians and publications, a ban on labor strikes, and a massive shift of legal jurisdiction from civil to military courts. Marcos himself estimated that, by November 1975, about 50,000 persons had been arrested and detained under martial-law authority. Amnesty International has reported at length on the torture of martial-law detainees and on the role of some U.S.-trained officers in the torture centers.[96] Suppression of dissent extended to the United States, where Marcos's agents apparently harassed and, in at least one instance, killed his opponents. U.S. authorities evidently knew of these agents' activities.[97]

Under international pressure, martial law formally ended in 1981. But the abuses went on. Preventive detention for one year continued to be used by the regime to arrest and re-arrest those whom it wanted out of the way.[98] A number of clerics who worked with the rural poor were murdered, apparently with the military's approval.[99] That proved to be a profound error in a predominately Catholic country whose church leaders had aligned with the poor.

The political and economic situation in the Philippines was thus ripe for change in the mid-1980s. But other dictators have survived in similar circumstances. And in Marcos's case, he had the advantages that accrue to a leader who is fighting communist guerrillas and is host to major foreign military bases (the U.S. naval base at Subic Bay and the air base at Clark). Marcos had always been able to count on U.S. support based on Realist strategic interests. Why he was toppled nevertheless, and with the United States giving him the final push, is a story worth pondering for its potential global implications.

U.S. disenchantment with Marcos clearly stemmed from the conviction that his excesses and ineptness could no longer be rationalized away. He had outlived his usefulness. The Aquino movement promised a fresh start: It had won the election, it promised an end to human-rights abuses, and (probably most significantly from the standpoint of U.S. interests) it gave no indication of wishing to alter military or economic relations with Washington. Corazon Aquino could hardly be branded a leftist—the fate usually suffered by opponents of U.S.-supported regimes—when the NPA urged a boycott of the election and former Marcos military loyalists defected to her side.

But Marcos's demise was sealed, not determined, by the United States. It was above all the popular strength of Aquino's movement that made it impossible for him to govern. The extraordinary feature of that movement was its ability to mobilize a wide spectrum of the Filipino urban middle class, people who were prepared to defy the thugs, police, and military personnel to ensure that their democratic decision at the polls would not be overturned. Nationwide, Filipinos loyal to Aquino guarded the ballot boxes, some at the cost of their lives. When Marcos proclaimed his intention to stay in power, Filipinos heeded Aquino's call to boycott Marcos-controlled newspapers and businesses and withdraw money from his cronies' banks. And in his final hours, thousands of her supporters surrounded the barracks of rebellious military leaders, putting Marcos's officers in the predicament of having to create a bloodbath in order to impose order. They would not.

Will a new government in the Philippines mean new social and economic priorities? Aquino starts out with an enormous reservoir of popular support and high public expectations. But a program aimed at attacking inequalities has yet to be outlined. Powerful interests that profited under Marcos are likely to put up strenuous resistance to major reforms. The military will surely want to cash in on its late-hour support of Aquino, which could mean opposition to reforms and a high priority to quashing the NPA. Whether or not "people power" can ward off politics as usual will be crucial to the ability of the country, and its millions of impoverished people, to create "another development." Citizens of other similarly situated Third World countries will doubtless be watching the Philippines closely.

South Korea: The Contradictions of an "Economic Miracle"

South Korea, along with Brazil, is one of the most frequently cited examples of successful capitalist economic development in the Third World. Both have enjoyed periods of high growth rates, both have high average incomes, and both rank at the top among underdeveloped countries in average levels of health and education. The overall performance of South Korea—officially, the Republic of Korea (ROK), as distinct from the socialist Democratic People's Republic of Korea (DPRK) in the North—is all the more impressive when we consider that its population is five times less than Brazil's. But to call South Korea an "economic miracle," as it frequently is called, overstates economic reality and ignores the country's politics. For in South Korea, again as in Brazil, one finds major inequities in the distribution of the rewards of economic growth and, consequently, serious human-rights problems.

From 1962, the year in which the government in Seoul introduced its first five-year plan, to 1983, the GNP of South Korea rose from $2.3 to $75 billion. The South Korean government anticipates that the GNP will rise to $100 billion by 1988. Per capita GNP in the same period rose from $87 to $1,800. A striking feature of this income increase is its relatively broad distribution: "the income share of the bottom 40 percent of South Korea's population is comparable to that of Yugoslavia, . . . while the relative gap between the top and bottom quintiles in Korea is less than one-third that of Brazil."[100] At first glance, therefore, it appears that the ROK leadership has found a way to achieve both rapid economic growth and social equity.

The driving force behind this economic growth is the rapid expansion of industrial production for export, which was the cornerstone of the development strategy adopted in 1962. As a result, the weight of the manufacturing sector in the economy has steadily increased. Mining and manufacturing account for over 31 percent of GNP in the 1980s as opposed to 16.2 percent in the 1960s. Ninety-three percent of exports are manufactured goods. Their value rose from $15.3 million in the early 1960s to $24.4 billion in the early 1980s, accounting for almost one-third of total GNP. To many observers, looking at the quality of South Korean electronics, steel, and small automobiles, the country resembles the Japan of not so many years ago.

The first complicating factor in assessing South Korean economic advances is the growing neglect of agriculture. South Korean peasants, once the backbone of the economy, have been hard hit by export-led development. Prior to 1962, peasants had benefited from a large-scale land-to-the-tiller program and state intervention to ensure adequate prices, fertilizer, and credit. Since then, state investment in agriculture has sharply declined, and so have agricultural production, employment, and income. The social consequences are by now familiar to us.[101] Peasants who were not forced into tenancy migrated to the cities, taxing the resources of government and industry. Between 1960 and 1982, South Korea's urban population leaped from 28 percent to 61 percent of the total population.[102] High urban unemployment, shantytowns, and prostitution have become commonplace. Increased grain imports, U.S. rice in particular, have reduced the ROK's once high self-sufficiency. Social services and education are far less available in the rural than in the urban areas.

The actual distribution of income in South Korea may be much less equitable than the official statistics would suggest. It has been argued, for example, that the surveys used to develop the income data were biased by their exclusion of whole categories of the wealthiest and the poorest families. Furthermore, official figures reveal sizable changes in income share over time: up, for the top 20 percent of the population; down, for the bottom 20 percent.[103]

Export-led development has also had unfortunate consequences for urban workers, notwithstanding improvements in employment and public services overall. Wages and working conditions are poor in comparison with other industrialized societies. South Korean industry has one of the world's worst safety records. Its workers, according to a 1980 survey by the International Labor Organization, "worked the longest hours per week of any nation surveyed." Yet various Korean surveys report that upwards of 65 percent of these workers earned well below the minimum monthly costs of living. What is happening is that increased labor productivity is not being rewarded with increases in real wages.[104]

Why? For one thing, wages in export industries are deliberately kept low to keep down the price of Korean goods. For another, female labor is exploited. Women constitute about 50 percent of the industrial work force, and from 70 to 90 percent in such export industries as electronics, clothing, and textiles. Their pay is substantially lower than that of a man performing comparable work. Many skilled males have been sent abroad to scarce-labor countries such as Kuwait. Another basic reason for low wages is that the ROK government prides itself on maintaining a "disciplined" work force. It runs its own unions, as in the DPRK and other socialist countries. The independent unions are kept weak (where they are allowed to exist at all) by laws that proscribe social activism and sharply limit the right to strike. These unions are subject to removal of their leaderships and outright abolishment if their behavior does not conform with government definitions of the social good.

With these controls on wages and workers, as well as special tax and other incentives to TNCs, it is hardly surprising that foreign investors have been attracted to South Korea. The main investing firms are from Japan (about 47 percent) and the United States (29 percent). Yet, unlike Taiwan and Singapore, where direct foreign investment is by far the key source of external capital, South Korea relies on loans, mostly from U.S. sources. Foreign investment accounts for less than 6 percent of the total.[105] South Korean growth, as a result, has been financed with a high rate of foreign indebtedness that its people must eventually pay for out of their pocketbooks. In fact, the ROK is the largest borrower in Asia and the world's fourth largest debtor. Its $20 billion debt in 1982 represented about 28 percent of its GNP (far higher than Brazil's ratio); by 1984 the debt had more than doubled to $41.8 billion, an awesome 60 percent of the GNP.[106]

We see here another weakness of export-led development: its dependence on the openness and strength of other economies to ensure a rising level of imports from countries like the ROK. When trade between South Korea and the United States, its number-one trading partner, was growing at an average of 20 percent annually between 1961 and 1983, the Korean economy could register impressive GNP figures. But when protectionist legislation was enacted in the United States, as happened in the mid-1980s against textile and color television imports, Korean industry was hard hit. A senior ROK trade representative reminded the United States that both sides would be hurt, including "the American banking industry, because they have exposure in Korea."[107] In other words, reduced Korean exports means reduced debt repayments.

A final area of economic weakness is the concentration of market power among very few giant firms.[108] Ten conglomerates in South Korea dominate sales, exports, and bank loans, pointing up the government's central role in economic planning. Korea may be a *growth* miracle, but it is certainly not a miracle of the free market. For Korean consumers, who pay higher prices for the same goods exported abroad, and for Korean small businesses, which have increasing difficulty competing with the conglomerates, state capitalism means reduced opportunity and competition.

While the ROK is thus among the higher-income and best-performing Third World economies, it is far from being a model of equitable development. An additional reason this is so is the country's substantial spending on the military: over 6 percent of GNP (in North Korea it is about 22 percent) in the 1980s and over 35 percent of the government budget. Despite the Korean armistice of 1953, armed clashes on land and at sea occur periodically. Each Korea draws extensively on the resources of its major-power partners—the United States for the South, the USSR and China for the North—to acquire the latest military hardware. A state of war exists throughout the peninsula, justifying not only arms buildups but also widespread domestic repression. The national-security state in South Korea comprises an extensive police and intelligence apparatus that employs the "communist threat" to intimidate, jail, and torture political opponents. South Korea is a much more open political system than is North Korea, as evidenced by many years of student demonstrations and the parliamentary elections of 1984. But the ROK remains a highly authoritarian system.

Political repression is a part of the South Korean "miracle" that even proponents of human rights sometimes downplay.[109] South Korea's need for domestic "order," either to ensure continued economic development or security against threats from the North, becomes a justification for a wide range of well-documented government acts: the arbitrary arrests and detentions of dissenters, official controls on campuses and intellectual freedom, muzzling of the press, use of military courts to dispense justice, harsh treatment of labor agitators, and the torture of internees. U.S. representatives have often had to excuse the shortcomings of Korean democracy—not only the abuses of human rights but also the Korean government's junta-like conception of politics—in the name of the alliance and its common anticommunist commitments. The essential weakness of that approach, its inability to take account of how fragile is a stability that relies heavily on repression, became plain in the remarkable events of 1987.

President Chun had promised to step down at the end of his term in February 1988. The Olympic Games scheduled to take place in Seoul in the summer of 1988 would be a personal and national triumph. Chun's error was to assume that his successor as party leader would automatically also become the next president—that neither opposition leaders, such as Kim Dae Jung, nor Korean citizens and students could effectively challenge Chun's reliance on an electoral process that virtually ensured victory for the ruling elite. What actually happened is that student demonstrations throughout Korea for direct presidential elections were widely supported, notably by the middle class and the Buddhist, Anglican, and Catholic churches. When the demonstrators were assaulted and gassed by the police and army, public sympathy went entirely over to the opposition movement. Even U.S. officials publicly questioned Chun's legitimacy. In an extraordinary development, Chun's heir-apparent pressured him not only to support a constitutional revision that would allow for direct elections, but also to release some 2,000 political prisoners, to commit to honoring civil liberties, and to free Kim Dae Jung from house arrest.

The high drama of events in South Korea may only be a prelude to further confrontations. Whether or not free elections will actually take place, whether or not the military will stay out of politics, how cohesive either the student movement or the opposition party will be—these are among the key issues yet to be resolved. Whatever the outcome, however, one lesson is already clear: Only when the rewards of rapid economic growth are widely shared and are coupled with advances in political and social justice can we legitimately speak of a development "miracle." Chinese modernizers and Filipino reformers alike need to ponder that lesson along with Koreans.

CHAPTER FIVE

Arms and Insecurity in the First World

The two superpowers lie in the same bed, but they do not dream the same dreams.

— China's Premier Zhou Enlai

Security in the nuclear age means common security. Even ideological opponents and political rivals have a shared interest in survival. There must be partnership in the struggle against war itself. . . . International peace must rest on a commitment to joint survival rather than a threat of mutual destruction.

— Independent Commission on Disarmament and Security Issues

. . . if we [the United States and the Soviet Union] cannot end our differences now, at least we can help make the world safe for diversity."

— John F. Kennedy

THE MILITARY CRISIS OF THE FIRST WORLD

There is no Third World problem that is not also a problem in the other two worlds. To be sure, people in the First and Second Worlds are not starving or unemployed in the same staggering proportions we observed in the Third World. But significant numbers of Europeans, North Americans, and Japanese are hungry and jobless. And they face other problems not faced in most Third World countries: living in or near nuclear targets; running a high risk of contracting certain diseases (such as cancer and stroke) and of being victimized by crime; having constant concern for the health and safety of children; being disconnected (alienated) from self, community, and nature. Many such problems are the peculiar consequence of *over*development: superabundance, fast-paced living, technology outrunning thoughtful evaluation. Others are problems we have associated with *under*development, such as the manufacture of toxic chemicals in areas populated by poor minorities. "Institute is like Bhopal—we're in the Third World," said a black teacher when a Union Carbide gas leak occurred in her town of Institute, West Virginia, not long after the same company's tragic accident in India.[1] The millions of people who live in the peripheries of the industrialized world can also become victims of structural violence.

Most all analysts would agree that human needs in the industrialized world *could* be met with existing technical, logistical, and monetary resources. That state leaders of the most "advanced" social systems *choose* not to mobilize these resources for that purpose is a political matter which must be explained in terms of their higher priorities. None is higher than preparedness for war—"national security"— even at the cost of domestic and international political-economic disorder. As a United Nations report stated in 1982, "the world can either continue to pursue the arms race—or move consciously and with deliberate speed toward a more sustainable international economic and political order. *It cannot do both*. The arms race and development are thus in a competitive relationship." The report cited President Eisenhower, who drew the same conclusion in 1953: "Every gun that is made, every warship launched, every rocket fired, signifies, in a final sense, a theft from those who hunger and are not fed, from those who are cold and are not clothed."[2]

This chapter on First World international politics will examine the dangers and costs of the arms race. Nuclear weapons will receive primary attention, although the superpowers' interventions, alliances, and military transfers (such as arms sales) are no less important components of the war crisis. From 1960 to 1981, these activities together absorbed over $3 *trillion* in combined U.S. and Soviet military spending.[3] U.S. and Soviet allies in the Second World are also deeply enmeshed in the war crisis. The European members of NATO and the Warsaw Pact spent over $1 trillion in the same twenty-year period, for example. They themselves are major arms producers and sellers as well as recipients, and together they host most of the U.S. and Soviet troops stationed abroad—roughly 900,000 out of a total of well over 1 million.[4] The next chapter shows, however, that the drive for increased political and economic autonomy by these Second World allies and their preoccupation with developmental concerns such as the environment and energy are the main focus of their global politics. For them, the strategic arms race is to a large extent an imposition.

THE NUCLEAR DANGER

The nuclear question is the subject of an enormous literature that is often complex and even surreal in its discussion of strategy, weapons physics and characteristics, and the outcome of a nuclear exchange. In global perspective, however, answering two questions may help us to rise above the clutter of numbers and arcane language: Do nuclear weapons in fact promote national security, *military* security in particular? Here, we accept the reality of these weapons and challenge their usefulness on their own terms. We then ask, What are the social and economic costs of escalating military expenses, nuclear and otherwise, and how do those costs affect the real security of the superpowers? Once again, we employ an expanded definition of what real security means.

Dealing with the war crisis inevitably begins with assumptions about the causes of war that should be explicitly stated. The Realists, for example, assume that the war system is a natural outgrowth of human beings' innate inhumanity and the corruption of the state system by, among other things, the enemy's expansionist ideologies. To them, nuclear weapons are a necessary evil, the logical outcome of technological sophistication which evolved to deter future (nuclear) war between the two great nuclear powers. Nuclear weapons paradoxically have both heightened and diminished the war crisis: They lend stability to the global balance of terror.

I find this view neither logical nor factual. It tells us we should learn to live with a weapon which all agree must never be used and, if used, might well mean the end of life as we know it. It assigns technology, rather than political economy, the central role in driving the arms race. It perpetuates the myth that nuclear weapons are merely defensive. And it helps sustain the belief that nuclear weapons can be "controlled," when the evidence shows that arms control is far behind the pace set by weapons development and strategies for using them.

My view is that the war crisis, and the nuclear arms race in particular, have their roots in the domestic insecurity of the superpowers. Possessed of a particular way of looking at the world (a global ideology), and harboring the kinds of values previously identified, state leaders in the First World are driven by self-preservation and expansionism. The social systems over which they preside contain vested bureaucratic interests in "national security"—the military-industrial complex—that exist *independently of any actual threats to national survival*. The combination of ideological self-righteousness, conflict-oriented values, and bureaucratic momentum makes preparedness for war a dominating feature of political life, regardless of the system's economic structure. It leads to deliberate exaggeration of the other side's *capabilities* ("We overstate the Soviets' force and we understate ours, and we therefore greatly overstate the imbalance," said former U.S. Secretary of Defense Robert McNamara in 1982).[5] It creates fears about the other side's *intentions* and lofty presumptions about one's

own. It prompts *planning* for the worst case, which maximizes opportunities for *miscalculation* and *misperception* of the other side's
actions.

Ultimately, cold-war politics generates an *expansionist interpretation* of the national interest, leading to ever-larger military budgets,
incentives to develop more deadly weapons, disincentives to negotiate
arms reductions, increasingly tight identification of the work force and
education with the military, restrictions on information and civil liberties in the name of national security, and constant efforts to attract allies to one's side in the worldwide struggle against "them." As we
witness in the U.S.–Soviet arms deadlock today, each side sees itself
embarked on a noble crusade that of necessity must be justified in stereotypic images. "We" are always the epitome of virtue, while "they"
are evil incarnate: angels versus devils. Thus, in 1977, President Brezhnev declared that the USSR "will never embark on the path of aggression and will never lift its sword against other peoples"[6]—this, one year
before the invasion of Afghanistan—while in 1983 President Reagan
characterized the Soviet Union as the "focus of evil in the modern
world." Such mirror imagery has long been noted by psychologists; it
is one element of mutual reinforcement of the superpowers' domestic
insecurity, the specifics of which I come to shortly.

This way of looking at the phenomenon of war has specific relevance to understanding the purpose of nuclear weapons, the first
question posed above. It suggests that politics, rather than either technology developing independently of political will or careful calcula-
tion of the number and character of weapons actually needed for
national defense, is the driving force behind nuclear escalation.[7] But
still more fundamentally, this perspective leads us to question—and reject—the concept and morality of nuclear war itself. It is not thinkable.

The central issue of the nuclear arms race is not numbers of weapons and dollars, it is human life and the survival of the species. And
what makes nuclear war unthinkable, as Jonathan Schell pointed out in
The Fate of the Earth,[8] is that it is not *war* at all. For war is governed
and ended by political decisions, whereas the use of nuclear weapons
presages the end of politics and the onset of a global medical, ecological, and social catastrophe without foreseeable end.

There are enough nuclear weapons at the disposal of the superpowers to incinerate every populated area in the two countries down
to the level of a town of 1,500 people, and still have an ample reserve.
The U.S. and Soviet arsenals include thousands of warheads in each
part of their so-called strategic triad: long-range ICBMs, intercontinental bombers, and submarines. Any one of these parts—in fact, even the
warheads delivered by a few submarines—could effectively obliterate

another society. Figures inevitably vary on how many people might be killed instantly, die later of radiation poisoning, or be disfigured, genetically mutated, blinded, and so on. Comparisons with the experiences of Hiroshima and Nagasaki are absurd, since today's one-megaton bomb (1 million tons of TNT) is equivalent in destructive power to eighty Hiroshimas. In addition, weather conditions and the number and location of the weapons dropped will determine the extent of casualties. Suffice to say that a nuclear exchange involving at minimum several thousand megatons of weapons would cause appalling numbers of deaths—perhaps 200 million in the United States and the Soviet Union alone—injuries in the range of 60 million persons, and disease and destruction of unparalleled, hence unimaginable, scope.[9]

But that is not all. For we are dealing here with a phenomenon that transcends the great physical destructiveness of war. Soviet and U.S. physicians have underscored the unprecedented and unmeetable demands a nuclear catastrophe would place on a society's medical resources, beginning with the oft-forgotten fact that a nuclear attack would kill doctors and nurses along with everyone else. To them it would be the "final epidemic." Hospitals, blood transfusions, pain killers—these and numerous other resources would be exceedingly scarce precisely where they would be most needed, in heavily populated areas.

Beyond the medical problem lies "nuclear winter": the long-term consequences for the entire planet, and not just the targeted countries, of a large-scale nuclear exchange. Enormous clouds of dust and smoke would be hurled upwards by the bombings and resulting firestorms, blotting out the sun and turning day into prolonged darkness. As scientists have attempted to chart the consequences, nuclear winter holds a hellish prospect for survivors: toxic soil and water as well as months without sunlight, hence mass starvation and poisoning; the elimination of numerous forms of wildlife, insects, and plants; long-term cold and, with the return of sunlight, the onset of harmful ultraviolet rays due to the damaging effects of the thermonuclear blasts on the earth's protective ozone layer. And beyond that would be the loss of the knowledge and resources for technological living to which the Northern Hemisphere's people have become accustomed.[10]

Yet official and, to a great extent, public debate on the nuclear issue is dominated by arguments about numbers: Which side has more weapons, the biggest weapons, the highest military spending? Such arguments had merit when the United States had a nuclear monopoly (1945–1949) and then clear superiority over the USSR (1949–1962). Once the USSR started to catch up, however, the numbers game distorted far more than it revealed. For by then, according to Robert

McNamara, in spite of maintaining a strategic superiority over the USSR of "at least three or four to one"—enough to destroy a third of the Soviet population and half its industry with only a fraction (about 400 bombs) of the U.S. stockpile—the United States could still be "effectively destroy[ed]" by a Soviet retaliatory blow.[11] And that has continued to be the case. "What in the name of God is strategic superiority?" asked Henry Kissinger in 1974. "What is the significance of it, politically, militarily, operationally, at these levels of numbers? What do you do with it?"[12]

Indeed, what *do* you do with so many weapons? McNamara and his boss, President Kennedy, were among those who recoiled at the unusable capability for overkill, particularly targeted against cities. Yet the change that came about was not to stop the production of nuclear weapons but to move toward a different mixture of targets. A "counter-cities" nuclear force became "counter-value" (directed mainly at economic targets) and still later "counter-force" (directed at military, communications, and political targets as well as economic assets). And as the number of all these targets grew—to about 40,000 in the 1980s from 2,600 in 1960 and 25,000 in 1974—the number of warheads and weapons needed to "cover" the targets also mushroomed.[13] The "rationality" of such planning had lost touch with reality: Many millions of civilians would still be killed even in the most "selective" nuclear attacks (since nonmilitary targets, after all, often are located near population centers); the number of warheads (in the *hundreds*) actually needed for deterring attack (convincing an enemy, that is, that it would be destroyed if it attacked the United States) was *thousands* fewer than the number available; and the targeting of several or more warheads on a single industrial plant, city, or other facility defied imagination.

Not only did target lists and weapons arsenals grow, they also, perhaps inevitably, became more refined. Military planners and scientists, foremost in the United States, began emphasizing the technical characteristics of nuclear weapons and the means of delivering them. "More" would have to be coupled with "better." And so for nearly two decades now, the decisive military factor in the U.S.–Soviet strategic competition has been the relative *technical quality* of the weapons: their accuracy, reliability for delivery, and vulnerability to attack. It is the advances in weapons technology that in recent times account for the dangerous new threshhold of the arms race. For despite the widely held view, which this analysis shares, that the United States and the Soviet Union have roughly equivalent strategic striking power—each side has enough to destroy the other several times over, and neither side has a usable margin of superiority over the other—they are both deploying

weapons that move beyond deterrence of attack to potentially offensive capabilities.

Let us look first at the weapons themselves.

What Chart 5.1 reveals goes beyond mere numbers. It tells us that,
although the Soviet Union has deployed many more strategic weapons
(*launchers*), the United States has many more *warheads* it can deliver.
(If so-called "tactical" nuclear warheads are included, the U.S. lead is
about 24,000 to 15,000). The chart also shows that Soviet strength is in
land-based intercontinental missiles—about 73 percent of its strategic
force—which are far more vulnerable to attack than the U.S. strategic
force, roughly half of which is deployed on virtually invulnerable submarines. Finally, Chart 5.1 points up the biggest U.S. advantage of all:
the greater accuracy of U.S. missiles, reflecting a decided technological
advantage which U.S. military leaders acknowledge but rarely mention
in public discussion. They prefer to focus on the Soviet advantage in
destructive potential due to more and bigger bombs. That aspect is real
enough, but it is secondary in importance to the ability to deliver
bombs on target. Smaller is better in this case. In fact, the upcoming
generation of weapons, such as the U.S. MX and Trident II (D-5) and the
Soviet SS-18-X and SS-X, will drastically increase the probability of a
direct hit and thus make land-based missiles sitting ducks, no matter
how hardened their silos might be.

A few additional points not reflected in the chart deserve mention.
The U.S. submarine advantage is heightened by the fact that the U.S.
fleet is at sea far more frequently than the Soviet fleet. Both sides
maintain substantial nuclear weapons in close proximity to potential
battlefields. For example, the U.S. has over 6,000 warheads stored in
eight countries (West Germany, Britain, Italy, Turkey, Greece, South
Korea, the Netherlands, and Belgium),[14] creating so-called nuclear trip-
wires. Soviet nuclear weapons are deployed throughout Eastern Europe. Finally, the United States can count on the independent nuclear
forces of Britain and France, and possibly China, in a nuclear confrontation with the Soviet Union. The Anglo-French force is formidable: It
includes 272 single-warhead submarine-launched weapons in a total
arsenal of over 700 nuclear warheads.[15]

If one can speak of advantage when so many deadly accurate
weapons are so widely deployed and can be delivered in several ways,
it belongs to the United States, largely due to its submarines. More generally, the advantage lies in a technological lead in nuclear-weapons development that the United States demonstrated over Japan in 1945 and
has never relinquished since.[16] Consciousness of their *relative* nuclear
inferiority to the United States has been a key factor in the rapid Soviet
buildup of nuclear weapons since the early 1960s,[17] just as it has been

Chart 5.1: U.S. and Soviet Nuclear Arsenals in 1983

	Weapons Deployed	Total Warheads	Total Yield in Kt. (fallout area in sq. mi.)	Accuracy of Best Weapon[a]
ICBMs (land)				
U.S.	1,049	2,149	1,766,535	730
USSR	1,398	5,862	4,094,400	851
SLBMs (sea)				
U.S.	520	4,800	288,000	1,520
USSR	969	1,865	1,356,000	3,040
Bombers (air)				
U.S.	328	2,626	1,485,200	304
USSR	245	345	345,000	n/a
Subtotals				
U.S.	1,897	9,575	3,539,735	
USSR	2,612	8,072	5,795,400	
Total Tactical and Intermediate Range Forces				
U.S.		14,342	3,874,604	
USSR		6,795	3,098,850	
Grand Totals				
U.S.		23,917	7,414,339	
USSR		14,867	8,894,250	

[a]Accuracy defined as distance (in feet) from target within which half of missiles will hit.

Source: Coalitions for a New Foreign and Military Policy, "U.S. and Soviet First-Strike Capabilities," Washington, D.C., February 1984, pp. 2–3.

in the U.S. buildup of the 1980s to maintain a lead. The Soviets have always been playing catch-up, since most of the technological breakthroughs in weapons design (from the intercontinental bomber and the submarine-launched missiles to the multiple-warhead and the cruise missiles) have been U.S.-made.[18] The nuclear race has thus proceeded unevenly, explaining why Soviet Foreign Minister (and later President) Andrei A. Gromyko spoke of his country's quest for "the holy of holies . . . the principle of equality and equal security" in arms negotiations.[19]

The nuclear competition is also more than the sum of its parts. The net *strategic* result of nuclear-weapons development has been to alter the logic that underpins it: deterrence. Nuclear deterrence refers to the ability of one side to make a nuclear attack on it too costly for an opponent to contemplate rationally. In theory deterrence is achievable because the defending side can sustain a nuclear attack and still have the ("second-strike") capacity to retaliate devastatingly against valued targets of its opponent — population centers, industry, strategic and other military assets, and the leadership itself. But even in theory, deterrence is a weak reed on which to rest the planet's survival. It is largely a state of mind; there is no certainty about the military forces needed to deter an adversary until (possibly) *after* being attacked, at which point deterrence has failed. Precisely what deters the Soviets from attacking the United States or its allies, and vice versa, is a matter of conjecture, of educated guesswork; and from conjecture springs the belief that increasing numbers and types of nuclear weapons are essential to deterrence. It is an irresistable logic for rationalizing continued research and development of additional nuclear warheads and weapons. For no one, the argument goes, can be certain how much is enough to ensure deterrence.

But if such logic is irresistable, it is also deadly. There is an ultimate irrationality about relying on nuclear weapons to deter attack. Consider: Country A is theoretically deterred from an initial nuclear strike against Country B or its allies—assuming both countries to have accurate nuclear weapons—by A's belief it will be devastated in return. Yet B recognizes that a nuclear retaliation will subject *it* to annihilation from A's counterattack. Are A's leaders crazy enough to take the chance, for example, of launching a "small" nuclear attack? Or maybe of initiating an all-out attack? And would B's leaders be crazy enough to retaliate, or would they surrender? If these questions seem absurdly theoretical, note that the situation sketched above essentially describes the U.S. and NATO strategy in Europe in the event of a massive Soviet conventional attack. Deterrence in that case has long rested on the threat of a massive *nuclear* response to the USSR, "even if actually to carry out the threat [as an early classic on deterrence said] would be irrational because of the enormous costs we [the United States] would suffer from Soviet counterretaliation." The only deterrents in such a case, then, are "Soviet uncertainties about whether or not nuclear retaliation is rational for us, and about how rational we are."[20]

So much for theory. In the real world, deterrence is fast eroding because of the nuclear technology itself, with respect to the U.S.–Soviet competition and the proliferation of that technology worldwide. Deterrence rests on a certain stability akin to mind over matter, rational planning over technology run amuck. In a deterrence relationship, what must work is *confidence* on all sides in the reality of deterrence. And this confidence is precisely what advances in nuclear weapons have undermined, since the more accurate, destructive, and widespread nuclear weapons become, the more unpredictability of control and use they create.

Technological advances in strategic weapons evidently are creating in the minds of some high-level leaders (particularly, but surely not exclusively, on the U.S. side[21]) a conviction in the ability to fight, contain, win, and survive a nuclear war. Such careless thinking, even though discounted by other top U.S. officials (such as the commander of NATO forces), has alarmed many in Western Europe, one potential locale of a nuclear exchange. Both Soviet and U.S. leaders have periodically deplored the concept of a nuclear victory—former Soviet President Leonid Brezhnev, for instance, called it a "dangerous madness" that could only stem from a suicidal impulse[22]—but both sides have nevertheless invested considerable resources in planning for a postnuclear future: improved communications among remaining national leaders, civil defense, and postattack economic and social recovery.

Dr. Desmond Ball of the Australian National University has offered perhaps the most decisive rebuttal of the logic of limited nuclear war.[23] He emphasizes the context in which *any* use of nuclear weapons might occur. Instead of a "relatively smooth and controlled progression from limited and selective strikes" to larger attacks and counterattacks, Ball observes the numerous difficulties a political leadership will have in maintaining control. Perfect rationality is hard to imagine when communication and command facilities have been disrupted or destroyed (and these are priority targets in a "counterforce" strategy, it will be recalled); when decision processes have become chaotic; and when popular feelings of confusion and hatred have run rampant. Indeed, as four former senior U.S. policymakers have contended, "there is no way for anyone to have any confidence that [a small-scale] nuclear action will not lead to further and more devastating exchanges."[24] Rather than accept the notion that limited nuclear war is a viable step between conventional war and all-out war, they urged U.S. adoption of a no-first-use nuclear-weapons policy in Europe and, like Ball, improvement of conventional defenses.

Beyond limited nuclear war, weapons accuracy may also be making more conceivable a nuclear first-strike, meaning the ability to decimate an opponent and not suffer a crippling retaliatory blow. One might think that the days were over when, as Robert McNamara reported of the period just before the October 1962 Cuban missile crisis, the U.S. Air Force could believe in its ability to carry out a disarming first-strike on the Soviet Union.[25] But technology, as demonstrated by the U.S. MX and cruise missiles, has reopened that possibility. This has specific relevance to strategic targets that can be pinpointed, namely, land-based ICBMs that the Soviets count on for most of their nuclear strength. Great accuracy could create in the minds of one set of leaders the fear that unless its country attacks first, it will lose its ICBMs. In the minds of their opponents, it could create the belief that, unless *they* strike first, their missiles will have nothing to hit but empty silos. Either circumstance may already be compelling the adoption of a launch-on-warning policy to ensure that missiles will not be caught in their silos. Can a threatened, fearful national leadership then *afford* to believe in deterrence?

Deterrence also depends on knowing the capabilities of each side's weapons. When capabilities change or become undetectable, deterrence erodes. The U.S. cruise missiles have what might be called virtues—by everyone but a Soviet planner—of being highly accurate, very difficult for radar to detect due to their smallness, and launchable from land, sea, or air. Nuclear-armed cruise missiles cannot be distinguished from non-nuclear ones, making them unverifiable under arms-control agreements. Here is only one example of a new weapon that may simultaneously make larger weapons and existing arms agreements obsolete, thus stimulating further rounds of "defensive" and "offensive" deployments by each side to counter them.

Still another threatened aspect of deterrence is assured communication in a nuclear crisis. Daniel Ford's research on Pentagon command and control of nuclear weapons has led to the disturbing conclusion that communication among U.S. military and civilian leaders would be so fragile and uncertain in the event of a nuclear attack as to "reinforce the idea that a first strike is, by default, the preferred military option in a real showdown with the Soviet Union."[26] Soviet military forces may share this problem, particularly their submarine force, which, if it functions at all like the U.S. force, would only be able to receive a few words at deep depths from its leaders in a nuclear crisis. Scientists can only speculate on the effect of different kinds of nuclear explosions on the earth's electromagnetic field. But a frequent conclusion is that it could be wiped out by only a few large weapons exploded in the atmosphere, literally bringing all forms of communication and transportation to a halt, including the means of negotiating a cease-fire.

Deterrence can also be subverted by accident. Drug and alcohol abuse among U.S. missile personnel responsible for nuclear weapons have been reported over the years. Computer failures are becoming all too commonplace. For example, over 800 false alarms in the U.S. strategic warning system occurred between 1979 and 1983.[27] U.S. strategic forces went to high alert three times during a seven-month period in 1979 to 1980 because of computer failures in the North American radar system. In one instance the failure left only four minutes for a decision on how to respond to a Soviet "attack."[28]

The dangers of technical and human breakdowns are all the more ominous because of the decreasing time between a missile launch and its arrival on target—only six minutes in the case of U.S. Pershing II missiles based in West Germany, or less than ten minutes for a Soviet submarine off the U.S. coast. With increased interest, presumably on both sides, in a launch-on-warning policy, the decision time on a nuclear response to *apparent* attack becomes highly compressed. In August 1983, Soviet commanders took about two hours to track a Korean Air Lines passenger jet before ordering it shot down in the belief the aircraft was on a spying mission.[29] So little time to distinguish between a real and an imagined threat may mean that the grave decision to execute a nuclear strike will be delegated to military officers on the spot or even "loaded" into computers that automatically trigger a retaliation. That President Reagan was apparently not notified about any of the three computer-generated alerts mentioned above is an ominous sign of decentralized authority over nuclear weapons.[30]

Over the years, accidents involving nuclear weapons—though none in which a nuclear weapon has been detonated—have occurred. In 1981 the Pentagon reported on twenty-seven such accidents since 1950, most involving aircraft crashes.[31] A reasonable prediction is that the increased number of nuclear weapons and their frequent transportation to widely dispersed locations will add to the list of such accidents. Six of the previous U.S. accidents occurred in foreign waters or over foreign territory. Deterrence theory takes no account of how one state's leaders may react to a reported nuclear accident in a highly tense period of cold war.

The proliferation of nuclear weapons adds yet another uncertainty to the nuclear-war issue, perhaps a larger one than the U.S.–Soviet rivalry itself. For the prospect of as many as thirty-five nuclear powers by the year 2000 is an awesome one. Several such nuclear-capable states—South Africa, Pakistan, Libya, Iraq, and Israel (which probably already has a small stockpile of weapons)—are closely tied to one of the superpowers and are involved in hostile relations with neighboring countries. A conflict involving one or more of the near-nuclear states could embroil a superpower partner. Israel's June 1981 bombing of Iraq's French-built nuclear reactor did not lead to that point, but a similar future raid on a country's nuclear installations could. The Soviet Union apparently tried to win U.S. approval of an attack on Chinese nuclear facilities in the early 1960s. President Nixon stated that he considered, but rejected, the use of nuclear weapons in two potentially explosive situations: in the 1971 India-Pakistan conflict over Bangladesh's independence, when he believed both the Soviets and the Chinese were threatening to become directly involved; and in 1973, when the Nixon administration concluded the Soviets were prepared to intervene on Egypt's side in the war with Israel.[32]

International cooperation in the United Nations by Moscow and Washington has sought to prevent the emergence of new nuclear states, but with mixed results. Since the 1968 Nuclear Non-proliferation Treaty (NPT) and its regulatory body, the International Atomic Energy Agency (IAEA), have come into force, no non-nuclear member state has gone nuclear. (The treaty is essentially a promise by signatories, numbering over 130 at the end of 1985, to "pursue negotiations" to end the arms race and achieve "nuclear disarmament." In exchange for agreeing not to acquire, manufacture, or seek technical assistance concerning nuclear weapons, non-nuclear states are promised access to nuclear-energy technology. The agency's purpose is to inspect atomic facilities and ensure that adequate safeguards have been installed to prevent the diversion of nuclear fuel to weapons manufacture.) But three of the six nuclear powers—China, France, and India—have not signed the treaty; and neither have five near-nuclear ones—Argentina, Brazil, Israel, Pakistan, and South Africa.

The line between peaceful and military uses of atomic power, which once seemed clear to many, is no more: "*every* known civilian route to bombs involves *either* nuclear power *or* materials and technologies whose possession, indeed whose existence in commerce, is a direct and essential consequence of nuclear fission power."[33] The IAEA is poorly equipped to deal with that problem. It lacks the enforcement powers, the personnel, and the right of unimpeded access that would make it an effective oversight agency. When, for example, Israel bombed the Iraqi reactor, which the IAEA had inspected, the agency could neither punish Israel nor absolutely refute Israel's charge that Iraq was diverting nuclear fuel for bomb-making purposes.

The related problems of theft and covert acquisition of plutonium are even farther beyond the IAEA's ability to control. Several cases of theft have been reported from U.S. nuclear plants, for instance. More ominously, the international availability of plutonium is nearly out of control. One creditable estimate by the Nuclear Control Institute based in Washington, D.C., is that in the noncommunist countries alone there was enough plutonium in 1983 from conventional nuclear power plants to produce "at least 6000 bombs, if separated out of spent fuel in reprocessing plants." And that amount could increase fifteen times by the year 2000.[34]

But the most grievous weaknesses of the nonproliferation regime lie in the contradictory and hypocritical behavior of the superpowers, the United States in particular. Of all the NPT signatories, they have been among the least responsible, for they have failed to meet their commitment under the treaty to take "effective" steps toward an "early" end to the arms race and nuclear disarmament. Yet they want to universalize membership, supposedly to deny nuclear-weapons technology to the non-nuclear states. As Samuel Kim observes, "It is difficult to explain logically why nuclear weapons are good or safe in the hands of the great powers but bad or unsafe in the hands of the small powers."[35] An even greater hypocrisy is that the United States, in order to promote the faltering fortunes of its nuclear power industry and maintain good relations with Third World allies, has provided several near-nuclear states with nuclear materials. It has also looked the other way when, by hook or by crook, agents of these states have surreptitiously exported such materials from the United States or elsewhere.[36] Here we have another example of how Realism and Corporate Globalism come together to undermine a vital global interest. The U.S. government does not want U.S. corporations such as Westinghouse, General Electric, and Bechtel to lose out in the competition with French and German nuclear-energy companies; nor does it want to slap the hands of its "strategic" friends, the Israelis, the Argentines, the Pakistanis, the South Africans and the Chinese. So Washington has done virtually nothing to prevent their moving closer to, actually acquiring, or expanding a nuclear capability—and, in fact, the U.S. government has sometimes facilitated matters.[37]

Considering the failure of the United States and the Soviet Union to reach agreement on a range of meaningful arms-control and arms-reduction measures (such as a comprehensive test ban, a freeze on nuclear-weapons deployment, or a global halt to commerce in plutonium) and their inability to exercise mutual restraint in Third World conflicts, it is pointless to expect that nonproliferation will make more progress. In fact, the cause is going backwards, with Washington and

Moscow leading the retreat by their actual practices.[38] Thus, we find deterrence weakened by horizontal (among countries) as well as vertical (by types of weapons) arms races.

In such dismal circumstances, along comes strategic nuclear defense to pose as an alternative to the mutual balance of terror. Both superpowers have begun investing heavily in space-based weapons that can shoot down enemy satellites (ASATs) and direct powerful lasers to knock out offensive missiles as they leave the launching pad or en route to targets. Ballistic missile defense is hardly a novel idea; the anti-ballistic missile (ABM) to defend land-based missiles was a major political issue in the United States when it was first proposed in the mid-1960s. But under President Reagan's "Strategic Defense Initiative" (SDI), it has emerged as the technological breakthrough that assertedly will solve the problems of deterrence:

> As strategic defenses make it increasingly unlikely that Soviet offensive forces can accomplish their mission, the incentive for new Soviet investment in them is reduced. We thus enhance Soviet willingness to join us in deep reductions of offensive forces.[39]

The far greater likelihood is that nothing of the kind will occur and that, to the contrary, "strategic defense" will deepen the contradictions of deterrence.

For the purposes of this study, it may suffice to enumerate the most prominent criticisms of the SDI, or "Star Wars," concept.[40] First, its proponents admit that it cannot be totally effective against enemy missiles, as was originally claimed. A *perfectly* functioning strategic defense system can only protect against ICBMs, not submarines or bombers. Even at 99 percent effectiveness, the system's worthiness becomes suspect. A nuclear attack by a mere one percent of the current Soviet (or U.S.) force—meaning perhaps 100 missiles—would wreak incalculable damage. Second, to the extent such a system is considered effective (that is, *threatening*) by the other side, it will surely be answered with deployments to offset it, such as submarines and cruise missiles, and by intensification of antisatellite weapons development to shoot the system down. A further escalation of the arms race and not negotiation from an inferior position has always been the pattern of the U.S.–USSR competition. Now the prospect looms of space warfare to control the "high frontiers."

A third major objection to strategic defense is that such a system, initially announced as being purely defensive and non-nuclear, in fact may be applied to offensive purposes, like all allegedly defensive weapons. One such application is by directing lasers at military and economic targets on earth. Another is by fitting the system with nuclear weapons.

Other criticisms relate to the cost and technological limitations. The projected cost of the system runs into the hundreds of billions of dollars. But countermeasures, such as laser-resistant coating on missiles and use of dummies, are likely to be very cheap in comparison. There are, moreover, numerous technical problems that may never be resolved, such as the inability of lasers to pierce cloud cover and the extensive reliance on computer software that can only be adequately tested in actual combat.

Depending on how far beyond the research stage SDI goes, it will very likely be a breakout from at least one major arms control agreement, the 1972 Anti-Ballistic Missile Treaty. It prohibits the development, testing, and deployment of sea-based, air-based, space-based, or mobile land-based antimissile systems and their components. Only the development and testing of fixed land-based ABM systems and components are permitted. The treaty is a central element of arms control precisely because it flatly stops the evolution of a weapons system at the point of field testing. Should Washington decide to abrogate the treaty by developing SDI outside the laboratory—a distinct possibility during the Reagan presidency—it would probably have a devastating impact on prospects for U.S.–Soviet arms negotiations across the board.

Since SDI may take twenty years to be deployed, what will each side be doing in the interim? Further research and development of new strategic weapons with increasing first-strike potential is the likely direction. So, rather than break the mold of deterrence, strategic defense is likely to reproduce some of its worst features: the cycle of action and reaction when new technology becomes available to one side, and increased reliance on high-speed computers. Strategic defense at bottom exemplifies one of the fundamental flaws of First World politics: the faith in technology's ability to resolve problems that the pursuit of power have created. The more it is left on its own, the more technology will add to the problems, possibly accelerating a doomsday scenario in which decision time is reduced to a few minutes.

The search for absolute security thus rests on the mistaken belief that more is better and certainty is achievable. But so long as both superpowers share the same reasoning, the logic of deterrence must eventually collapse. Advances in weapons accuracy and survivability, which should make many *fewer* weapons necessary for deterrence, instead are part of the larger rationale for expanding the number of warheads, launchers, and targets. Yet a complete understanding of what accounts for this enormous overinvestment in strategic weapons requires that we go beyond the counterintuitive logic of deterrence. We need to consider as well the deep institutional stakes the United States and the Soviet Union have in maintaining the arms race, and the political uses to which nuclear weapons can be (because they have been) put.

On the institutional side, each social system has created its own variation of the military-industrial complex. In the United States,[41] this grouping of public and private institutions is tightly interlocked: government agencies, the military services, and industries depend on one another for weapons research, planning advice, manufacturing, testing, and sales; many Congressional districts are economically and politically dependent on military bases; and roughly 9 million people directly or indirectly depend on the military budget for their livelihoods. The process transforms "national security" into more commonplace matters: careers, jobs, profits, and therefore political backscratching and manipulation. The Soviet system unites party, industrial, and military leaders in a similar common interest.

This situation of reinforcing interests, operating largely outside the business rules of the civilian economy, creates a separate (state-run) command system in both countries.[42] It enables both sides to commit a large portion of their GNP to the military (since 1960, an average of 6.5 percent by the United States and 10.9 percent by the Soviet Union).[43] Each government devotes the bulk of its research funds to military work (close to 70 percent in the United States). Each maintains huge military forces and numerous bases abroad: for the United States, about 2 million service personnel, of whom about 284,000 are at sea and 460,000 are stationed overseas in 360 major bases; and for the Soviet Union, about 3.6 million soldiers, of whom over 700,000 are stationed (or fighting) abroad in twenty-four countries.[44] And the superpowers control well over half the world market in arms exports.[45]

Command of such resources creates bureaucratic and economic power that is the essence of the national-security state. Secrecy is one measure of such power. The separate military economies contain top-secret, so-called "black" weapons programs within them. On the U.S. side, some of these programs are so tightly guarded that even their existence is rarely acknowledged.[46] Another measure is the political and economic functions performed by military spending. Comparative research suggests that, despite the great differences in the way U.S. and Soviet politics operate, military spending is used for similar purposes in both countries.[47] It responds to the needs of a powerful interest group, the military and civilian professionals who work on national security matters. It can be used to affect overall economic performance and thus either to influence elections (in the United States) or intra-leadership disputes (in the USSR). And in either society military spending can be a quick fix to promote employment and increase or decrease consumer demand. (Arms exports, for example, have accounted for over 5 percent of total U.S. exports and over 10 percent of Soviet exports in the 1980s.[48]) Add to this list the inevitable military service rivalries, which lead each service to covet a strategic role and the budget to sustain it, and we have the key elements of a deep-seated structural bias in favor of more weapons.

In the United States, the high cost and profitability of weapons and military technology supply added political and economic incentives for more arms. The latest-model Trident submarines cost over $1.5 billion each. The B-1B long-range bombers have a price tag of about $400 million each. Every ground-launched cruise missile costs over $6 million.[49] Contracts for such expensive weapons are dominated by the major military firms, companies such as General Dynamics and Lockheed (the main Trident contractors), Boeing (cruise missiles), and Rockwell International (the B-1B) that do the bulk of their business with the Pentagon, including conventional arms, electronic components, and overseas sales. Cost overruns, government research and lobbying subsidies, and tax benefits add to the profit margins of the weapons. And with hundreds of thousands of jobs at stake and with the economic lifeline of specific communities (such as Seattle, Washington) and entire states (such as California) tied to those jobs, it is no wonder that the major military industries are politically active at election time. They have every incentive to pressure legislators for more and better weapons regardless of the actual military need.

Take Star Wars, for example. Most of the major military contractors are the leading recipients of Star Wars research money and are on line to be the prime contractors if a strategic defense system is produced and deployed. They, along with many smaller research and production firms, view Star Wars as a golden opportunity to get ahead in scientific and profit competition. Potentially involving hundreds of billions of dollars, the brief political history of SDI is already similar to that of other weapons systems: the recruitment by military industry of former Defense Department officials to advise, direct, and sell its programs; the lobbying of members of Congress and foreign governments to support SDI as sources of jobs and research funds; and the awarding of SDI contracts overwhelmingly to "states or districts whose Congressional representatives sit on committees with the most power over weapons acquisition and funding."[50]

"National security" is the inevitable rallying cry of any military-industrial complex. They are the worldwide code words for ensuring a lion's share of a national budget—and for undermining those who might challenge high spending for defense. Because the business of national security is, moreover, esoteric and secretive; because it is heavily influenced by leadership ideology; and because it contains so many imponderable, unpredictable factors that lead to worst-case planning, enough is never enough for "defense." In addition, national leaders sometimes believe, as Reagan said in an interview in 1982, that they can spend their opponents into submission.[51] Such wisdom is music to the ears of military industrialists; it means a virtual blank check on weapons research and production. And to judge from the leaps in U.S. and Soviet military spending of the 1980s—an eight-year, projected $2 trillion buildup under Reagan; annual Soviet military budgets of roughly 12 to 15 percent of total spending—a blank check comes close to describing what the military-industrial complex has gotten. ·

These institutional forces go far toward explaining the consistent surge forward of nuclear and overall military spending and deployment. Still, the explanation is incomplete. It is not as though a technological monster has been unleashed and now is subject only to the availability of dollars and rubles. Just as political priorities determine military spending, they also determine how nuclear weapons can be used.

True, nuclear weapons are built in hopes they will never be used *in war*. But U.S. presidents have several times threatened to use them against other governments, mainly the Soviet Union's and China's. Apparently the first instance was in 1948, when President Harry S. Truman ordered atomic-capable bombers moved to bases in Britain during the first Berlin crisis. A second instance occurred in the final stages of the Korean War. According to President Eisenhower's memoirs, the United States conveyed to China its preparedness to employ nuclear bombs against it if the armistice talks dragged on. Eisenhower also had tactical nuclear weapons sent to Taiwan in 1958 during a crisis with the PRC over the Taiwan Strait. President Kennedy ordered nuclear-armed B-52s to prepare for a strike against China in 1961 during the crisis over Laos. It is also well known that Kennedy considered using nuclear weapons against Moscow during the 1961 Berlin crisis and the missile crisis over Cuba in 1962. President Nixon revealed in a 1985 interview that he had considered using nuclear weapons four times during his tenure. On at least one of those occasions—the 1973 conflict in the Middle East, in which the Strategic Air Command's B-52s were placed on full alert for twenty-nine days—he let Soviet leaders know he would use those weapons.[52]

U.S. leaders privately pondered the nuclear option in several other conflicts.[53] So far as we know, Soviet leaders have not directly threatened the United States with nuclear attack, although on occasion they have engaged in nuclear saber rattling of an ambiguous nature. Atomic diplomacy has apparently been the peculiar mainstay of the United States. A policy of first-use of nuclear weapons has long been in force in case of a Soviet *conventional* attack in Europe or a North Korean invasion of South Korea. The belief has persisted in high U.S. circles that nuclear weapons have had an "extraordinarily salutary effect" for both superpowers in helping restrain conflicts between them. But such "restraint" has merely channeled conflict into other countries at a high level of violence.[54]

The political utility of nuclear weapons, which the three military services compete to control,[55] not only helps to account for their ongoing production (far beyond conceivable need), it also enables us to understand U.S. resistance to arms reductions. We can clearly date this resistance to the onset of cold-war internationalism in 1946 when (as was discussed in Chapter 2) a high-level government consensus evolved against nuclear-arms talks while the United States had a monopoly of mass-destruction weapons. The U.S. government was far from reaching an agreement with Moscow that might put the nuclear genie back in the bottle, as some scientists were urging. The prevailing view, epitomized by then Army Chief of Staff Dwight Eisenhower in a top-secret memorandum of January 1946, was that "if there are to be atomic weapons in the world, we must have the best, the biggest and the most."[56]

The political effect of such advice, which Truman and all his successors accepted, was twofold. One was to present the Soviets with proposals for limiting nuclear arms or tests that they were certain to *reject*. Examples are the Baruch Plan of 1946 for internationalizing control of nuclear weapons, Eisenhower's proposals in 1955 for "open-skies" and on-site inspection of nuclear facilities, and Reagan's proposals in the early 1980s for mutual cutbacks of launchers. Each of these offers would have been to the U.S. advantage and, in the Soviets' eyes, would have frozen the Soviets into an inferior position.

The second political effect of the consensus on arms control was to reach agreement *only with assurances to the military-industrial complex of support for the next generation of weapons*. Agreements such as the Nuclear Test Ban of 1963, SALT I in 1972, the Vladivostok agreement of 1974, and the never-ratified SALT II in 1979 were acceptable to the U.S. national-security establishment precisely because of their modesty: They left large loopholes for budgeting increases in weapons research, production, and deployment. The test ban, for instance, permitted underground explosions, of which there have been over 700 by the superpowers since the treaty was signed. SALT I largely limited antimissile systems, ICBMs, and SLBMs. At Vladivostok the Soviet and U.S. leaders (Ford and Brezhnev) put a cap on certain categories of strategic launchers and the number of them that could be fitted with multiple warheads (MIRV'd). SALT II did much the same thing. But all of these agreements allowed ample room—which has since been filled—for building *up* to the specified limits, for continued testing underground, for weapons research and deployment in categories not covered (such as cruise missiles), for vastly increased spending, and for unlimited production and replacement of nuclear warheads (there are nearly three times as many warheads now as there were before the SALT treaties).[57]

All this is not to say that the Soviets have acted on the basis of different rules of national and bureaucratic self-interest. Their having had to catch up in nuclear technology accounts in part for their rejection of various U.S. offers. But now that they *have* caught up in second-strike (if not yet counterforce) capability, the argument of self-preservation is not so compelling. Some general Soviet arms-control proposals of recent years—such as for a mutual nuclear freeze on weapons testing, production, and deployment; for a U.S.–Soviet pledge of no first use of nuclear weapons; and for a unilateral moratorium on nuclear tests that would continue if the United States also declared one—have been interesting and ought to have been pursued by U.S. leaders. But Moscow undermined its case with a rapid, strategically unjustifiable buildup to over 400 intermediate-range missiles aimed at Europe. It seems safe to assume that a weapons lobby dominates nuclear policymaking there as here and, therefore, that arms control, not to mention arms reductions, will continue to be outpaced by weapons development. This circumstance, along with historic Soviet mistrust of the West (dating from allied intervention in the Russian Revolution) and the ideology and values of Soviet leaders, account for the paranoid style of Soviet, as of U.S., nuclear policy.

In summary, the superpowers' nuclear weapons race has brought the world to a dangerous threshold because of the global pretensions and ambitions of their leaderships, the combined driving force of weapons technology and an open-ended strategic doctrine (deterrence), the powerful, vested institutional interests in weapons, and the political uses to which nuclear weapons can be put. These factors are an answer to the first question raised in the beginning of this section: The proliferation of nuclear weapons has very little to do with national defense. They in fact undermine military security, national and global. They *"serve no military purpose whatsoever. They are totally useless—except only to deter one's opponent from using them."*[58] They contribute far more to destabilizing global political relations and hastening the day of planetary suicide than to easing the crisis of world conflict. As discussed below, with reference to the second of our questions, nuclear and other kinds of military spending in the United States and the Soviet Union distort the entire concept of "security," adding to military arsenals while weakening social and economic cohesion.

THE HUMAN COSTS OF THE NUCLEAR GAME

The nuclear game features very few players and very high stakes. But even if the game is never played to a conclusion, its impact has been deeply felt in both Soviet and U.S. society. Planning and spending on "national security" have long occupied prominent places in their national budgets, industrial production and research, labor forces, and the conduct of social life. All these requirements draw resources from other sectors. And since this process has been going on for over forty years, with each system seeking global hegemony, its cumulative impact has been immense. "Superpower" is an apt term for the United States and the Soviet Union with respect to military spending and weapons, in which they rank first and second. But it does not fit so well when we consider some fundamental social and economic weaknesses and inequities within these countries that flow, sometimes directly, from military supremacy. Again, President Eisenhower: "The military establishment, not productive of itself, necessarily must feed on the energy, productivity, and brainpower of the country, and if it takes too much, our total strength declines."[59]

This section examines the social costs of the arms race in terms of its direct impact—how military spending affects Soviet and U.S. economies, and its indirect impact—how military spending siphons money away from other social sectors in which human need is great and growing. Setting the stage for this undertaking are brief portraits of the Soviet Union and the United States in the mid-1980s.

The Soviet Union

In March 1985, leadership in the Soviet Union transferred to Mikhail Gorbachev, who soon unveiled a reform program—*glasnost*, or openness—that, in his view, would be as sweeping as the Bolshevik Revolution. Considering the enormous internal problems facing Soviet leaders, *glasnost* comes none too soon. Before noting what *glasnost* promises, we need to take a hard look at Soviet political economy in the mid-1980s.

The Soviet system is showing the strains of aging leadership, economic wastefulness, and the high price of maintaining empire—the

huge sums (perhaps $50 billion annually in the mid-1980s) it pays be-
yond "national defense" to maintain its military forces abroad and sub-
sidize the economies of Vietnam, Cuba, Angola, Afghanistan, and
Eastern Europe.[60] Although the land is rich in energy and mineral resources (such as oil, gas, coal, chromium, uranium), the economy is
plagued by poor national economic management, inefficient alloca-
tion of labor, transportation problems, and administrative inflexibility.
And despite abundant cropland, Soviet agriculture is characterized by
low productivity and rigid collectivization of production.

Overall, the USSR produces half as much as the U.S. in terms of
GNP, and allocates less than half as much per capita of GNP.[61] It is a
small factor in world trade, with combined imports and exports about
one-third that of the United States and also far below West Germany
and Japan.[62] As Chart 5.2 summarizes, based on a wide range of social
and economic performance indicators, the Soviet Union on average
ranks only twenty-fifth in the world. That is far below its number-two
ranking as a military power.

Against a background of underdevelopment, revolution, and two
world wars, Soviet communism has achieved some remarkable gains
for its people. The chart reveals some of them in education and health;
others are in science and technology, industrialization, women's rights,
and improved educational and work opportunities for rural dwellers
and ethnic minorities (who now account for about 48 percent of the
total population). The Soviet people have gone through some painful
experiences in war and politics yet have attained a fairly high living
standard in about seventy years.

But there are serious problems, many inherent in the political-economic system. Agricultural inefficiency is one of them. Since the huge
1972 wheat deal with the United States, the USSR has been the world's
largest grain importer. Mismanagement, low incentives to produce, inefficient use of fertilizer, and inattention to soil erosion are responsible
for low production and long food lines in the cities. As in the United
States, feeding grain to beef cattle adds to Soviet requirements.[63] Consequently, the Soviet Union puts major demands on the world's grain
supply and upward pressure on grain prices.[64] It also pays for its grain
with oil—an increasingly expensive trade that, in the future, may convert the USSR to an oil importer.

Like other heavily industrialized systems, that of the Soviets is ex-
periencing the usual contradictions of development: water pollution;
excessive use of a major fishery, the Caspian Sea, for water; air pollution that is affecting large areas of forest land; and inefficient industrial
technology (steelmaking in particular) that wastes energy in production.[65] Soviet officials may be finding, as some U.S. economic man-

Chart 5.2: Economic and Social Ranking of U.S. and USSR Among 142 Countries (1980)

GNP

	Economic/Social Standing	Per Capita		Public Expend. Per Capita	
	Average Rank	Rank	$US	Rank	$US
U.S.	9	16	11,347	16	571
USSR	25	34	4,564	31	231

Education

	% School Age Pop. in School		% Women in Total Univ. Enrollment		Literacy Rate	
	Rank	%	Rank	%	Rank	%
U.S.	1	85	12	49	1	99
USSR	60	59	9	50	1	99

Nutrition

	Calorie Sup. Per Capita	
	Rank	No.
U.S.	5	3,652
USSR	21	3,389

Health

	Public Expend. Per Capita		Population Per Physician		Population Per Hospital Bed		Infant Mortality		Life Expectancy	
	Rank	$US	Rank	No.	Rank	No.	Rank	Rate	Rank	Years
U.S.	13	439	26	550	34	171	19	13	8	74
USSR	37	113	1	270	8	82	47	36	38	70

Source: Ruth Leger Sivard, *World Military and Social Expenditures 1983*, Table III, pp. 36–37.

agers have found, that declines in economic efficiency go hand in hand with excessive investment in military production.

Human rights stand out as the Soviet system's greatest shortcoming. The worst excesses of the Stalinist political terror have receded. But the leadership's Gulag syndrome, captured in Solzhenitsyn's writings, remains: the internal exile of political opponents and peace activists; the tight control of religious, media, and artistic expression; the pervasiveness of the secret police; the rejection of free emigration for Jews and other groups. All these actions violate provisions of the 1975 Helsinki Accords signed with the United States and the European countries. The 100-odd Soviet citizens in the Helsinki Watch Committee who attempt to monitor their government's compliance have often been officially silenced. Such widespread repression can be attributed to an extremely insecure and conservative party leadership, one that is rigidly hierarchical, hostile to reform, and fearful of the working class in whose name it rules—hence, its crackdown on Czech liberalism in 1968 and its pressure on the Polish authorities to drive Solidarity underground. Soviet officialdom has been fairly characterized as a privileged class bent on self-perpetuation.[66] There is no room under Soviet-style socialism for alternatives to officially sanctioned and controlled forms of political and economic power—except, of course, underground.

A few other social problems deserve mention. As a multi-ethnic society, the Soviet Union shares with numerous other states, including the United States and Canada, unresolved problems stemming from "bilingualism, assimilation, ethnic intermarriage, affirmative action, regional autonomy, . . . and the geographical mixing of ethnic groups through migration . . ."[67] Political leadership typically is in the hands of Russians, not minority persons. The higher birth rate among non-Russians than among Russians evidently worries some Moscow officials.

Soviet women have made great strides beyond traditional rules; but discrimination is still widespread in employment, politics, and the home.[68] Social alienation, evidenced in widespread alcoholism (which affects over one-third of Soviet workers and has become the main public health problem)[69] and popular dissatisfaction with the limited avenues for upward mobility, is a major problem that the leadership acknowledges in its press commentaries.

As previously noted, Soviet (and, for that matter, East European) socialism on a transnational level is, in the words of a radical critic, "increasingly an integral part of the capitalist world economy."[70] Promoting that trend was, in fact, part of Henry Kissinger's announced strategy for achieving detente in the 1970s, a strategy welcomed by Brezhnev.[71]

Although it petered out beginning in the second half of the Carter administration, when trade ties with the USSR were cut back, the longer-term development remains: a substantial growth in the importance to the Soviet and East European economies of trade and credit from Western Europe and the United States. As traced by Andre Gunder Frank,[72] East-West trade was the fastest growing segment of the socialist East European countries' total trade by the mid-1970s. The Soviets and their East European partners in COMECON (the Council of Mutual Economic Assistance) are importing technology and grain in return for fuel and raw materials. (In the Soviet case, these imports amounted to 35 percent of all imports in the early 1980s, compared with 20 percent in 1965.)[73] But this exchange has been increasingly uneven and has led to large annual trade deficits—in 1975, for example, a $4.8 billion deficit for the USSR—that are only partly reduced by a surplus in trade with the Third World. Financing their increasing imports from the West has put the COMECON countries, the USSR included, in significant debt to West European and U.S. banks: over $58 billion in 1981.[74]

In terms of debt and trade patterns, the Soviet Union and Eastern Europe resemble the Third World NICs: They occupy a similar middle position in the so-called international division of labor. As Frank outlines it,

> the East imports advanced technology manufactures from the industrially developed capitalist countries, paying for them with raw materials and incurring a growing trade deficit. In exporting less sophisticated manufactures to the underdeveloped countries, the socialist countries run up a trade surplus, part of which they use to reduce their trade deficit with the West, also not unlike the subimperialist [newly industrializing] capitalist countries.[75]

The result for the Third World is similar to the result of its trade with the industrialized West: a trade imbalance and increased indebtedness. Inasmuch as the socialist bloc needs the capitalist world's trade and credit far more than it needs the Third World, the USSR has consistently sided with the United States and Western Europe on NIEO issues such as a debt moratorium, international control of seabed exploitation, and increased aid to the Third World.[76] The COMECON countries have also been increasingly receptive to cooperative undertakings with Western TNCs in the form of joint ventures, technology transfers, coproduction, and licensing arrangements. Such forms of multilateralism yield hard (convertible) currency for the socialist governments and relatively cheap, "disciplined" labor and large markets for the transnationals.[77]

What we see here, in short, is an economic picture that is quite different from the military side of East-West relations. In keeping with the Corporate Globalist vision of world order, the Soviet Union and Eastern Europe have become increasingly interlinked with the global economy—at the very time when Realist anti-Soviet hardliners such as emerged in the Reagan administration were emphasizing the military competition and the consequent need (which they attempted, largely unsuccessfully, to implement) to weaken COMECON's access to Western credit and technology. These two quite distinctive approaches to dealing with the Soviets probably resemble infighting among factions in the Soviet leadership itself. For in the reforms launched by Gorbachev we see Realist and Globalist forces arrayed in a major contest over the USSR's basic directions in society, economy, the arms race, and human rights.

Gorbachev's *glasnost* seeks to draw the USSR away from the precipice of great-power obsolescence.[78] He appears to be convinced that real Soviet security has been emasculated by official corruption, loss of individual effort and initiative, a stifling party-state hierarchy, excessive military spending, and intolerance of intellectuals. Without dismantling the party or state machinery, Gorbachev challenged it to create a "reformation"—*perestroika*, a radical change in the way it does business. In Gorbachev's first two years, many old-line officials were removed, a number of dissidents (some quite prominent, such as the physicist Andrei Sakharov) were freed, literature and film began to reflect a new realism (especially about the Stalin era), and the first steps were taken to make state factories more autonomous and responsive to workers. *Glasnost* thus has some of the earmarks of China's opening—minus significant foreign involvement in internationalizing the economy.

Gorbachev has also called for *perestroika* in foreign affairs. He has shown sensitivity to "global problems" that transcend class and national interest, such as the environment and (after Chernobyl) nuclear energy. He has asserted that "security can only be mutual," and that "there can be no security for the USSR without security for the United States." Gorbachev consistently took the initiative in arms-control proposals, including a nineteen-month unilateral moratorium on nuclear testing and acceptance of the principle of on-site verification of agreements.

These startling reversals of traditional Soviet policy have their detractors inside as well as outside the USSR. *Glasnost* clearly threatens the ideological and career interests of many well-entrenched bureaucrats who have thrived on state control and a hard-line military policy. Soviet reformism also bothers some Western Realists who refuse to believe Gorbachev is all that serious or, if he is, are concerned he will "win over" European and U.S. publics with his personal charm and rhetoric on arms reductions. Whether Gorbachev gets the respite he apparently seeks from the cold war to institute his reforms, promises to be a central issue in international politics in the years just ahead.

The United States

How America illustrates birth, muscular youth, the promise, the sure fulfillment, the absolute success, despite of people—illustrates evil as well as good, The vehement struggle so fierce for unity in one's-self . . .

—Walt Whitman, "Thoughts" (1860)

The United States approaches the year 2000 a nation deeply divided between wealth and poverty, new and old economic and political forces, the concentration of power in the center and its evisceration in the periphery. In a nation of such extraordinary diversity and shifting moods, it is always hazardous to identify trends. But the Reagan years have been such a distinct departure from the moderate liberalism of previous administrations, Republican as well as Democratic, that their imprint on U.S. political economy is more clear-cut and likely to be more lasting than any previous period since Franklin Roosevelt's New Deal. Reagan's crusade against communism is not the new ingredient, even granting the vigorousness of its pursuit. What is new has happened within the country: the determined effort to dismantle the welfare state, including its leading role on behalf of civil liberties, environmental protection, and equal opportunity; the alignment of conservative politics with New Right fundamentalism (the "Moral Majority"); the open identification of state power with big business and the wealthy class; the often doctrinaire application of supply-side economics to basic human problems such as workplace health and safety, unemployment, and education; and, as previously discussed, passage of the largest peacetime military budgets in U.S. history, alongside equally unprecedented budget deficits.

With all these departures, a fairer assessment of the Reagan years may be that they intensified, rather than created, economic inequalities and social problems that had been around for some time. One example is the United States' indebtedness. The national debt, as measured by U.S. government budget deficits, increased about $250 billion under Jimmy Carter's leadership. In Reagan's first term, however, the debt went up about $750 billion and is generally expected to be about $2 *trillion* by the end of his tenure in 1988. Meanwhile, the

U.S. international debt also skyrocketed. In 1985 the United States became a debtor nation for the first time since 1914: Total financial obligations to foreigners exceeded their obligations to the U.S. government and its citizens. In 1986 this indebtedness, representing a pivotal turnaround from the traditional U.S. position as a creditor nation, was roughly $250 billion and was increasing by about $100 billion a year. By 2000, the U.S. foreign debt is expected to reach $1 trillion, or a crushing 15 percent of GNP.

Growing poverty and wealth provide a second comparison. Although the existence of a "permanent underclass" in the United States was documented in the 1960s (at the time of President Lyndon Johnson's "war on poverty"), it grew by over one-third under Reagan. In 1983, 35.3 million persons—roughly 15 percent of the total population—lived below the government-established poverty line of $10,178 in annual income for a family of four. A striking 40 percent of those persons were children. The poverty rate was highest for blacks (35.7 percent) and Hispanics (28.4 percent) and their children.[79] Unemployment figures followed this pattern: Overall official unemployment was about 7 percent in the mid-1980s, but for nonwhites the rate was much higher, including nearly 50 percent of young blacks. The structural nature of poverty in the United States is best gauged by observing that it took place at a time of increased wealth among the upper class and rising median income as a whole. A 1984 Federal Reserve Board study found that the richest 2 percent of families collected about 15 percent of all income, and that the income share of the top 10 percent had risen to 33 percent.[80]

This discussion again raises the matter of discrepancies in average figures on prosperity. Chart 5.2 indicates an overall U.S. economic and social ranking of nine, in itself reflective of a problematic gap between military power and domestic achievement. But careful examination shows how the actual gap is much greater. The top rating for literacy, for example, pertains to the most elementary form of education and not to functional (job-related) literacy, in which the United States ranks 49th of 158 UN members.[81] In health care, despite its national wealth, the United States rates poorly on the chart. (Particularly disturbing is the ranking in infant mortality.) But the rating would be much lower still if it took into account about 12 percent of the population (mostly the poor) who lack medical insurance, which some specialists believe to be the key indicator of access to health care.[82] Skyrocketing health costs (especially for the elderly, who pay twenty cents of every dollar for health care), would also lower the rating, as would such environmental hazards as the 71 billion gallons of toxic waste annually produced and often disposed of in several thousand unmonitored landfills, threatening the water supply of numerous communities.[83]

Hunger, a basic cause of poor health, affects up to 20 million Americans; in the most comprehensive report on hunger in 1985, a physicians' group called it a "public health epidemic."[84] Yet, the nutrition ranking for the United States as a whole is high. Equally misleading is the chart's picture of education: The top ranking on school-age population belies a number of national educational surveys in the early 1980s that were sharply critical of the public school system. One of them, issued in April 1983 by the National Commission on Excellence in Education, went so far as to declare that "if an unfriendly foreign power had attempted to impose on America the mediocre educational performance that exists today, we might have viewed it as an act of war."[85] Finally, the chart inaccurately portrays the status of women: Although women make up nearly one-half of total university enrollment, that figure does not describe the failure of (male-dominated) state legislatures to pass an equal rights amendment to the U.S. Constitution, the unlikelihood that a woman (with or without a university degree) will earn a salary comparable to a man's, and such longstanding frustrations as inadequate child-care facilities and unequal work and training opportunities.

There are other social "epidemics" in the United States, crime being principal among them. Lawlessness at every level—crime in the suites as well as crime in the streets; crime by, and especially, against children—dominates all media and affects an increasing proportion of citizens. The overall crime rate is one of the world's highest, and the rate of imprisonment stands behind only that of the Soviet Union and South Africa.[86] A murder takes place every twenty-three minutes—also among the world's highest rates.[87] Women are especially vulnerable: A commonly cited figure is that an average of one of every 2.3 women will be a victim of violence, most likely rape, in her lifetime. Yet white-collar crime is no less rampant—and several times more costly to society than street crime. These factors contribute to staggering problems of justice and administration.[88] Almost inevitably, the rate of conviction and term of imprisonment vary greatly, often depending on the socio-economic background of the defendant. The overcrowding of prisons has also become a major problem, one not likely to be solved by constructing new penitentiaries with high price tags and little room for the huge numbers of new inmates. Finally, society is increasingly aware of the special problems associated with children: their neglect, abuse, abduction, molestation, as well as their (equally criminal) impoverishment.

These problems of personal insecurity have a counterpart in the economic domain. There, too, an entire middle sector—small businesses, small banks, the family farm—is being squeezed and shrunk by economic forces that strengthen the upper stratum while weakening the lower level. This development, which has international implications, is, again, long-term; the "Reagan Revolution" accelerated it. The main elements of this concentration of benefits and power are:

First, inequities in the tax system—multibillion-dollar tax breaks for the largest corporations for depreciation, investment, and research;[89] continuation of the post-World War II trend of increased federal revenues from personal taxes and decreased revenue from corporate taxes (48 percent from the former, 5.9 percent from the latter in 1982); and the failure of numerous large corporations to pay any federal tax despite showing hefty profits;[90]

Second, abuse of tax investment incentives by their largest beneficiaries, who use them either to absorb other businesses or to pay larger dividends to stockholders, in neither case benefiting the economy;[91]

Third, a record pace of corporate takeovers in the multibillion-dollar range, leading to further concentration of control of manufacturing and banking assets and, correspondingly, to

Fourth, increasing numbers of business failures, such as 530 small business failures a week in 1983, and about 1,600 farm closings a week (the U.S. farm debt stood at $215 billion in 1985);[92]

Fifth, the sharp downturn of the U.S. trade position, made so by long-term neglect to modernize basic industries, retool management and labor for a changing world economy, and bring the budget deficits to a halt so that U.S. farm and manufacturing exports can be competitively priced;

Sixth, the shaky position of the banking system, whose record post-Depression failures and high interest rates in the 1980s reflect not only the huge demands of the federal government and indebted businesses but also risky loans, such as those to Third World governments, amounting to over one and one-half times the major banks' total equity.[93]

"Who will bail out the United States?" asked President Ford.[94] The doubling of the national debt under Reagan, the heavy obligation of interest payments on that debt (about 14 percent of the total budget), the soaring trade deficit, and increased foreign investments in the United States meant that by the late 1980s, the U.S. "debt should exceed all the Latin American megaborrowers put together."[95] So long as U.S. consumers use more than they are willing to pay for, they will be living dangerously—borrowing from abroad and paying interest, and borrowing from the future, when the approximately $6 *trillion* in government, business, and personal debts will have to be paid off.[96] Absent so far is the political will to make major changes in government spending and tax policies that would keep families, communities, and the nation from paying the painful price of being a poor risk. Because at some point, as economist Lester Thurow warned, "the party [on borrowed money] stops and the work of repayment begins. The larger the borrowing, the harsher the period of repayment. If one wants to know what happens when countries are forced to begin repayment, go to Mexico or Brazil and look."[97]

These critical observations should be considered in the context of both the American dream and the American reality. To many millions of people abroad the United States still represents a land of opportunity and personal freedom. The ongoing, huge flow of refugees into the country attests to that, although in economic bad times many U.S. citizens erroneously see the refugees as competitors for scarce jobs and as a net drain on public funds. And the United States continues to possess enormous talent, energy, and youthful dynamism, as Whitman's poem says. Even its most vociferous critics give credit to the country's history of social activism and openness to dissent and cultural diversity. But the divisions within society and the economy are growing; the appearances of wealth and power are both real and deceiving. At the political center is a growing sense of paralysis about what to do—and a striking lack of political imagination to break clear of old shibboleths, left and right, in search of a new consensus appropriate to real security in a world in crisis. The costs of empire hang like a dead weight over the country, as they do over the Soviet Union, obstructing opportunities to make such a break.

The Price of Being Number One

We can now examine the direct and indirect costs of the arms race in light of the serious social and economic problems the superpower societies share. Because the availability of pertinent data is limited to the United States, the discussion will deal only with it. But in view of the similar rules of the game that the military-industrial complexes in the two countries operate under, a reasonable assumption is that what is true about the impact of the arms race in the United States is also true in the USSR.

Any discussion of the real costs to a society of "national security" must consider the full dimension of military spending. Some figures for the United States and the Soviet Union have already been given concerning the most obvious kinds of expenditures: weapons, armed forces, and bases at home and abroad. But other line items should be added, such as nuclear energy, veterans' benefits, the military component of space programs, the military reserve, and interest payments on the national debt from past wars. The defense department budgets of both countries hide these costs in the budgets of other agencies. When they are added to the bottom line of "national defense," they account in the United States for over 50 percent of all federal general spending out of tax revenues.[98] It may be even higher in the USSR.

The most glaring set of economic consequences of such profligate spending in the United States is in relation to indebtedness, interest rates, and taxes. Past and present military obligations have contributed far more than any other kind of public spending to the U.S. national debt.[99] (Equally obvious to many observers is that only a sizable reduction in military spending can make a dent in the debt.) Economists generally agree that huge budget deficits drive up interest rates; and in the mid-1980s the military, having the largest claim (about 60 percent) on government borrowing, helped to keep interest rates high. Individual taxpayers were therefore being hurt in two quite direct ways from high levels of military spending. First, as consumers, they were paying high interest on credit purchases, from home mortgages to clothing. Second, the four-person family with a $25,000 annual income (in 1986) could expect to pay 57 percent of its income taxes—about $172 a month—for military spending alone.[100]

A second set of direct costs of military spending pertains to economic productivity and competitiveness internationally. Here is the point of direct conflict between U.S. political-military predominance and the erosion of U.S. international economic hegemony. As Seymour Melman, among many others, has frequently pointed out, the Pentagon's inefficient way of doing business over many years — and, one should add, the congressional toleration, if not encouragement, of it— has been a major factor in the loss of industrial advantage to the Japanese and the West Europeans. Large cost overruns, lack of competitive bidding on all but 8 percent of prime contracts, seemingly endless amounts of money to spend, and scandalous waste and overcharges all add up to very expensive military equipment very inefficiently produced by a very large sector of the economy—in short, low productivity and over-priced goods.[101] It is no accident that the high-productivity societies are also the ones with relatively low military spending and, as in the case of Japan, a massive trade surplus (about $60 billion in 1986).

Low productivity and a poor trade position are also the result of the previously noted drain of U.S. research money and talent into military work. In 1982, U.S. research spending for nonmilitary purposes was only 1.9 percent of the GNP, considerably less than for West Germany (2.6 percent) or Japan (2.5 percent).[102] Simon Ramo, former president of TRW, a major military contractor, puts the issue succinctly: "In the past thirty years, had the total dollars we spent on military R&D been expended instead in those areas of science and technology promising the most economic progress, we probably would be today where we are going to find ourselves arriving technologically in the year 2000."[103] Military work in the United States employs over 25 percent of all scientists and engineers, including 30 percent of all mathematicians, 25 percent of all physicists, 47 percent of all aerospace engineers, and 11 percent of all computer programmers.[104] "If the brightest engineers in Japan are designing video recorders and the brightest engineers in the United States are designing MX missiles," Lester Thurow observes, "then we shouldn't find it surprising that they conquer the video-recorder market."[105]

Military spending is a two-edged sword in a third area: jobs. That it creates employment is self-evident. But the *kind* of employment created—skilled technical work for the most part—cannot tap into the much larger pool of semiskilled and professional workers that nonmilitary employment can. Thus, several studies comparing the number of jobs brought about by every $1 billion of government spending found that money used in (for example) education, public transportation, and health and police services produces thousands more jobs than spending on military development.[106]

While it is often argued on behalf of military spending that it contributes to the civilian sector through the technological spin-offs of research, notably aircraft and computers, there seem to be absolute limits to civilian applications.[107] In a word, the prospects for reducing unemployment in the United States, or anywhere else, are going to depend on the development of civilian goods and services. And when it comes to cutting into hard-core unemployment among the least-skilled, education and the expansion of human services, not military service or production, are the most effective remedies.

The military's absorption of resources represents yet another large social cost. Murray L. Weidenbaum, chairman of Reagan's Council of Economic Advisers, said in criticism of the 1980s military buildup: "What worries me is that these crash efforts rarely increase national security. They strain resources, create bottlenecks."[108] The U.S. military's large-scale consumption of strategic materials such as oil and chromium adds up to two unpleasant possibilities: the use of force to gain or preserve access to valuable resources, or, as in the case of South Africa, U.S. government and corporate alignment with an oppressive regime that supplies the resources. As a big user of resources, moreover, the military is a big waste-producer—in fact, by far the largest creator of nuclear waste. Overall, then, a solution to the problem that would be in both the national and global interest would be to develop mineral and energy substitutes, to conserve and recycle, and to reduce the military's needs for weapons and resources.

As Eisenhower's remark quoted earlier suggests, excessive military spending indirectly draws human and material resources away from socially productive purposes. At precisely what point military spending becomes "excessive" is, of course, always a matter of debate. But when national security is redefined in Global-Humanist terms, it becomes possible to see the transfer of resources from military to civilian purposes as a contribution to defense. Sharp declines in industrial productivity, massive budget and trade deficits, childhood poverty, and a "mediocre" educational system surely count as indicators of declining real security for generations to come. When these and other socioeconomic problems can be traced to particular causes, such as unprecedented levels of military spending, there is reason for judging the spending excessive and injurious to the national interest.

When Eisenhower, in his farewell address, issued his famous warning about the military-industrial complex, he specifically included two other areas: civil liberties and democracy. "We must never let the weight of this combination endanger our liberties or democratic processes," he said. "We should take nothing for granted." The warning is well-taken. The shrouding of government activities with the mantle of "national security" has been detrimental to the American way of life in many instances, taking such form as secret warfare against other states, for example the early years of U.S. intervention in Indochina; bolder, partly hidden involvements abroad led by the Central Intelligence Agency, such as the Iran Contragate hearings revealed went on in the Middle East and in Central America between 1984 and 1986; secretive contractual ties between federal agencies and academic institutions; suppression of information that would embarrass and cause public criticism of government officials, rather than subvert national security; the prosecution of prominent former employees-turned-critics; extra-Constitutional actions designed to avoid congressional oversight and debate; the denial of entry from abroad of persons and films critical of U.S. policy; the insistence on a right of prior restraint on scientific and academic exchanges with persons from socialist countries; and the infiltration of groups that peacefully protest U.S. policy, such as churches that offer sanctuary to refugees from Central America. The Founding Fathers foresaw this danger of the national-security state. "Perhaps it is a universal truth that the loss of liberty at home is to be charged to provisions against danger, real or pretended, from abroad," James Madison said in 1798.

The Prospects for Peace

The 1980s have been inconclusive so far as U.S.–Soviet arms talks are concerned. Two summit meetings between Reagan and Gorbachev gave hope of a major accord that would eliminate U.S. and Soviet medium- and short-range nuclear missiles from Europe. But actually being able to settle on terms that each side's military-industrial complex can live with—while each remains free to pursue research and testing of other strategic systems in space and at sea—is another matter. The late 1980s could yield the first significant reduction in nuclear weapons— or be known as the time when an unusual opportunity for containing the arms race was lost.

Which road is taken depends, as the concluding chapter argues, on how the leaders of the superpowers define security. The agenda is a long one and goes considerably beyond the tough questions of weapons, the character of the military economy, and the substance of arms agreements. "Today," Anne O'Hare McCormick has said, "the real test of power is not the capacity to make war but the capacity to prevent it." War prevention would seem to deserve far more than the infinitesimal resources currently being devoted to it by the major powers. Beyond that, U.S. and Soviet leaders, as heads of the most "developed" and certainly the most militarily powerful states, ought to begin investing in building trust rather than constantly adding to the prospect of binding hatred. Another presidential farewell address is worth pondering in this connection: George Washington's. In the face of increasing opportunities for the use and spread of nuclear weapons, Washington's call for restraint has immediate relevance:

> Nothing is more essential than that permanent, inveterate antipathies against particular nations and passionate attachments for others should be excluded, and that in place of them just and amicable feelings toward all should be cultivated. The nation which indulges toward another an habitual hatred or an habitual fondness is in some degree a slave. It is a slave to its animosity or to its affection, either of which is sufficient to lead it astray from its duty and its interest.

CHAPTER SIX

The Quest for Autonomy and Security in the Second World

At the end of dinner Mr. Honda was asked, "In your opinion, what will happen to industrial companies that don't accept the same method you have adopted and remain in the present capitalist system?" Honda did not hestitate: "They shall all perish."

— Quoted in Jean-Jacques Servan-Schreiber,
The World Challenge

THE NEW MEANING OF POWER

When the history of the twentieth century is written, we can be certain that the rebirth of Europe and Japan after World War II will be a prominent chapter. One of its themes is familiar: The transformation of war-ravaged economies into the world's most dynamic centers of business. Another theme, still in the making, is less frequently noted: How advanced political economies whose fates are closely tied to the First World seek to assert their independence and contribute to easing the world's military, economic, and ecological crises. To study the Second World—which includes Canada, Australia, and New Zealand—is to study the constraints and possibilities of innovative policymaking in countries caught between the Third World's demands for a new economic order and the First World's insistence on political allegiance.

The Second World's politics has given new meaning to power. Its economic and social performance has demonstrated what can be accomplished when military considerations are not permitted to become dominant. This is not to say that Second World countries are minor participants in the global arms race. Thirteen of the top twenty-five countries in military spending in recent years are in the Second World. France and West Germany head the list with total spending of about $26 billion each in 1980. Second World countries are right behind the Soviet Union and the United States in arms exports, led by France (11.5 percent of world deliveries in 1983), West Germany (4.8 percent), and Britain (4.3 percent). West Germany and France also maintain armed forces of about a half-million members, and France has nearly 60,000 troops stationed abroad. (Discounting NATO forces in Germany, Britain, with about 94,000 troops overseas, is the only other Second World country with a large foreign military presence.)

On the other end of the spectrum, however, are very large economies that have small military budgets and armed forces. Japan officially spends about 1 percent of its $1 trillion GNP on the military. Its armed forces number about 241,000. Canada devotes less than 2 percent of its GNP to the military, which numbers 79,000. And Australia, with a GNP considerably larger than Belgium's, devotes less money to its military and has about 15,000 fewer troops, even though both are allies of the United States.[1]

The heart of the matter is that, from 1960 to 1981, while the United States was spending an average of 6.5 percent of its GNP on the military, and the Soviet Union was spending 10.9 percent, their European allies in NATO and the Warsaw Pact were spending, respectively, 3.7 percent and 3 percent of their GNPs.[2] The superpowers have been subsidizing their partners' defense—the United States in that period accounted for two-thirds of NATO military outlays, and the USSR for about 90 percent of Warsaw Pact outlays[3]—and therefore also their economic growth. This situation evolved from the solidification of the cold war beginning in the late 1940s, when Moscow and Washington coalesced their spheres of influence in Europe around military and economic alliances. They paid the price of cold-war politics, not simply in hardware, but far more heavily in stunted economic performance. Each practiced "military Keynesianism," which helped its partners to take off economically (far more so, of course, in Western than in Eastern Europe).

The consequence, as has been noted previously, was a decline in the U.S. trade balance in manufactured goods that became permanent in 1968. U.S. transnational firms moved to Europe, a powerful Eurodollar market emerged as more and more dollars found their way into European banking hands, and West European and Japanese industries began to outperform their U.S. counterparts.[4] The superpowers got what they wanted —the military dependence of their allies in the great East-West strategic competition—but in the long run they sacrificed much more. The United States helped create economically competitive allies whose industries became more productive, innovative, profitable, and better-managed than their benefactors'.[5] The Soviets, meanwhile, helped spawn some economies more efficient and flexible than their own, such as Hungary's, and some massive headaches, such as Poland.

Chapter 1 noted the increasing share of world exports being taken by Japan and the European Economic Community (EEC) of West European states. The share of West Germany (12 percent) alone surpassed that of the United States by 1978. Growth in trade fueled a good part of these countries' growth in GNPs, which since 1950 have risen at a far faster rate than that of the United States.[6] Europe and Japan are highly dependent on trade for economic growth. In 1977, for instance, international trade was 13 percent of Japan's GNP, 24 percent of West Germany's, and 25 percent of Britain's, whereas it was only 6 percent of the U.S. GNP.[7] Therein lies strength, but also vulnerability. Dependence on oil imports exemplifies the latter: The 1979 oil shortages, for example, drained Western Europe, Canada, and Japan of about $400 billion in that year alone to pay for higher-priced oil and reduced economic activity.[8]

Since the late 1960s, whenever major recessions or inflations have occurred in the United States, they have become transnationalized; that is, their effects have been quickly felt in Europe and Japan, either in high unemployment and high interest rates, or in high unemployment and inflation ("stagflation").[9] And that is why, in the mid-1980s, European and Japanese leaders, as much as Third World leaders, pushed the United States to reduce its enormous budget deficits. Their economies were being hurt by weaknesses in the U.S. economy, even though their exports were being helped by an overvalued dollar.

Despite these vulnerabilities, the EEC countries and Japan have proven quite adept at resisting U.S. pressures to reduce tariff and other barriers to trade, eliminate government subsidies (such as on European agricultural products) that may unfairly price exports, and substantially increase their shares of military spending—all measures that U.S. administrations have argued would help reduce trade and budget deficits. Periodic, serious strains in the Western alliance have resulted from these perceived inequities. In the 1980s, for instance, they inspired strong protectionist sentiment in the U.S. Congress and led to pressure from the president on Japan and the EEC to "open up" their economies to a long list of U.S. products. Neither side in the dispute would admit to exaggerating its claims and scapegoating the other. For the reality would seem to be that Japanese and European markets *are* much more protected against other countries' products than they care to admit,[10] and that U.S. trade problems are *much less* the result of such protectionism than of a long-term U.S. neglect of its industrial base.

The EEC countries, Japan, and Canada are challenging U.S. predominance on another international economic front as well: transnational investments. Collectively, EEC-based TNCs, led by British firms, accounted (in 1980) for about 37 percent of total direct foreign investment worldwide. Canadian-based firms invested nearly 4 percent of the total, and Japanese TNCs over 7 percent. (The U.S. share then was about 41 percent.) Two facts about this development stand out: the rate of growth of global market investments by these Second World economies has significantly outpaced that of U.S. firms in recent years; and, like U.S. firms, those of the Second World invest mainly in each other's manufacturing sectors, secondarily in the NICs (such as Brazil and Singapore), and least of all in the most underdeveloped Third World economies.[11]

The erosion of U.S. leadership and competitiveness in world trade has, as stressed above, coincided with its enormous investment in arms and global alliances. In Chapter 5 we observed the social and economic costs for both the United States and the Soviet Union of this investment. In contrast, the Second World countries, led by the market economies, have put a significant portion of their savings on the military into long-term economic investment and social well-being. Consider, for instance, how research and development (R&D) money is allocated. The United States and the Soviet Union spend much more on scientific research, as a proportion of GNP, than any other industrialized country. Yet U.S. and Soviet industrial productivity rank very low in comparison, one reason clearly being that they invest such a high proportion of R&D in their military establishments.[12] Industrial productivity in the United States has also been hindered by failure to modernize equipment and production methods, inefficient energy use, top-heavy management geared to short-term profit-making, and low capital investment—all opposite of what Japan and West Germany experience, particularly in basic industries (such as steel and auto).[13] No wonder, then, that Western Europe and Japan have so consistently outperformed the United States (and, of course, the USSR even more so) in GNP growth, productivity, entrepreneurship, technological innovation, and, in many cases, wage levels.

Social spending reveals similar differences of emphasis. Whereas public spending in the United States declined (as a percentage of Gross Domestic Product) from 35.4 percent to 29 percent between 1961 and 1981, it rose significantly everywhere else: in Canada, for example, from 30 percent to 41.4 percent; in Japan, from 17.4 percent to 34 percent; and in France, from 35.7 percent to 48.9 percent.[14] Based on several indicators of public health (including nutrition and water quality), education, and economic performance, the United States ranks below Denmark, France, West Germany, Iceland, Norway, Finland, Sweden, and Australia. And the Soviet Union, despite its social and economic gains since World War II, still ranks below every Second World market economy, as well as below East Germany.[15]

These social and economic gains suggest that Second World countries have learned from and taken advantage of conditions in the First World. But sizable problems remain. One of them is respect for human rights. The problem is most acute in Eastern Europe, as seen in the statement of Charter 77 in Czechoslovakia and as the following case study of Poland discusses further. Deprivation of civil liberties is a serious problem as well in Romania, Albania, and East Germany. The capitalist Second World states have some human-rights problems too. Japanese women, for example, are only beginning to receive an equal voice with men in politics and in the work place. The excerpts (in Chapter 3) from two American Indian protests could as readily have come from Indian tribes in Canada. Blacks, West Indians, and other minority groups in England are frequently victims of social injustice.

An entirely different set of problems is the Second World's military and economic vulnerability to the troubles of the superpowers. Having suffered through two world wars, Europe is again a prime target, this time of a nuclear exchange that might escalate from a conventional conflict. In 1982 approximately 10 million soldiers, about equally divided between NATO and Warsaw Pact forces, were on active duty in Europe.[16] NATO deploys about 6,000 nuclear weapons there, including about 2,000 nuclear artillery shells that are of questionable military value;[17] and the USSR has deployed a similar number of "tactical" and intermediate-range nuclear weapons in Eastern Europe.

For as long as nuclear weapons have been deployed in Europe, there has been controversy over whether and how they might be used in the event of war. The central issue has been European confidence about U.S. willingness to put its own cities at risk in the event of a Soviet non-nuclear attack on Europe. (Why the Soviets would do that and risk complete destruction by British and French nuclear forces is a question frequently ignored.)[18] Perhaps inevitably, the more the Soviets built up their European theater nuclear forces to offset the U.S.–NATO advantage (to the point of superiority today), the more European confidence eroded. To be sure, the North Atlantic Treaty (Article 5) invokes the principle that an attack on one member shall be considered an attack on all. And every U.S. administration has conveyed assurances to its NATO partners that the United States will risk its own destruction in the event of Soviet aggression.

But both the credibility and the wisdom of such assurances are in doubt. High-level U.S. officials, including President Reagan, have openly discussed the possibility that, should conflict with the Soviets erupt, nuclear weapons could be "limited" to use in Europe. Europeans consider that idea preposterous and dangerous; it implies that targets in the United States might be spared at their expense. And what if U.S. leaders really do mean to retaliate with nuclear weapons? Said Henry Kissinger in Brussels in 1979: "The European allies should not keep asking us to multiply strategic assurances that we cannot possibly mean, or if we do mean, we should not want to execute because if we execute, we risk the destruction of civilization."[19]

Here was one of those all too infrequent admissions of an ultimate reality: The weapons which are designed to deter attack will destroy all of Europe, and much else besides, if they are used. Europeans understand that full well. The costs of a "limited" nuclear conflict in central Europe have, after all, been known since 1955, when NATO war planners ran a simulation which found that a mere 335 nuclear weapons, mostly detonated in Germany, would cause *immediate* casualties of about 5 million people dead or wounded. Later studies, which take into account the increasing number of nuclear weapons deployed in Europe, have greatly increased the predicted level of casualties and contamination.[20] The "nuclear allergy" that the Japanese have applies across the political spectrum in Europe too. As then Chancellor Helmut Schmidt of West Germany was moved to remark in 1981, at a high point of massive popular demonstrations against the deployment of neutron weapons in Europe, "the intense fear that Europeans have—in some situations it seems that Europeans are even more afraid of the Americans than they are of the Russians—is not a very healthy state of affairs."[21]

One result of European concerns has been to question the value of NATO from time to time. But the only defection has been that of France in 1966—and it was a limited defection at that, since France remains a member of the North Atlantic Council and continues to engage in military cooperation with NATO, even though French forces are no longer part of the joint command. (Spanish voters, in a 1986 referendum, agreed to their country's continued membership in NATO with similar limitations, such as pulling out of NATO's joint command and prohibiting the stockpiling of nuclear weapons on Spanish soil.) Other Europeans have raised the prospect of a "neutral," "Finlandized" Europe, disengaged from the United States, and of a nuclear-free zone in central Europe. But these ideas, which would certainly redefine the Second World's place in world politics, have yet to receive sustained interest by European publics.[22]

The nuclear disarmament movement, on the other hand, has had some success in Western Europe—and its efforts have carried over into the East. Massive demonstrations in the Netherlands, West Germany, and Britain greeted the NATO decision to accept U.S. deployment of Pershing and cruise missiles in 1983. The demonstrations did not alter the decision, but they did spur parliamentary oppositions to adopt antinuclear platforms, and they showed that popular support of groups like the Greens and the British Campaign for Nuclear Disarmament extended to the middle class. In Eastern Europe antinuclear sentiment was not restricted, as Moscow had hoped it would be, to opposing only U.S. missile deployments. Antiwar demonstrations, church meetings, and protests have taken aim at Soviet deployments as well. The common call has been for serious U.S.–Soviet negotiations and mutual force reductions, most strenuously in East Germany, where nuclear anxieties are linked to identification with German pride and national independence. Summarizing these developments in Eastern Europe, one analyst argued that "a regional peace movement could one day challenge Soviet control even more broadly than did Poland's now-banned independent trade union Solidarity."[23]

Economic interdependence between Western and Eastern Europe has become the key counterpoint to political and military tensions. Its manifestations include economic ties between East and West Germany that grew out of Willy Brandt's *Östpolitik* (referring to Eastward-looking detente) in the 1960s, the major investments of West European banks in the East, Hungarian and Romanian membership in the IMF, and the previously discussed economic relations between a technology- and capital-hungry USSR and an energy-hungry Europe. These forms of interpenetration fly in the face of old-fashioned Realist geopolitics, which has always looked for ways to exploit East-West differences for strategic advantages. Various U.S. administrations have regarded Eastern Europe's dependence on the West as a source of political leverage, either to "mellow" Soviet behavior or to punish Soviet wrongdoing. As a result, U.S. trading firms have often faced government-imposed limitations on trading with "the enemy," for example, denial to the Soviet Union of most-favored-nation status (which keeps tariffs high on Soviet exports) and of substantial credits to facilitate Soviet imports. Because in Western Europe East-West trade is important both economically to growth and employment, and politically, to reduce cold-war tensions, West European (and Japanese) firms do not face similar trade restrictions. They have been willing to follow through on large commercial ventures (such as a gas pipeline from the USSR to West Germany and joint Soviet-Japanese development of Siberia) in spite of U.S. objection and even (in the gas pipeline case) U.S. efforts to prevent the use of its technology.

Another kind of European economic initiative with long-term implications is the planned conversion of unprofitable industries to nonmilitary, "socially useful" production. The model program was developed in the mid-1970s by workers at Lucas Aerospace, Britain's largest defense industry, in response to the threat of large-scale layoffs.[24] Although Lucas management rejected the proposal—which included the creation of prototypes of profitable alternative products, job retraining, and work reorganization—the "Lucas Plan" gained widespread attention in Britain and on the Continent. It generated activity in a number of directions: a major employment program by the city council of Sheffield, England, to convert unused factories for production of useful items (such as dehumidifiers to combat building mold); conversion of a shipyard in Landskrona, Sweden, which resulted in the opening of forty new businesses and the saving of over 1,600 jobs; and campaigns by West German workers in military industries to interest management in turning existing technology to new purposes rather than closing the plants.[25] To Mike Cooley of the Greater London Enterprise Board, the British labor leader who was instrumental in the Lucas proposal, conversion is the way to reverse a government's priorities while saving and creating jobs. "What must happen," he says, "is that we force the government to make kidney machines and the arms manufacturers go around collecting pennies to produce arms."[26]

The following studies of Japanese, Canadian, and Polish cases give further evidence of Second World efforts to strike out on its own. Energy independence and environmental and economic self-protection have provided powerful incentives to do so. To what *extent* such considerations will promote greater political and military autonomy is a key question; that they *do* is undeniable. Every act of disaffection by an alliance partner holds the potential to put the entire partnership on a new foundation. New Zealand made the point in 1985 when it decided to bar U.S. nuclear-powered or nuclear-armed ships from visiting its ports. The New Zealand government reaffirmed its commitment to the ANZUS agreement, but the U.S. government acted as though the alliance had become permanently altered—and therefore it had. Like the West Europeans, including many political conservatives, New Zealanders simply do not share U.S. citizens' pervasive sense of threat from the communist world, any more than Eastern Europeans (with some exceptions, such as the Albanian and East German leaderships) buy the Soviets' paranoia about the imminent dangers of capitalist penetration. And therein lie the seeds of major political changes that might decisively alter the complexion of the cold war.

SOME SECOND WORLD CASE STUDIES

Japan: Between Interdependence and Dependence

Japan presents the anomaly of being an economic superpower while retaining economic and military dependence on other countries. It has the world's second-largest GNP, a per capita income comparable to that of the United States, and number-one status as a world lender. Japan is also close to surpassing the United States as the leading exporter. As Japan begins what has been called its third structural economic transformation—from textiles in the early 1900s, to heavy and chemical industries between the 1930s and the mid-1960s, and now to knowledge-intensive production[27]—it has demonstrated, perhaps better than any other society, an ability to adapt to global economic interdependence. Yet Japan must still rely heavily on resources from abroad and on the United States for protection from attack under terms of a 1960 security treaty. As the only victim of atomic attack, Japan has a deeply ingrained "nuclear allergy" that has led it to forswear producing nuclear weapons even though it has the ability to do so. Article 9 of the Japanese constitution forbids warmaking as a national policy. This provision has been interpreted by successive governments to permit the maintenance of so-called Self-Defense Forces (along with U.S. bases), but to restrict their role to defense of the home islands. As a result, Japan's total military expenditures are high, but not as a percentage of GNP, leaving it with considerable added spending power.

Observers have attributed the global surge of Japanese industry to many factors.[28] In the early postwar period, the imposition of a democratic system, partial elimination of the *zaibatsu* (finance-business combines) and their replacement by an interlocking government–big business–banking complex, and the establishment of a U.S. protectorate enabled Japan to concentrate on economic growth. Japan also took advantage of its being a latecomer to use the newest technologies in rebuilding its industrial base. Leftist labor unions were contained or crushed, providing a period of enforced stability. Domination of national politics by a single party, the Liberal Democrats, has lent continuity to the political system. By the early 1960s, Japan was prepared to take off economically, moving quickly from mere imitator and absorber of technology to producer of some of the highest-quality goods on the world market. Spurred by the vision of Yoshida Shigeru, who was prime minister from 1946 to 1954, Japan opted for a reactive foreign policy, including limited rearmament, but aggressive pursuit of economic growth.

In this strategy to win the peace even though having lost the world war, investment in human resources and energy alternatives has been as critical a factor as any other. The Japanese work force is the world's best educated, for example. A paternalistic relationship between corporations and labor affords job security for a substantial portion of the work force, and promotes productivity. The Japanese have a high rate of domestic savings that contrasts sharply with the U.S. penchant for buying on credit. A great deal of this money flows abroad in pursuit of higher returns than are available on investment at home. Energy-saving measures, such as extensive recycling of aluminum and use of compact refrigerators, go along with investment in a diversity of energy sources, including nuclear power.

The quality of life in Japan is quite high, reflecting a sense of national purpose that is seldom encountered elsewhere. Still, Japan has its share of social and political problems. Its political system, for example, is tightly controlled at the top levels. Big business is seldom regulated. Employment for many workers and farmers is not secured by lifelong tenure. The status of women remains low. The cost of housing and food is astronomical. Environmental issues are serious: air pollution is hazardous in the major cities; Japan is the only industrial nation without an antismoking campaign; land-use laws are weak, accounting for the disappearance of forests; and Japan's opposition to a worldwide moratorium on commercial whaling puts it in a class by itself.

Japanese adaptability and farsightedness have not, however, been the only factors shaping their international perspective. Economic nationalism and a strong (some might say exaggerated) sense of vulnerability are equally important. They account for a major contradiction in Japan's approach to foreign trade and investment: working for an open world economy, but putting Japanese economic interests first. The dominant view in Japan is that the contradiction is necessary. Resource dependence is one reason: Japan relies on imports for about 50 percent of its food and over 85 percent of its total energy (including nearly 100 percent of its oil), making it vulnerable to the political stability and trading practices of others. Another reason is that, while Japan enjoys a large surplus in trade with the United States, its senior partner, circumstance creates dependence on the openness of the U.S. market to Japanese products. (In 1981 more than one-quarter of Japan's exports went to the United States, as against about 9 percent of total U.S. exports that were shipped to Japan.) Likewise with Western Europe, to which over 12 percent of all Japanese exports were sent in 1981, as against only 2 percent of European exports imported by Japan.[29]

When it comes to foreign involvement in Japan's economy and to Japan's overseas investments, self-preservationism again prevails. Japanese leaders lean toward monopoly control rather than unfettered competition. They tend to promote the most efficient and technologically advanced firms, national and transnational. Foreign ownership of domestic companies and foreign access to financial and equity markets are severely restricted, whereas Japanese investment abroad is heavily promoted.[30] The figures confirm the success of this strategy— and the reasons for U.S. and European chagrin over Japan's "neomercantilism." For in comparison with the U.S. and Common Market economies, Japan's is indeed quite closed: Only 1.5 percent of direct stock investment worldwide in the industrialized countries went to Japan in 1980, compared with 15.5 percent to the United States, 10.3 percent to Canada, and 10.2 percent to Britain. Comparing direct investment flowing into and out of a country, Japan allows in a mere 4 percent of what it invests abroad, whereas the figure is 31 percent for West Germany, 46 percent for Canada, 59 percent for Britain, and 48 percent for the United States.[31]

In overseas investment, we can best see the Japanese pattern by contrasting Japanese with U.S. practices. Japanese TNCs invest far more extensively than their U.S. counterparts in the Third World (about 42 percent to 25 percent), where they concentrate on the Pacific Basin and Southeast Asia. Japanese TNCs generally promote, rather than discourage, technology transfers there in the expectation of building new markets for the next generation of Japanese products. Japanese firms accept minority ownership more often than not, make investments part of a "development assistance package," and encourage exports back to Japan of the manufactured product. Overall, these investment practices seem to benefit both home and host country: For Third World hosts, they fit with the usual desire for more control over foreign investment, for greater employment opportunities, and for increased exports of processed goods; for Japan, they mean access to land and labor that are in short supply at home, and they compel the constant upgrading of Japanese production to meet competition which its own investments have helped to create.[32]

An important exception, however, should also be mentioned: banking. Japan is a major contributor to the World Bank and various regional multilateral banks, such as the Asian Development Bank. But Japanese commercial banks, the world's largest, only hold half or less of Third World debt. This reflects their preference for investing where capital is most profitable, in the industrialized world, rather than where it is in desperately short supply. Only in 1987 did Japan indicate a major new commitment of funds to Third World development.

Despite all these innovations, Japan's leadership is uncomfortably aware of the country's junior status. For it has frequently placed constraints on Japanese foreign-policy independence, primarily in relations with the United States. In the 1950s, for example, U.S. nuclear weapons were secretly stored in Japan, and in the 1960s, U.S. air bases in Japan were crucial to the bombing of North Vietnam. Until the start of U.S.–China diplomacy in the 1970s, various Japanese governments had been under pressure from the United States to minimize economic ties with the PRC. All these forms of deference to U.S. policy posed domestic political problems for Japanese leaders. Dependence on the United States has also put pressure on Japan to increase military spending and either liberalize its trade and domestic investment policies or face rising barriers to Japanese exports to the United States. Occasionally, Japan's second-rank status has been reinforced by surprise moves by the United States, such as Kissinger's secret trip to China in 1971 and the "Nixon shock" the same year that imposed import surcharges and reduced U.S. exports of soybeans, a staple of the Japanese diet. Surprises make for resentment when, as in Japan's case, a nation is frequently told how valuable an ally it is and then is neither consulted nor informed in advance about key decisions.

We should expect that the Japanese would be debating the politics of dependence and how in particular it should affect their relations with the United States. One Japanese analyst has portrayed the debate in terms similar to those employed in this book.[33] "Passivists," like many American Realists, argue for continuing Yoshida's reactive strategy: a narrow pursuit of Japan's national interests. They emphasize Japan's weakness, a priority to domestic problems over foreign-policy assertiveness, and therefore a low-key, case-by-case diplomacy. On the other side are the "activists," Japan's Corporate (and other) Globalists. Nakasone Yasuhiro, prime minister since 1982, is their leading figure (although 1987 marked his last year in office). They see the necessity for Japan to contribute directly to shaping a world community that is being most profoundly altered by economic interdependence. Japan must shake off the image of "Japan, Inc." and become a force for peaceful cooperation and a new world order. Japan's ability to secure Middle East oil in the early 1970s, independently of U.S. policy, was a landmark for activists, who want to encourage Japanese international self-reliance whenever possible. In fact, Japanese Globalists like Nakasone believe that the nuclear stalemate, interdependence, and an emerging global consciousness will make the twenty-first century distinctly Japanese. Nationalism and racial pride will be expressed through international superiority.

"Passivism" clearly dominates in official Japanese thinking. But especially since the oil crisis, Japan has become more activist. It was Japan's prime minister, and not the U.S. President, who was first to normalize relations with China (in 1978) by signing a peace treaty that accorded the PRC diplomatic recognition. It was the Japanese leadership which, reflecting the strong pull of resource diplomacy, broke with the United States over Iran's seizure of U.S. hostages in 1979 and decided to continue importing Iranian oil. Japan has proven adept at resisting U.S. pressure from time to time for it to adopt a more expansive interpretation of Article 9 that would justify its assuming a greater military burden in the Pacific. This, despite recent signs of a loosening of traditional restraints on military deployments and spending, such as a sharp increase in participation in joint military exercises with the United States and its allies and (in 1986) adoption of a military budget that for the first time exceeded one percent of the GNP.

Other indications of Japanese foreign-policy independence are their ability to ignore pressure to become a larger importer and supplier of military equipment; to align with China and others against the Soviet Union and forego long-term economic cooperation plans (which began in 1975) with the USSR on Siberian development; and to transform its domestic economy to allow in more U.S. capital and technology. Japanese government and business leaders have thus far judged that such steps would be politically and economically dangerous. They would create enormous domestic division, resurrect the specter (above all in China and Southeast Asia) of a Japanese military revival, and curtail economic growth.

Japan's energy policy exemplifies the leadership's single-minded pursuit of national objectives in an interdependent economic world. Since energy is not just a commodity in trade but a strategic resource for Japan, assurance of its continued supply must be planned as part of a comprehensive economic strategy. That explains why, in pursuit of its own energy needs, Japanese independence has often run afoul of U.S. policies, whether with respect to Middle East oil or Soviet gas or U.S. supplies to Japan of nuclear fuel and technology.[34] As Japan further develops its knowledge industries, its energy priorities will be changing. Electronic and microprocessor goods will be research-intensive, therefore less resource- and energy-dependent (and less polluting) than previous kinds of production, which are being transferred abroad.

Still, in the immediate future, Japan will continue to rely heavily on oil and nuclear imports to meet growing electricity demand. It will probably seek to diversify energy sources by focusing on the Pacific Basin and by gaining greater control over the entirety of the nuclear process. But in the longer run we can expect to see even greater stress being placed on energy efficiency and conservation, with which Japan has had considerable success,[35] and on vigorously exploring renewable energy sources, such as solar and geothermal.[36] Government and industry will not be alone in making such decisions. Since the late 1960s, citizen-activists in local environmental and other protest groups in Japan have been instrumental in pushing an alternative energy agenda that reflects postindustrial values.[37] In important respects, therefore, Japan's future is at the cutting edge of growth policies among the major industrialized nations.

Canada: Resources and Sovereignty

From afar, it is remarkable that two countries, Canada and the United States, which have so much in common historically and culturally, which share a long and quiet border, and which have similar and closely intertwined political-economic systems, should perceive one another so differently. Whereas the United States has always taken Canada's friendship and cooperation for granted and probably devotes fewer resources to studying it than to Mexico or Brazil, Canada has for many years intensely debated its U.S. partnership. The perennial issue is Canadian sovereignty: Can it be preserved? Is it already lost? Or is a certain amount of dependence on the United States inevitable and desirable in an interdependent world economy? I want to explore this issue with particular reference to resources and the environment, not in order to arrive at a crisp definition of Canada's status, but to observe both the opportunities and the limitations that close interdependence affords a major Second World society.

"Of all the industrialized nations, Canada is probably second only to Japan in the degree to which its economy depends on a healthy world economy and active world trade."[38] The centrality of Canadian–U.S. economic ties warrants making it our first order of business. With a total bilateral trade of about $120 billion in 1984, the two countries represent the world's largest trading partnership. Canada's share is slightly greater; but with over 70 percent of both exports and imports being sold to or taken from the United States, Canada is highly dependent on the U.S. market.[39] In large part, the trade involves an exchange of Canadian resources—minerals and forest materials in particular—for U.S. manufactured products. The United States is a voracious consumer of resources (in 1975 they were nearly 53 percent of total imports), and Canada supplies many of the ones the United States most uses. For example, in 1975 Canada accounted for "15 percent of U.S. imports of petroleum [and currently under 5 percent] . . ., virtually all imported uranium and natural gas, 85 percent of forest products, 73 percent of nickel, 51 percent of zinc, 49 percent of iron ore, 48 percent of copper . . ." It is important that, as the source for these figures goes on to note, "the capital for developing Canadian raw materials production was supplied predominantly from the United States, and the book value of U.S. direct investment in such production multiplied 26 times [by the mid-1970s]."[40]

Therein lies a fair portion of the debate over Canadian sovereignty: the question whether or not Canada's economic, hence also its political, independence is threatened by the large and growing U.S. stake in its resources; and the related issue of who benefits, in either or both societies, from the potential depletion of Canada's natural resources.[41] A prominent Canadian official, Walter Gordon, worded the issue sharply in 1967:

> During the last fifty years we have freed ourselves of traces of colonial status insofar as Britain is concerned. But having achieved our independence from Britain, we seem to have slipped, almost without knowing it, into a semi-dependent position in relation to the United States. . . . If present trends are allowed to go unchecked . . . then, as I've intimated, Canada may not exist as a separate and independent nation in another 100 years. . . . Already, in my view, we have surrendered too much ownership and control of our natural resources and our key industries to foreign owners, notably those in the United States. And history has taught us that with economic control inevitably goes political control. This is what colonialism is all about.[42]

Gordon's remarks may be considered unduly alarmist. For one thing, Canada's foreign investments and trade have expanded beyond North America to Western Europe and Latin America, respectively. Like the United States, Canada has attracted much more capital into the country than it has invested abroad. But in Canada's case the trend is toward greater overseas investments.[43] The growth of state-run enterprises in Canada also may be seen as diminishing its dependence on foreign (mainly U.S.) corporations. As a result, the foreign sector's share of total Canadian corporate assets (about 28 percent in 1978) and profits (about 38 percent) has dropped appreciably.[44]

Even with these changes, two circumstances stand out: Canadian foreign investments and trade remain overwhelmingly with the United States; and foreign-owned businesses in Canada (of which U.S. ones account for 74 percent of assets and 87 percent of sales) dominate key sectors of industry—including, so far as resources are concerned, 69 percent of petroleum and coal, 90 percent of rubber, 59 percent of mineral fuels, and 35 percent of mining.[45]

There can be little doubt that such tight economic ties with the United States have imposed limits on Canadian sovereignty, limits that have led to Canada's being described, by Canadians, as a "rich underdeveloped economy."[46] Economically, for example, there has been a considerable net outflow of capital as Canadian money is used to finance foreign subsidiaries. Technological dependence on foreign corporations is substantial and growing. Certain activities of U.S. corporations in Canada, such as trade with communist countries, have been restricted by U.S. law, resulting in a reduction in Canadian exports. The processing of Canadian raw materials prior to export to the United States has been harmed by high U.S. tariffs. And mounting U.S. protectionism to meet its balance-of-payments problems has penalized some Canadian exports. Meanwhile, since the Vietnam era Canadian administrations have occasionally criticized U.S. foreign policies, including prolonged interventions in Southeast Asia and Central America and the enormity of the 1980s nuclear buildup, which increases Canada's own vulnerability. But these criticisms have hardly amounted to a break with longstanding Canadian support of overall U.S. objectives. As a former Canadian prime minister, Lester Pearson, once conceded, for his country to depart from traditionally friendly relations with the United States would risk economic retaliation that Canada simply could not afford.[47]

A lingering question is how much independence of decisionmaking Canada will exercise when U.S. resource demands conflict with the perceived requirements of Canada's own population. Will Canada continue to be able to resist U.S. inquiries about the export of water?[48] Of more immediate relevance is energy. The extent of U.S. corporate ownership of Canadian mineral fuels may raise some troublesome issues in the future. Such a situation is made all the more difficult because the two countries' oil and gas pipelines are linked to reduce costs. Actually, at different times Canadian exports to the United States of oil and natural gas *have* been cut back. The same could happen to other resources in which U.S. investments are substantial.

Thus far, the two governments have been able to reach agreements on most resource issues. But Canadian nationalism might well heighten resistance to the export of precious resources in the future. Increased Canadian ability to finance investment in resource extraction and greater conservation of nonrenewable resources would diminish the need for U.S. dollars. It could even lead to expropriation of U.S. companies. Increased Canadian consumption of energy could reduce its export to the United States. On the other side, expanding U.S. demand for a resource that is in short supply, increased control by U.S. corporations of Canadian energy resources, and Canada's aspirations for energy self-reliance all provide fertile ground for tension.[49]

Environmental politics might prove to be the pivotal issue for Canadians in deciding whether to pursue a resource trade and investment relationship with the United States that is based more on nationalism or on interdependence. For while importing increased amounts of Canadian resources, the United States is also exporting pollution. And corporate interests, U.S. and Canadian, bridge the two concerns.[50] Acid rain buildup centered in the Great Lakes–Ohio Valley region stands out as the latest, and most serious and well-publicized, irritant for Canadians.[51]

Acid precipitation consists mainly of sulfur dioxide from metal smelters and coal- and oil-fired power plants and nitrogen oxides from auto emissions. Fifty million tons of acid rain falls over the region every year. A U.S.–Canadian scientific fact-finding group reported in 1979 and 1980 that U.S. sources account for 80 percent of the sulfur emissions and 90 percent of the nitrogen oxides. The reports warned of the serious damage being done to Canadian forests, crops, and lakes— damage that was becoming irreversible. The industries believed most responsible for the pollution and the local governments whose economies would be affected by new environmental regulations naturally reacted by challenging the reports' methodology and conclusions. But the two governments forged ahead, with Canada taking the lead. In August 1980 they signed a Memorandum of Intent that recognized the problem and made a commitment to reach a formal agreement on reducing transboundary air pollution.

Since then, the U.S. government has done little, slowed by the anti-regulatory bias of the Reagan administration and, even more so, by the seemingly unquenchable thirst for energy and other resources. This, despite the firm conclusion of the administration's own scientific commission that industrial pollution from U.S. plants would need to be brought quickly under control in order to prevent "grave" ecological damage.[52] Most Canadians, with the main exception being those who stand to profit from environmental exploitation, wonder how much they must continue to sacrifice on the altar of U.S.-led industrialization. The solutions are no secret: energy conservation, a shift of energy sources away from fossil fuels, and, in the interim, use of more efficient and cleaner production methods. But such a major (and costly) undertaking requires U.S.–Canadian cooperation. For what is at stake in such a complex interdependence is not only the preservation of a regional ecosystem, but also the economic viability of Canada and the entire tenor of U.S.–Canadian relations.

Poland: Human Rights Underground

For a time after the death of Josef Stalin in 1953, Paul Sweezy suggests, "there was much optimism in the international socialist movement . . . that the worst was over and the future would bring an evolution of socialist values and institutions." But "these hopes gradually faded," he wrote.[53] No more so than in Poland, where the political and economic brutalities of everyday life make a mockery of Marx's concept of working-class leadership. Here, a communist party makes the rules, Soviet tanks ensure their enforcement, and democracy exists only underground.

Like every other European society, Poland's contemporary political economy was fundamentally altered by the devastation of World

War II. The country lost 22 percent of its resources. The old ruling elites were removed in favor of pro-Soviet partisans who came to power in the wake of the Soviet Red Army's drive westward. Protests from the West that this process violated the Big Three (U.S.–USSR–Britain) accords at Yalta (February 1945) were to no avail; Poland was drawn into the Soviet sphere of influence.

The new communist regime adopted the Soviet economic model, with its emphasis on heavy industrial development and centralized planning. Investment in consumer goods and agriculture, which was the mainstay of the prewar economy, was sadly neglected. Today, Poland ranks tenth in world industrial production, led by its extractive industries (coal), iron and steel, and machine building. But a high percentage of factory equipment is obsolete. Meanwhile, collectivized farming has performed poorly: food shortages and sudden food price increases are frequent. Public facilities such as urban housing, transportation, heating, and sanitation are decaying and inadequate. Although Poland's health care and nutrition rank high worldwide, the precipitate decline of public services has created serious air and water pollution, and therefore worsening public health.[54] A report of the Polish Academy of Sciences offered the somber prediction that "the long limitation of investments may have in the near future social and ecological consequences on an unimaginable scale."[55]

Access to a higher standard of living comes with political power, which means membership in the Polish Communist Party. The higher one's position, the greater one's privileges: better opportunities for jobs, higher income, the purchase of scarce goods (both in urban and rural areas), social standing, and justice. The contrast with nonparty people is striking. Intellectuals who are not party members are barred from higher job classifications. But unskilled workers earn roughly half the pay of an intellectual, and live accordingly.[56] Justice is based on a "two-class legal system," according to Lech Walesa, Solidarity's leader. While most Poles are "bound by the legal norms and have to obey them, . . . there is a caste of people who are above the law."[57] What we have in Poland, therefore, is not the traditional Marxist struggle to end class conflict, but rather its perpetuation in a quite different form: a party elite versus the working class.

Inequities of these kinds and deteriorating economic conditions have prompted five major periods of social protest: in 1956, 1968, 1970, 1976, and 1980 to 1981. The last of these was the most dramatic and far-reaching. For the first time anywhere in Eastern Europe, an independent trade union, Solidarity, was officially recognized and granted the right to strike. But the workers were joined now by intellectuals and the church, representing Poland's 95 percent Catholic

population. Their collective call for improved wages, worker participation in decisionmaking, more food, and free speech struck at the
heart of Communist party authority. The situation proved intolerable,
to Moscow as well as to the Polish leader, General Wojciech Jaruzelski.
In December 1981 he declared martial law and brutally put an end to
Solidarity's run as an open political force.[58]

But the imposition of "law and order" in Poland has proven extremely costly to the authorities, and it has failed to alleviate the country's critical economic problems. The Communist party has the least
public confidence, by a very wide margin, of any institution. The
church, Solidarity, and the army rank highest, in that order.[59] In the
aftermath of the workers' movement, some 181,000 party members
were expelled, another 240,000 turned in their party membership
cards, and thousands of party officials were convicted of mishandling
funds. Poland's economic woes are a major reason for this destruction
of the party's credibility. Its external indebtedness, already about $27
billion in 1981, rose close to $30 billion in 1985. According to pub-
lished estimates by the U.S. Central Intelligence Agency, "93 cents of
every dollar of Polish export earnings [went] to pay interest and principal on the country's hard currency debt, and 85 percent of its new
borrowing was used to roll over maturing debt."[60] As they have done
with their loans to Third World countries, West European and U.S.
banks pressed Poland's leaders to invest in export industries (to earn
more foreign exchange) and to reduce price supports on food staples
such as sugar and meat. These steps have added to the people's anger.

Poland's dependence on Western banks has important implications for human rights: It has produced an unholy alliance between the
banks and the Soviet Union, both of which want labor "stability" and
reduced public consumption in Poland to ensure that the country will
not go bankrupt. Interdependence, Corporate-Globalist style, out-
weighs East-West conflict as far as TNBs and Moscow are concerned.
As one West German banker said shortly after martial law was declared, "I now see the chance for Poland to return to a more normal
working schedule and this could be a good thing for the banks."[61] Soviet leaders said nothing of the sort publicly. But it is clear that with
about $6 billion of their own money poured into Poland in 1982 alone,
the Soviets had to be concerned about the prospects of a Polish default, which would harm the international credit standing of every
Eastern bloc country, theirs included.

Although martial law was formally lifted in mid-1983, it continues
in fact. Solidarity spokespersons call the numerous laws that legitimate
repression in Poland today a "legislation of terror." Among these laws
are:

an amendment to the constitution that gives to the Committee of the Defense of the Country the right to establish a state of emergency if the commmittee alone finds it appropriate; new provisions in the penal code that impose strict sanctions on all people who engage in any oppositional activities, even people who participate in meetings in private homes; . . . a so-called anti-parasite law; and a work-referral law that institutionalizes forced and compulsory labor as a means of worker discipline, political constraint and economic development. The same is true of a juvenile delinquency law that allows the punishment of young people who exercise the right to free assembly; a censorship law modified in order to reinforce strict governmental control of publications and performances; and a law on trade unions that eliminates the workers' right to free association and collective bargaining, and transforms the only officially recognized trade union into a driving belt of the Communist Party.[62]

Amnesty International has added to this list in its reports.[63] Strikes, demonstrations, and factory occupations are banned. The media are strictly censored. And, on grounds of a public emergency, the Polish government informed the UN secretary-general that it would not adhere to provisions of the International Covenant on Civil and Political Rights governing basic freedoms such as personal security, assembly, speech, and movement. "Legislation of terror" in Poland is precisely what George Orwell portends in *1984*: "People can now be persecuted not because they act directly against the party or communism, but because they violate the existing law."[64]

Official leadership in Poland seems to be at a dead end. Solidarity, however, has "created an unprecedented underground network of cultural, educational, publishing and other activities" involving an estimated several hundred thousand people.[65] This sharply focused human-rights struggle is likely to come to a head again, and, when it does, European and probably world politics will again be significantly affected. For if repression by the Polish authorities proves ineffective, direct Soviet intervention may, unlike in 1981, become the only alternative to liberalization. In that case, Soviet–U.S. and Soviet–West European relations would probably go through another tortured round of cold war. The global challenge posed by the politics of Poland is how the international community can assist in the struggle for economic and political justice there without legitimizing a brutal authority.

CHAPTER SEVEN

In the Human Interest:
An Agenda for
Transforming World Politics

The only thing we have to fear is fear itself.
—Franklin D. Roosevelt

The ability to reach unity in diversity will be the beauty and the test of our civilization.
—Gandhi

Harold: You sure know how to get along with people.
Maude: They're my species.
—from the film *Harold and Maude*

LESSONS FOR THE FUTURE

In his inspiring book on developing an "equilibrium economy," James Robertson proposes five possible futures for the major economies: "Business-As-Usual," a continuation of present-day policies and practices; "Disaster," a series of ecological and economic catastrophes; "Totalitarian Conservationist," in which neofascist regimes arise in response to massive crises; "Hyper-expansionist," the push for maximum growth with heavy emphasis on technological fixes; and "SHE," the preferred "Sane-Humane-Ecological" alternative, which would "give top priority to learning to live supportively with one another on our small and crowded planet."[1] Like Robertson, I search here for a new realism that can address the multifaceted global crisis in positive ways—politically pluralistic, economically just, and ecologically sensitive.

What, in a nutshell, have we learned thus far? We can begin by offering two general lessons. One stems from the enormity of the problems we have covered, their interconnectedness, and their transnationalization. These problems can probably only be ameliorated by global approaches, and only resolved by global system change. Unless the overarching crisis of unfulfilled human needs is transformed—and soon—we can expect violent upheavals and environmental catastrophes to become the norm in world politics. The need is urgent, as the Brandt Report has said, for state leaders to develop a sense of "global responsibility."[2]

We have also learned that the process for achieving "idealistic" objectives—peace, environmental protection, the meeting of basic needs, the spreading of democracy—should be both humane and grounded in political reality. Neither the theoretical argument for Global Humanism nor the program for attaining it should dogmatically ignore the contributions that Realism and Corporate Globalism have to offer. The global crisis will not end by appeals to conscience; nor by excessive reliance on trust between ideological adversaries in the state system; nor, finally, by the development of elaborate models of new global institutions and world governments. It *will* end when consciousness of the human condition, the political will of national leaders, openness to increased trust, and new global structures cohere around concrete political-economic programs that have widespread popular support. That such support is evolving can be seen not merely in the growing body of research and activity along Global-Humanist lines, but just as importantly in the arguments of Realist and Corporate-Globalist practitioners for human-interest policies such as major arms reductions, the dismantling of apartheid in South Africa, a negotiated settlement of the Central American crises, energy conservation, and equity in North-South trade and investment ties.

Realism, grounded in the values and practices of power politics, reminds us of the necessity to deal with the world as it is and not only with the world as we would like it to be. Global changes will require the agreement of governments. It will also require major policy reorientations at the national level, above all with respect to the use of force and threats. State interests and state sovereignty, the chief pillars of Realism, will need to be satisfied even as change that may undermine the nation-state occurs. Here is the overriding challenge of Realism to Global Humanism: How can the national interests of the First and Second World states be made to coincide with the global interests of humankind, when any erosion of the nation-state system will threaten those state and private interests that have, up to now, been the principal beneficiaries of the unequal global distribution of power?

One answer, which emerges out of the Japanese experience and the economic reforms of Gorbachev and Deng Xiaoping, is that Realist decisionmakers may be driven toward globally meaningful change by self-interest. The territorial state, as Richard Rosecrance's recent study argues, is already an anachronism; the trading state (the one which displays adaptability, entrepreneurship, and cooperativeness in its domestic as well as its international policies) is best suited to the era of global interdependence.[3] As state leaders come to appreciate the nonmilitary threats to national security, they may invest proportionately more in dealing with them, and eventually more in cooperative responses to problems (such as debt, employment, and pollution) that are transnational in scope.

Corporate global power offers a different kind of realism that must also be taken into account in developing a human-interest agenda. Just as the use of force is a fact of international life, so is the increasingly concentrated control by global corporations of the movement of food, energy, information, capital, and other tangibles of political-economic power. Are there ways to make that power more decisively and immediately serve human ends? (I assume here that "abolishing" transnational corporations is neither possible nor feasible in an interdependent global economy.) Considering the successes and failures of contemporary capitalism and socialism, what combination of private incentives and public (governmental) welfare seems to hold promise of meeting human needs and enhancing overall world security? The growing dependence of the socialist economies on (capitalist) transnational bodies suggests that a Global-Humanist program should pay attention to how they operate, including their relative efficiency in comparison with governments and national firms.

These general lessons are backed by several more specific ones that ought to be incorporated into a human-interest agenda:

• *First*, a new world politics begins at home. The domestic enhancement of personal and collective well-being, improving human rights in the fullest sense, strengthens a leadership's ability and willingness to deal positively, and globally, with the great crises of our time. As Franklin D. Roosevelt once said, "America's own rightful place in the world depends in large part upon how fully [basic human] rights have been carried out in practice for our citizens. For unless there is security here at home there cannot be lasting peace in the world."[4] The more successful a national leadership is at creating real security at home, the less is it likely to seek security through expansion abroad.[5] That is why the success of Gorbachev's *glasnost* is important to the world and not only to Soviet citizens.

• *Second*, mere increases in the means of global welfare (aid, food, refugee relief) not only are very unlikely to solve problems of inequity but are more likely to reinforce their structural foundations.

Preventive approaches are preferable to constantly treating symptoms. Among them, increased self-reliance, in the First and Second Worlds as much as in the Third World, may be the single most important. Gandhi's maxim that "there is enough for every man's need, but not enough for every man's greed" provides a sensible guideline.

• *Third*, specific human-interest policies will need to reflect a diversity of ideas and priorities. No single formula or blueprint can adequately speak to the complexity of the human condition, no matter how humane its intent. Both public and private mechanisms and incentives will need to be considered in all societies. Economic growth that creates jobs and enhances life can proceed along with protection of the environment and conservation of resources. "Zero growth," or something like it, seems to be as untenable politically and as implausible economically as ignoring ecological considerations is shortsighted.

• *Fourth*, because state leaderships are likely to withhold support of human-interest policies for as long as possible, the most decisive force for humane change will probably continue to be popular, broadly based national and transnational movements. But humane changes will certainly also occur at the personal, local (community, tribal), national, regional, and global levels. Education will be a crucial source for promoting global awareness and Global-Humanist values at each of these levels. The cumulative impact of all these efforts, not one of them alone, will determine the course of world political change.

• *Fifth*, converting military-industrial complexes to research and production that meet human needs is essential to stopping the arms race. Among the many groups whose support is necessary for a conversion program to work are those persons whose jobs would be directly affected by the elimination of weapons contracts.

• *Sixth*, modest, workable programs that produce clearly beneficial results are preferable to grandiose schemes backed only by high ideals. Nor should the power of positive example be understated. Human-interest policies must widely be seen to serve everybody's interests rather than the interests of one segment of society, however numerous its members may be.

• *Seventh*, the various elements of the global crisis are primarily the result of interlinked national and transnational political-economic forces; they are not mainly caused by haphazard occurrences in nature, "backward" cultural traditions, the wrath of God, or some singularly nefarious political doctrine. Awareness of the political roots of the crisis is grounds for both pessimism and optimism: pessimism about the historically powerful interests that must be confronted if the global crisis is to be resolved; optimism that what has been made to happen can also be made to transform.

THINKING GLOBALLY

In this section I put the above lessons to use in outlining a human-interest policy agenda. I want to take note of the many positive achievements in creating human security that have occurred, and are being created now, worldwide.

Toward Humane Economic and Social Development

Humane development embraces values such as equity, self-reliance, and community, and norms such as decentralization, self-determination, and basic needs. To discuss development in these terms is to cut to the heart of the question of inequitable distribution and wasteful use of resources, some of which (for example, oil) will soon run out at present rates of consumption. If development can be redefined to take account of both real and planned scarcities and of its human impact around the planet it may reward societies politically and economically. Humane development may be regarded as low-cost, preventive medicine for terrorism and mass revolution—and as a preferable alternative to counterterrorism and repression.

The highest priority of human development is fulfillment of the *right to food*. Once that right is accepted as a global priority—and it has taken the African famines of the 1970s and 1980s to push world hunger to the top of the global agenda—it opens the door to debate about the political-economic forces behind hunger: unequal land ownership, dependence-creating international aid programs, and oppressive national and transnational authorities. The previous discussion has addressed these questions in the context of global underdevelopment and environmental destruction. We can now turn to some policy implications of these findings.

Setting the conditions for food *self-reliance* may be the single most important human objective in world politics today. Giving people their own land offers hope of dramatic improvements in public health; of ending control of food for profit and political extortion; of new opportunities for small farmers, farming communities, and women; of the restoration of ecologically sound, energy-conserving farm practices (such as minimization of soil erosion and labor-intensive irrigation and plowing); of curtailment of the export of protein and overuse of cropland for export purposes, and, instead, use of local resources for local needs; of the establishment of a better rural-urban balance in the resources provided by governments; and, finally, hope of reversal of the pattern of high population growth, unemployment, and migrations to cities and across borders that typically accompanies hunger. Such a food-first strategy[6] would be frankly revolutionary, which accounts for the resistance to it by numerous authoritarian governments, landed oligarchies, and, oftentimes, transnational corporations. But the experiences of China and Nicaragua, for example, suggest that the road to food self-reliance has major payoffs, including, so far as world politics is concerned, reduced dependence on external suppliers of grain and money.

Clearly, the key factor in moving to a food self-reliance strategy is the attitude of elites, their perception that, as a matter of self-interest and/or nationalism, ending hunger and malnutrition is vital to national security. Successful programs and international policy changes can influence that perception. Home food production, such as Jamaica carried out in its "Grow Our Own Food" campaign, can sharply reduce malnutrition.[7] Lending money to low-income farmers, who repay the loan as their projects (the purchase of a cow, for instance, or a small shop) make a profit, has worked well in Bangladesh (where a private, voluntary organization, the Grameen Bank, provides the funds).[8] Providing farmers with credit as well as a supply of high-yield seeds, fertilizer, and agricultural advisers has enabled Zimbabwe to make dramatic production gains.[9] Shifting from large-scale governmental aid-giving to people-to-people programs that teach food self-reliance is yet another approach; among the global organizations that stress grassroots development are Oxfam International, Grassroots International, the Plenty Project, and Church World Service.[10]

At the international level, administering world emergency food surpluses—and devising a method for compulsory food contributions by those nations and corporations which consume and transport most of the food—is another possible step. Tax regulations governing TNCs could be changed to reward those corporations that invest in labor-intensive, energy-saving technology, promote women's and peasants' farm cooperatives, and offer opportunities for transferring patent and production rights to local ownership. Foreign economic aid could be conditioned on its use only for purposes that promote self-help in food production. Both international organizations and private nonprofit groups could disseminate the fruits of scientific research in biotechnology, plant pathology, energy conservation and other areas.[11] The benefits would belong to countries and regions with the poorest resources for food production, while the discoveries would not be monopolized for profit by TNCs, as has been the case with Green

Revolution seed varieties. Finally, internationalization of satellite technology, which has thus far been resisted by the major powers that lead in its development, could enable the poorest countries to gain access to information on weather and crop prospects for their own use.

No less important than food (and other kinds of) self-reliance in the Third World is greater self-reliance *in the richest countries*. One reason was given by the British economist E. F. Schumacher: "We must live simply that others may simply live."[12] Another is that successful experiments in resource self-reliance and conservation in the industrialized, high-consumption North would help deflect suspicions in the South that talk of simpler living is not just another ruse for keeping the underdeveloped countries underdeveloped.

First and Second World countries could make a major contribution to promoting a food-first strategy in the Third World by changing the way they treat food and food-producing resources. A conservationist approach could be of long-term benefit to everyone, but especially to the poorest consumers and small-scale farmers, North and South. In the absence of land and food reforms in the North, the world will have to reckon with the anomaly of rising production amidst widening hunger, declining land quality, and further concentration of land ownership and food distribution.

Specific changes in the richest countries would include: stable commodity prices, increased loans, and land tax advantages that give preference to the careful family farmer rather than absenteee land owners and the largest commercial farms; increased domestic production of food (such as many fruits and vegetables, fish, and beef) that is increasingly imported; reevaluation of the trend toward feeding animals food fit for human consumption; tax and other benefits to conserve soil and water and to prevent soil erosion, overuse of pesticides and fertilizer, and conversion of prime farmland to nonagricultural purposes; and increasing research support for and public interest in organic farming methods, grow-your-own-food programs, and new foodgrowing techniques (such as hydroponics, French intensive, and rooftop fisheries).[13] The practice, notably in U.S. foreign policy, of denying food aid to governments that oppose U.S. interests should be abandoned; it is unworkable and immoral. Finally, personal dietary changes in the food-rich countries away from excessive meat consumption for protein can also be important. Aside from the widely acknowledged health benefits, dietary changes on a large scale could reduce the use of land in the underdeveloped countries for the grazing of beef cattle.

Food self-reliance is also the principal element of *health* self-reliance. Mass preventive health-care programs, in which China and Cuba have pioneered, mobilize an entire society to ensure effective outreach. Prevention and social mobilization are now being emphasized by the World Health Organization and UNICEF with dramatic results, especially among children and in war zones.[14] Even in the poorest African societies (Tanzania, Gambia, and Burkina Faso) early immunization and breast-feeding campaigns have been successfully implemented.[15] These programs provide both low-cost *and* effective, on-the-spot treatment of the basic childhood and adult illnesses that are major killers. In the Andes mountain villages of southern Argentina, other successful preventive health programs are being carried out where medical attention had previously been unknown. Like the Chinese and Cuban programs, these include low-cost treatment, a pyramidal structuring of facilities, paramedical as well as professional providers, and an emphasis on basic health needs. WHO is already calling the Andes program a model for the Third World.[16]

Food and energy are intimately linked, as we have seen. The path of food self-reliance leads also to increased self-reliance in energy, along a "soft-energy path" popularized by Amory Lovins.[17] "Soft-energy" sources (solar, geothermal, hydro, biogas, and wind energy) have major advantages over the "hard" path of fossil fuels (petroleum, natural gas, and coal), and over nuclear energy. These soft sources are decentralized (many solar reflectors, for example, rather than a single giant utility), renewable and recyclable, job-producing, cost-effective, low- or nonpolluting, free of major health and safety problems, and far less of a drain on government treasuries and people's incomes because they do not require heavy subsidization. As with food self-reliance, the soft-energy path holds the promise—already fulfilled in many places[18]—of conserving precious global and local resources, strengthening community control, lowering user and government costs, and increasing productivity.

In the Third World, where the increased cost of oil and petroleum products (notably fertilizer) has been far more burdensome than elsewhere, a shift to soft-energy sources would clearly bring major benefits. Dung could again be used solely as a fertilizer, rather than also as a fuel. The enormous increase in tree-cutting for firewood, leading to deforestation and desertification in Africa and other places, could be brought to a halt, particularly if (as in Kenya) fuel-saving stoves were also introduced to farmers.[19] The migration of peasant labor to the cities could begin to be reversed as machinery took a less prominent place in agriculture—and on the assumption increased food output would become the local government's top investment priority. TNC investments in and transfers to the Third World of energy-saving technology and techniques, which their home governments' tax and trade policies could influence, would strengthen the attractiveness there of soft-energy strategies. These steps would likewise reduce the attractiveness of the nuclear option, with its high price tag in dollars and, potentially, in lives.[20] Other underdeveloped countries may emulate the Philippines in deciding not to use nuclear power (a difficult choice in that particular case, since the plant had already been built at a total cost of over $2 billion).

In the end an investment in food and energy self-reliance is an investment in national solvency: Fewer loans and less money spent on imported food and fuel means more money available for reinvestment and repayment of debts. China set an example of this approach when it adopted a self-reliant development strategy in 1958. Seven years later, it had repaid its debts to the Soviet Union. To be sure, few Third World countries have China's resources to carry out such a strategy. But many are in a position to experiment with selective delinking from an international political economy dominated by Northern interests. This approach calls for increased *South-South* exchanges, to the extent possible, in trade, transnational investments, technology and skills transfers, and even aid.[21]

Delinking might also include a moratorium on the repayment of debts, which have become a focal point of people's anger as human misery rises along with interest payments. During the 1980s, Bolivia and Ecuador put a moratorium on repayment. New governments in Peru and Argentina decided to limit repayment of external debts to a percentage of annual export earnings (in those cases, 10 and 30 percent, respectively). Brazil suspended payment of interest for a brief time. These actions forced several major international banks to increase their reserves to cover potential losses.

Selective delinking does not mean withdrawal from the international system. Nor does it mean any less vigorous pursuit through North-South negotiations of more equitable trade, loan, aid, information-sharing, and investment terms. But it does seek to minimize the worst consequences of international dependence that come from orienting Third World exports, capital requirements, and productive capacities to the needs and demands of remote capitals and board rooms.

Given the powerful pull of a globally interdependent economy, however, even a widely practiced selective delinking strategy is unlikely to improve conditions in the Third World as much as self-reliant trends in the richest countries. We may see this as we look at energy issues again. There is encouraging news of momentum in a self-reliant (and decentralized) direction in the North. Worldwatch Institute estimates that by 2000, 20 percent of the world's energy will come from renewable sources.[22] Nuclear power, while important to some major economies (for example, France, where it accounts for about 65 percent of total electricity, and Japan, about 25 percent), has become tainted by Three Mile Island, Chernobyl, and other major accidents.[23] Orders for new plant construction have plummeted; there have been none in the United States since 1979. Throughout Western Europe, nuclear plants are either being phased out or dismantled. Unfortunately, weak nuclear sales in the industrialized world have led the major nuclear-plant exporting countries (the United States, West Germany, and France) to push nuclear power in the Third World, adding "nuclear havens" to the list of dangerous exports.[24]

Coal has become a potential bridging fuel between a dwindling supply of oil and a non-nuclear energy future.[25] World coal reserves are "roughly five times the world's proven reserves of oil."[26] Coal's relative abundance, its many energy uses (for electricity, heating, and power), and the possibilities for exploiting it in synthetic fuels make coal superior to nuclear power as an oil substitute. But not a permanent or long-term substitute, for coal poses serious environmental hazards due to strip mining, acid raid from the sulfur dioxide generated, and carbon dioxide buildup that is already warming the planet's temperature. In fact, the three countries with the largest coal reserves, the United States, the USSR, and China, ought to have the biggest interest in moving away from fossil fuels, since their food-producing regions would be hardest hit by a global climate change.[27]

Conservation is the second element of energy self-reliance. It has gained momentum throughout the First and Second Worlds: for example, the recycling of waste paper, aluminum, and steel in Japan and Norway; the building of more efficient automobiles, household appliances (the refrigerator in particular), and heat-conserving homes and offices in Japan and Western Europe; the reduction of energy use in making steel, as in Italy and Spain; the shift to different fuels for automobiles, notably by Brazil to alcohol (creating, however, another set of problems: the use of food plants for fuel instead of for feeding people). As one authority has commented, the economic sensibility of energy conservation is enormous:

> A single decision in either the United States—to raise automobile fuel economy to 40 miles per gallon—or the Soviet Union—to produce steel as efficiently as Japan does—would save as much energy as Brazil now consumes. Just using the most efficient lights in the United States would save a third of U.S. coal-fired electric energy.[28]

Conservation, moreover, produces jobs while saving money for consumers and cutting down on bills for imported oil. These jobs will come from the new skills that will be in demand, from construction of soft-energy facilities, and from increased consumer spending with money saved on energy bills. As one example, in the Ruhr region of West Germany, employment patterns are changing as steel and coal, once the cornerstones of the economy, become uncompetitive. Today, businesses, local government, unions, and universities are combining talents to produce industrial environmental equipment (such as for water recycling) that is energy saving.[29] Similar stories are being heard from neighborhoods and communities throughout the United States, Canada, and Europe—for example, in programs to weatherize homes, convert from oil to solar heating, cogenerate heat and steam for industry, and reduce energy costs in hospitals and businesses through simple conservation techniques.[30] In the process, these programs are also demonstrating a Global-Humanist alternative to supply- and demand-side economics: end-use analysis, an approach to developmental issues that asks what the objective is before assuming that more is better.[31]

The third part of a program for humane development is *environmental protection*. As noted in the discussion of underdevelopment, the environmental costs of what Sunkel calls the "transnational lifestyle" are enormous—and they are hardly confined to the Third World or to specific localities of industrialized societies. Increasingly, in fact, the scope of environmental problems is seen to be regional and global, affecting ever-widening populations—as in the "greenhouse effect" of carbon dioxide buildup; nuclear and toxic waste dumping on land and at sea; and desertification and deforestation on every continent. All of these ongoing or potential environmental tragedies require a combination of regional, national, and international action. At the very least, they demand more interdisciplinary research and transnational monitoring, preferably at the international level, a course of action that space and computer technology now make possible.[32]

A very large part of the remedy lies in the shift to a pollution-free, soft-energy path discussed above. The adoption of a renewables-and-conservation strategy has only just begun, however; it will take considerable time to take hold worldwide and to become practical for large industries. More immediate preventive steps are called for, steps that would be sensible even if global environmental trends were to stabilize. Such steps include a multinational planet climate watch to detect and attribute the sources of changes, reforestation (such as the greenbelts in north China and Kenya) and other soil-protecting programs, improved water management, and development of crops more resistant to climate change.[33]

But it is timely to consider more immediate and even drastic preventive measures. These would include the outright prohibition of production of toxic chemicals and pesticides (unless demonstrated to be usable and disposable without danger to humans and wildlife); a global convention banning the ocean dumping of radioactive materials; a global moratorium on tropical clear-cutting in ecologically endangered areas; and national and international legislation that imposes heavy penalties on corporations that export (dump) dangerous chemicals (as well as products that contain them), chemical plants, or pollutants whose domestic production has been banned. There should be no more Bhopals, just as surely as there should be no more Three Mile Islands and Chernobyls.

It is interesting to note that global environmental problems have spurred the greatest advances to date in international cooperation. The London Dumping Convention regulates the dumping of radioactive wastes at sea. In 1982 most of the parties to it (but not the United States, Britain, France, South Africa, or Switzerland) agreed to an indefinite moratorium on oceanic nuclear-waste disposal. The Law of the Sea Treaty, signed by 119 nations in 1982, established an important globalist principle—that the planet's undersea wealth is the "common heritage of mankind"—and a new implementing regime, the International Seabed Authority.[34] The treaty includes measures that hold states liable for pollution of both territorial and international waters, that tax members for pollution cleanup, and that create a court for settlement of disputes.

At least three important concepts for dealing effectively with global issues emerge from these two agreements. One is international management of the planet's "common heritage," which ought to apply as well to food, energy, and other environmental and natural resources—not to mention peace. Secondly, taxation of offenders is a useful concept for punishing other crimes against the "common heritage," such as toxic waste disposal and acid rain, or for limiting against profit from the commons, such as exploitation of offshore oil and tropical forests by TNCs. Revenues from these violations could be used, as a group of Japanese environmental specialists has suggested, to set up an environmental trust fund. The fund would "purchase" conservation rights in, for instance, major forests to prevent their exploitation.[35] A third concept is the establishment of an international court. If it could have absolutely binding authority to settle disputes, which is not now the case, it would be a model for the settlement of numerous other forms of international conflict.

At the regional level there has also been progress on environmental protection. A reemergence of regional consciousness has occurred. In the United States it is referred to as bioregionalism, and in areas such as the Ozarks and the Great Lakes it takes activist political forms such as preserving watersheds and developing environmental policy platforms.[36] In a different vein, the United States and Canada subscribe to a long-established dictum prohibiting the carry-over of air pollution from one country to the other. (It remains to be seen, however, what concrete action Washington takes in accepting responsibility for acid rain over Canada from U.S.-based industrial plants.) The same principle, extended to all forms of environmental damage, is in the 1972 Declaration of the United Nations Conference on the Human Environment, signed in Stockholm. And in 1979, the thirty-four-member Economic Commission for Europe (under the UN) signed a Convention on Transboundary Air Pollution. But this effort to "limit and, as far as possible, gradually reduce and prevent air pollution" lacks the power needed to keep a major problem from getting out of hand. The convention does not establish pollution standards, lacks an enforcement mechanism, and does not stipulate accountability (such as in payment of damages) for polluting states or their corporations.[37]

The fourth component of equitable development is *employment*. We have already seen a few ways in which the unemployment crisis in the Third World can be addressed, starting with the redirection of government investment into agriculture and of transnational corporate investment into labor-intensive, energy-saving, ecologically responsible activities. Another approach is work cooperatives, one notable example of which is the Mondragon Cooperatives in the Basque region of Spain.[38] There, one finds local economic independence and control that has successfully incorporated democratic decisionmaking and worker ownership.

But employment is also a long-term structural problem in the advanced economies, especially in the United States. Jobs created in the service sector, by imports, and by military production simply cannot make up for those lost in manufacturing, agriculture, and exports. The need is urgent for the United States, given the central global role of its economy and banking system, to reinvigorate its domestic industrial base—not through trade protectionism, which is harmful to workers and consumers as well as to global economic cooperation, but through an overhauling of public spending priorities.

The discussion of the U.S. economy (in Chapter 5) brought out the main elements in its decline: concentration of economic power and wealth; Depression-level failures in banking, farming, and small businesses; huge government deficits leading to high interest rates, a monstrous trade imbalance, and the world's highest external debt; and a distorted conception of national security that has pumped up military spending far beyond actual defense needs. The kind of legislative agenda that would begin to base U.S. security on human priorities would therefore have to include: first, a major national program of job retraining and of corporate responsibility legislation to protect workers and communities in transition; second, sharp reductions in the military budget, particularly in new weapons procurement and through cost efficiencies; third, tax incentives to corporations and banks that invest in job-creating, productivity-improving activities at home—and disincentives to those that do not or that continue to invest in countries where labor is repressed and human rights are discounted; and fourth, increased public funding of education, family farming, small business, resource conservation, and renewable energy sources.

An equitable approach to North-South differences over *information* is the fifth component of humane development. There appears to be room for bargaining. Governments in the South might accept that the electronic media cannot be kept out and that restrictions on press freedoms need to be loosened. But they have a right to expect that foreign reporters will be sensitive to their societies' cultures and histories (which might be assisted by enrolling reporters in local universities when they arrive). Both sides would benefit from improved reporting on the Third World, with more attention to long-term issues of underdevelopment and to positive efforts by governments and international agencies to deal with them. An international convention on media rights and responsibilities that lays out an agenda of mutual benefit might be in order.

Toward Common Security

If movement toward a durable peace is to begin, the starting point must be the development of incentives for states to *avoid war* in their political conflicts. The end point is disarmament within a system of global security. In between, what must be constructed is what Karl Deutsch, in his classic study of West European unity, called "a sense of community," meaning a shared belief that "common security problems must and can be resolved by processes of 'peaceful change.' "[39]

The nation-state system has a long way to go toward becoming such a community. All its leaders pay lip service to the "peaceful settlement of disputes," but frequently resort to war and intervention to resolve conflicts. There has yet to emerge a shared perception among state leaders that international order—economic and social, not simply military—is in every society's best interests, and that maximizing armaments does not purchase real security or deter threats to it. Yet, unless state leaders have high confidence in alternative means of protecting their legitimate security interests, they will not agree to steps toward disarmament; nor will they give more than rhetorical support to international peacekeeping and arms reductions, all of which depend to a great extent on trust.

To create an agenda for moving to an alternative security system requires accepting certain fundamental premises. These flow from the previous chapters' argument about the nature of the global crisis of international conflict. One is that our field of concern is *the war system* and not merely one country's or one bloc's military program. Another is that we must take account of the bureaucratic and economic forces in all societies that propel the arms race forward. A third premise is that system change will evolve out of a process of successful experiments that have popular support. Neither technical fixes (such as setting limits on types of missiles) nor ambitious rearrangements of the future (such as global disarmament and world federalism) have worked or stand much chance of being widely accepted in the foreseeable future.

A fourth premise is that alternatives to the arms race must address insecurity at several levels, including people's deep pessimism and fear that to reduce arms will invite attack, mistrust between national leaderships built partly on long-standing grievances, and the structural violence of underdevelopment. Fifth, every change in global security policy should strengthen the ability of the global community to move beyond state conflict toward new forms of identification, representation, communication, defense, and conflict resolution.[40] This premise further means that each change should have real substance and not be mere window-dressing, as has often been the case with arms-control agreements.

Lastly, our agenda should rest on optimism that nuclear war is not inevitable. Rather, war has become obsolete. With a new vision, the goal of general and complete disarmament under effective forms of inspection and control is achievable.[41] At Reykjavik, Iceland in October 1986, the discussion between President Reagan and General Secretary Gorbachev on eliminating nuclear warheads in Europe, reducing strategic weapons by one-half, and working toward a total test ban showed that what is considered utopian one day can become a serious topic the next.

Promising steps to an alternative security system are presented here in terms of four key areas: communications between adversaries, military issues, nonmilitary issues, and the public's role. Because of the global impact that changes in U.S.–Soviet relations are likely to have, the emphasis is on superpower politics. But we should keep in mind that many of the proposed steps to improve that relationship are relevant to other conflicts, such as between Iran and Iraq, between India and Pakistan, and in Central America.

Communications. A helpful beginning to creating a momentum for peace is for adversaries to agree to emphasize the positive aspects of their relationship. In U.S.–Soviet terms, instead of constant efforts to score political points with U.S.- or Soviet-bashing, the two leaderships might note the numerous agreements (major and minor, over 100 in all) that they have abided by. A noted international legal scholar reminds us of what Soviet and U.S. leaders ignore: "how much international law and obligation applied and were effectively observed between the United States and the Soviet Union even when their relations were most strained."[42] Like it or not, these adversaries do trust each other all the time—to fulfill obligations under exchange programs and business deals, to keep military and political flare-ups around the world from escalating to a superpower confrontation, and especially to maintain nuclear weapons and communications in a fail-safe condition.

Some specific additional steps to facilitate communication would be:

1. Substantial increase in people-to-people exchange programs between U.S. and Soviet residents, both professionals and ordinary citizens. These would be supported by networks of coordinating groups in and between the two countries. "Space bridges," which use satellites to link groups of children, musicians, doctors, and simply concerned citizens in the United States and the Soviet Union, exemplify the new possibilities that technology is opening up.

2. Expansion of the sister-city concept that links Soviet and U.S. cities. Cities that are likely nuclear targets would be especially good choices.

3. Establishment of dates by the two leaderships for private ongoing consultations at high levels on issues of mutual concern. These might take place every two months. One specific function that such talks could serve would be to have each side spell out its interests in a disputed matter, its suspicions about the other side's intentions, and what action the other side might take to make it more trusted. (New approaches such as these need to be part of a comprehensive overhauling of the format and substance of negotiations so as to emphasize positive, trust-building techniques.[43])

4. Agreement by Moscow and Washington, or any two adversaries, to lower (if not eliminate) the level of invective, misrepresentation, and dehumanizing language in their public pronouncements. Looking back at the history of U.S.–Soviet arms talks, it is apparent that agreements occurred only when the name-calling and devil imagery had eased. Criticism should not be muted; but angry insults and politically inspired distortions would be—the kind of language former Ambassador Kennan decried as "the marks of an intellectual primitivism and naiveté unpardonable in a great government."[44] Despite ideological dif-

ferences, "we share the same biology," as the popular (and thoughtful) singer Sting reminds us. "The Russians love their children too."

Military issues. The question whether or not the USSR or the United States can be trusted to keep arms agreements overarches the problem of how to limit the weapons themselves. It is sometimes forgotten—and rarely commemorated—that among the U.S.–Soviet agreements that have been honored are more than twenty related to nuclear arms. The list begins with the 1961 Antarctic Treaty and includes the Limited Test Ban (1963), treaties governing outer space (1967) and nuclear proliferation (1968), the Seabed Arms Control Treaty (1971), the "hot line" agreements (1963 and 1971), the ABM treaty and protocol (1972 and 1974), and the Threshold Test Ban (1974) and Peaceful Nuclear Explosions (1976) treaties limiting the size of underground tests. The U.S.–Soviet record thus far has (remarkably in light of the cold war) been one of compliance.[45]

Violations of these agreements have occurred and undoubtedly will continue to occur. A foolproof verification system is hard to imagine. By the same token, satellites and other verification technologies are now advanced enough, many argue, to ensure that major violations (those that would give one side a clear strategic advantage) could not be concealed. Both sides, moreover, now accept on-site verification procedures. The nature of the reported violations, moreover, suggests that what most needs alteration is the precision of the language and the evidence presented to show breaches, rather than the practice of negotiating.[46]

Some important areas for negotiation and diplomacy are:

1. Improvement of the U.S.–Soviet crisis control system, in order to prevent panic from prevailing over calm good sense in moments of uncertainty. Exploring this issue, William L. Ury of the Harvard Negotiating Project has formulated several proposals, including establishment of round-the-clock crisis-monitoring centers in the two countries that would keep professional staffs in constant communication.[47] A 1986 agreement in Stockholm by the NATO and Warsaw Pact countries is an important precedent in crisis prevention. It seeks to prevent sudden military buildups or surprise attacks in Europe by providing for information-sharing on exercises and the right of on-the-spot military inspections. Confidence-building measures of these kinds are critical to successful diplomacy.

2. Conclusion of a U.S.–Soviet comprehensive test ban (CTB) treaty, negotiation on which began in 1977. A ban on all nuclear testing, and not (as at present) only on atmospheric, undersea, and space testing, would be a major breakthrough. No testing means no reliable

weapon to deploy, no certainty about one's weapons stockpile, and less incentive to do research on new weapons, such as those based in space. A CTB might also help to discourage the several near-nuclear states from taking the plunge.[48]

3. A U.S.–Soviet declaration, to which other states would be invited to adhere, of no first use of nuclear weapons. Parties making such a declaration would be agreeing to forego the nuclear threat. (The Soviet government endorsed the no-first-use concept in 1981; so have a number of former high-level U.S. officials.[49])

4. Inauguration of an agreement leading to a total ban on nuclear transfers. As a first step in that direction, a ban on selling or otherwise transferring nuclear materials and technology could be applied to states that have failed to sign the Non-Proliferation Treaty, such as China, India, South Africa, Israel, and Brazil. A second step, for which there was strong worldwide support after the Chernobyl nuclear accident, is to strengthen the International Atomic Energy Agency in its ability to monitor "civilian" nuclear power plants. Mikhail Gorbachev himself cited the need for an international "system of prompt warning and supply of information in the event of accidents and faults at nuclear power stations." The third step regarding nuclear transfers would be an enforceable international agreement banning plutonium exports, the use of plutonium for *any* purposes, and the reprocessing of spent fuel from civilian reactors. International specialists should also be brought together to find an acceptable final resting place for existing spent nuclear fuel.[50]

5. Establishment of an International Satellite Monitoring Agency within the United Nations, as the French government first proposed in 1978. Aside from its economic development uses mentioned earlier, such a system could oversee military movements and help verify arms agreements. Internationalization of satellite technology for peaceful purposes is long overdue and represents a positive departure from proposals to "weaponize" the heavens.[51]

6. A complete ban on weapons testing, production, and deployment. *Limiting* weapons and military activities is the most common—and, as has been suggested earlier, not the most effective—form of agreement between the major powers. At their best such agreements maintain a positive momentum in diplomacy between the parties. They may also be useful when they put geographic limits on arms, as in the ABM Treaty's prohibition of space-based defenses. More productive toward the goal of disarmament is actual *reduction* of arms. Even here, however, unless the reductions are substantial—on the order of, say, 50 percent—they will make a political and psychological impact rather than a contribution to global security. When, for example, Washington

and Moscow in 1987 discussed eliminating all their medium-range missiles, it was left unsaid that only about 4 percent of the superpowers' nuclear warheads would actually be destroyed. Their long-range capacity for total mutual destruction not only would be left intact; it might well be strengthened. This is why, from a global perspective, verifiable bans covering the testing, production, and deployment of categories of weapons and military activities—such as chemical weapons, space-based weapons, and antisatellite weapons—are preferable to limiting or reducing them. Governments are simply too clever at finding ways around incomplete restrictions and imprecise language.

7. Bilateral and multilateral pledges of mutual noninterference in the domestic affairs of other (namely, Third World) states. Pledges do not prevent conflict; but they may lessen the incentive to resort to arms or increase the incentive to stop fighting. (China's brief border war with India in 1962, despite their 1954 agreement of mutual noninterference and nonaggression, illustrates both the problems and the possibilities of this approach.) Concerning the conflicts in Central America, for instance, five governments in the region (Nicaragua, Honduras, Costa Rica, El Salvador, and Guatemala) agreed in August 1987 to implement cease-fires with opposing forces in their countries. They also agreed to end foreign military involvement and undertake democratic reforms as steps toward mutual respect for each state's self-determination. Another approach is for the major powers to limit agreement to a conflict in which they have few tangible interests at stake as a method of experimenting with noninvolvement.[52]

8. Unilateral military initiatives, which may perform the same function as negotiated agreements more efficiently, provided the other side reciprocates within a reasonable time. If the USSR halts nuclear tests, as it did for nineteen months beginning in August 1985, and the United States does likewise, an important step to bringing the arms race under control has been taken. (In that instance, however, the United States, apparently wanting to test components of its Star Wars research program, rejected making the testing moratorium bilateral.) Similarly, a government's unilateral declaration that it will reduce its military budget by a certain percentage, or refrain from a particular military act if its opponent also refrains, can create a positive atmosphere for reducing tensions and arsenals.

9. The creation of new or strengthened transnational institutions to monitor and enforce global standards of military (and nonmilitary) performance.[53] In addition to the ones discussed below, the new institutions might be a United Nations Disarmament Agency to supervise adherence to military agreements, including nonproliferation of nuclear technology, with information drawn from the kind of interna-

tional satellite agency previously proposed; a *permanent* global police force (unlike ad hoc UN peace-keeping forces); and an International Court of Justice with *compulsory* jurisdiction.

Nonmilitary issues. 1. Joint undertakings between adversaries in areas *outside* the arms race—a "search for common ground"[54]—are critical components of any peace process. The fate of arms talks should not govern the relationship between peoples or governments. That relationship can be improved along a second track, such as in agreements to combat childhood diseases and terrorism, to promote biotechnological research, or to make joint ventures into space. In fact, cooperation now takes place or is being considered in each of these areas and in many others. A proposal introduced in the U.S. Senate in September 1985, for instance, called for U.S.–Soviet cooperation to immunize the world's children against six major diseases by 1990, at a cost of a mere $500 million. A joint mission to Mars has also been discussed by the two governments and has strong scientific backing in both countries.

2. Increased use of mediators, specifically persons who do not represent governments. When hostages are taken and the lives of innocent persons having no official responsibility are at stake, unofficial mediators who can appeal on humane grounds may stand the best chance of succeeding. (Two examples: Reverend Jesse Jackson's successful mission to Syria in 1984 to free a downed U.S. pilot; and the efforts of Terry Waite, representing Britain's Anglican Church, to negotiate the release of hostages taken in Beirut by radical Islamic groups.)

3. The conversion of significant portions of military industries to nonmilitary production. What may seem like a pipe dream has in fact been attempted (with mixed results) in a number of U.S. communities, in Britain (at the Lucas Aerospace company, a prime military contractor), and elsewhere in Western Europe.[55] Conversion will occur when the kinds of military agreements mentioned above take hold, when communities become aware of the full costs of the arms race to families and towns, and especially when economic planning makes it possible for jobholders to shift over to nonmilitary employment. If, for example, a nuclear freeze were agreed upon, studies have shown it would result in savings of several hundred million dollars over a five-year period in the United States. But it would also put perhaps a quarter-million people out of work. Only a comprehensive economic strategy, worked out in partnership between governments, businesses, and communities, can make military conversion workable.

The public's role. The pervasiveness of war, its terrifying costs, and the slowness and weakness of the negotiating process have brought increasing numbers of people into the peacemaking arena. Popular rather than bureaucratic will is pushing the agenda of a non-nuclear, nonviolent world forward. Some national leaders recognize this human-interest potential. President Eisenhower once declared that people may one day "want peace so badly that governments better get out of their way and let them have it." And years later President Reagan agreed, saying in a letter to Brezhnev: "Sometimes it seems that the governments [of our countries] get in the way of the people."

The influence of citizens depends on education and involvement:

1. Education for a global citizenry. The incorporation of Global-Humanist values into world politics is conceivable only when large numbers of people, whether they are in policymaking positions or not, adopt a global perspective on national issues. That means educating people to think globally, on behalf of one planet.[56] Although this is a long-term project, it is already well underway. In the United States, for example, global education has taken shape in the introduction of peace studies to curricula at every level, in the founding of new conflict-resolution programs (such as Harvard's Negotiation Project), in Congressional funding of a U.S. Institute for Peace, and in a sizable increase in the number of teachers who use a global perspective in their courses.[57]

2. Proclamation of additional cities, states, and counties as nuclear-free zones. By 1986 over 100 U.S. cities and counties had either voted to become NFZ's (usually meaning that nuclear weapons cannot be based there or transported through them) or had proclaimed themselves nuclear-free (areas within which nuclear testing, manufacturing, acquisitions, deployment, and storage are prohibited).[58] Worldwide, about 3,100 communities have done the same. These are symbolic, but not empty, gestures: They reflect not only citizen concern, but also the political capacity to influence national policy. Forty countries and regions from Wales to Japan are nuclear-free. Treaties have also established outer space (in 1967), the Antarctic (in 1961), Latin America (in 1968), and the South Pacific (in 1985) as nuclear-free. Negotiations to do the same for other areas—for example, Africa, the Indian subcontinent, and ultimately Northeast Asia and the Middle East—may be prompted by all these activities. The sticking point in regions such as Northeast Asia and, of course, Europe is not the prohibition of nuclear-weapons manufacture or possession, which the Non-Proliferation Treaty already requires of signatories, but the major powers' use of certain territory as transit or staging points for their weapons.

3. Demonstration of Global Humanism in everyday life. The role of global citizen is also evident on a day-to-day basis: in neighborhood

and other decentralist programs of self-reliance and conservation (such as farmers' markets and household weatherization); in national and regional networks sharing information and ideas on environmental, economic, and other matters that are transnational in scope; in the many successful intentional communities that people have founded in urban as well as rural areas; in the increasing popularity of "socially responsible" investment programs (those that refrain from investing individuals' money in companies doing business in South Africa, for instance); and in conscious efforts by untold thousands of people to lead simpler lives and (as is discussed further later on) cultivate their most human qualities.[59]

4. Exploration of *preservative* means of defense.[60] The militarization of space on one hand, and the Philippines' experience of nonviolent takeover on the other, illuminate one of the great challenges to our imagination: finding ways of protecting societies while minimizing the likelihood of harming others—and destroying what one hopes to protect. Nonviolent resistance has a rich history that may be as relevant to the nuclear issue as it is to defense against tyrannies and foreign interventionists. Scientists who today refine instruments of war may tomorrow, working transnationally, develop nonprovocative instruments for repelling attack. In the meantime, it is left to citizens in threatened countries to act—and millions have, nonviolently, put their lives and positions on the line to say "no" to further violence.

Toward Democracy and Human Rights

In most of the world, political participation and accountable government (democracy, in short), respect for individual freedom and civil liberties, and adherence by public authority to domestic and international law are acknowledged human rights. They are also largely ignored. *All* forms of government give priority to order over law and centralization over democracy. The usual justification is either "national security"—a foreign threat, a rebellion—or the need to postpone constitutionalism (such as free elections) and the resumption of civil liberties until economic and social justice has been implanted. Granted, in some cases (Nicaragua today is one) threats to national security are real and economic and social development is a more immediate human need than, say, a free press. But the unpleasant reality is that governments which make a practice of ignoring, postponing, or trampling upon human political rights are highly unlikely to mend their ways. Which may explain Thomas Jefferson's famous remark that "a little rebellion now and then is a good thing."

Popular protests and movements for human rights have become the global counterpart in the 1970s and 1980s to revolution in the 1950s and 1960s. Contrary to the expectations of many, persistent mass activism can produce results and yet remain nonviolent and nonideological. We saw this in the demonstrations in South Korea that forced a strong-armed regime to make major concessions to democratic procedures. In the Philippines, Roman Catholic bishops declared the Marcos regime lacked a "moral basis"; a citizens' boycott was organized against businesses owned by Marcos' cronies; people protected the ballot boxes and surrounded the tanks; soldiers and diplomats defected—and suddenly the dictator was gone. In Haiti, what had seemed to outsiders to be a passive acceptance of the Duvalier family's tyranny turned, seemingly overnight, into demonstrations and the dictator's removal— all brought about largely by small clandestine networks of students supported by the church and slum dwellers. ("There were no Communists, no capitalists behind [the movement]—just the people with a desire for change," said a teacher.[61]) Even the most tightly controlled societies are vulnerable: In the USSR, the voices of Solzhenitsyn, Medvedev, Sakharov, and other dissidents have focused worldwide attention on human-rights abuses there.

Many other citizens' groups have yet to receive the attention due them for their heroic struggles on behalf of human rights in their own countries. Among them are Guatemala's Group of Mutual Support, a 650-member human-rights group that was begun by women; Poland's now underground Solidarity union; the Grandmothers of the Plaza De Mayo, parents of the "disappeared" children during Argentina's "dirty war" from 1976 to 1983; the whites of South Africa who are working to end apartheid; members of military establishments and military-industrial facilities who attempt to bring humane understanding to the arms race; the numerous coalitions devoted to working with the poor to build grassroots democracy and social justice (such as the great array of neighborhood and community groups, including the church, which came together in Brazil after official proclamation of a democratic *abertura*, or opening, in 1979); the Roman Catholic bishops of Canada and the United States, who have written astonishingly vigorous cricitisms of economic injustice in their countries; and the citizens of Long Beach and Oakland, California, and Seattle, Washington, which, for all their political dissimilarities, agree on at least one thing: the transit of spent nuclear materials through their boundaries is unacceptable.

Consciously or not, these diverse *national* groups and entities are part of a growing *transnational* network.[62] Citizens in one part of the world are taking action on behalf of victims of repression and injustice thousands of miles away. For example, in response to growing racial violence in South Africa, U.S. citizens and local officials were able to push through laws in the mid-1980s that barred their unions, cities, universities, and states from investing billions of dollars in pension funds in that country. A group called INFACT led many other national organizations in a worldwide boycott of the Nestlé Corporation, whose powdered milk was being widely used in Africa as a substitute for mothers' milk, with numerous infant deaths caused by combining the powdered milk with tainted water. Nestlé eventually acceded to a new marketing code adopted by WHO. And in Guatemala, workers for Coca-Cola struck and occupied the factory, demanding improved conditions. Helped by a broad-based coalition of U.S. church and labor groups, which pressured the parent firm to take responsibility for conditions in its branch plant, the strike was equitably resolved.

Then there are a number of well-established transnational groups, some activist and confrontational, others nonpolitical in their efforts to promote human rights and related causes. Among the best-known are two that have won Nobel Peace Prizes: Amnesty International, based in London, which issues periodic reports on political rights in particular countries and has successfully lobbied for the release of prisoners of conscience; and International Physicians for the Prevention of Nuclear War, founded by Soviet and U.S. doctors. Others are Greenpeace (nuclear-arms reductions and marine ecosystem preservation), International Physicians for Social Responsibility (the hazards of the nuclear arms race), Poètes, Essayistes, Nouvellistes (P.E.N.—a writers' association devoted to freedom of expression), Planned Parenthood (family planning), END (European Nuclear Disarmament, one of many Western European groups that has galvanized mass protests of Soviet as well as U.S. nuclear-weapons deployments), People-to-People International (international exchange), and Fellowship of Reconciliation (Christian peace and human-rights organization). Finally, we should include the Greens in West Germany, which as a political party, stands apart from the other groups. Its message of ecological balance and socioeconomic restructuring to reflect human needs has been taken up by similar groups elsewhere in Europe and in the United States.[63] Despite ideological factionalism, the Greens show the potential for translating human-interest ideas into politically workable programs.

Advancing the rights of women has also become a matter of transnational concern, as was dramatized in 1985 at Nairobi, Kenya, when women from all over the world convened to evaluate their progress and the long road yet to be traveled. Several international conventions to end discrimination against women have now been signed or ratified by the overwhelming majority of governments. But many governments have not done either. More to the point, discrimination against women persists, regardless of signatures and paeans of praise.[64] "Women hold up half the sky," the Chinese like to say. Clearly, human rights cannot be said to be advancing unless and until women's rights markedly advance.

Central to women's rights is an end to discriminatory laws concerning the acquisition, sale, and inheritance of property, and equality with men in marriage and divorce. Also critical are passage and enforcement of equal educational and economic opportunity laws, provision for child care for working women, and the right of women to vote and compete for any public office. These are among the rights already embodied in international conventions, but they need to be universalized and implemented. International, including corporate, assistance to women's businesses and cooperatives, as noted earlier, should strengthen the case for such laws. So should the appointment of many more women to positions in international organizations, which, by and large, have failed to put their own houses in order with respect to male-female balance. With progress in these areas will come increased (and equal) access to health care and food, and a generalized appreciation of the burdens of womanhood, especially in those parts of the Third World (the Moslem Middle East) where women have almost subhuman status.

The problems women have experienced in securing their rights illustrates an inescapable fact of world politics: the failure of governments to live up to their promises under international agreements, especially where human rights are concerned. It is easier for governments to engage in public posturing about human equality than to yield power, either to persons or to supranational bodies. That is one reason women, like other oppressed or disempowered groups, have found that activism is the most effective route to changing the behavior of states and of the international system. Among the examples of such successful activism are the human chain women formed around a British military base to protest the deployment of U.S. cruise missiles; the leadership of Randall Forsberg in the U.S. nuclear-freeze campaign; of Dr. Helen Caldicott in Physicians for Social Responsibility; of Winnie Mandela in the anti-apartheid movement in South Africa; and of Coretta Scott King in the United States; the many empowering workshops of women like Elise Boulding, Joanna Rogers Macy, and Chellis Glendenning to "re-vision" the future; and the role of ambassadors for peace played by children like Samantha Smith in her 1984 visit to the Soviet Union.

In fact, there is a resurgence of cynicism, from Globalists as well as Realists, about the usefulness, and even the desirability, of international organizations as vehicles of humane change.[65] Insofar as critics are concerned that tyrannical power might be vested in a world organization, the cynicism is understandable. But most of their fears stem from the

presumed "failures" of the United Nations as a peacekeeper and pres-
erver of human rights and from the use of the General Assembly by
Third World representatives as a forum for sometimes abusive criticism
of the industrialized countries. Forgotten is the fact that international organizations like the UN can never be more effective than their members
wish it to be. As Britain's Prime Minister Margaret Thatcher once remarked, the UN is merely a mirror of its members; they would do better
to reform themselves than curse the mirror if they don't like what they
see. Unless states consistently resort to international institutions, use and
abide by international law, and give international bodies greater powers
and the means of enforcing their charters and the law, it is unreasonable
to expect solutions to the global crisis to come from the supranational
level.

One would think that the superpowers, valuing political stability,
would take the lead in demonstrating adherence to international agreements and law. But while Moscow and Washington frequently cloak their
behavior in the language of world order, neither has shown consistent
respect for it when national interests are at stake. The USSR has a long
history of violations of political agreements with other states, notably
those involving the sovereignty of its bordering countries.[66] It has fla-
grantly violated human-rights agreements to which it subscribes, such as
the Universal Declaration of Human Rights, the International Covenant
on Civil and Political Rights, and the Helsinki Accords. Soviet officials
cavalierly dismiss inquiries about these violations with reference to interference in their internal affairs, the same argument used by South African defenders of apartheid and leaders of other repressive states.
Finally, the Soviet Union, like France, West Germany, and a few other
states, only accepts the jurisdiction of the International Court of Justice
(ICJ) on a case-by-case basis.

The United States' practice in these areas has not been much better.
It, too, has ignored international law and treaties. In Latin America, for
instance, the United States has consistently used force and threats to
overthrow legitimate governments or intervene in civil conflicts. Yet the
United States is a signatory of the Treaty of the Organization of American States (1948), which specifically prohibits any form of interference
in the internal affairs of states in the hemisphere. Its worldwide arms
shipments, like those of the USSR, contribute directly to human-rights
violations. U.S. air and naval attacks against Libya in 1986 were justified
on the transparent ground of "freedom of the seas" when, in fact, they
had no firm basis in international law. Its always qualified support of
compulsory jurisdiction by the ICJ (under the Connolly Amendment,
which enables a President to withdraw cases he judges to be "essentially
within the domestic jurisdiction" of the United States) became a formal

rejection in 1985 when the Reagan administration saw no other way to avoid losing a suit brought by Nicaragua over the mining of its harbors. In the 1980s the United States also withdrew from UNESCO, refused to approve the Law of the Sea Treaty, voted against the World Health Organization's ban on Nestlé infant formula, and agreed to Senate ratification of the 1948 Genocide Convention only with a reservation exempting the United States from being sued in the ICJ for genocide. Such behavior demonstrates a disregard for international cooperation that is extraordinary for a nation which prides itself on a historical commitment to the rule of law.

In terms of promoting the human interest, realism demands recognition *both* of the deeply ingrained resistance of state leaders to supranational authority *and* of the increasing need for strengthening it. Even when it is not possible to put teeth into global agreements and organizations—such as in the Law of the Sea Treaty, the various human-rights covenants, and the International Court of Justice, none of which can compel adherence by states—the establishment of global standards and of new structures may be worthy accomplishments in their own right. As the experience of the Law of the Sea Treaty shows, the first step is to gain *recognition* of the need for global action, then to piece together the means of *effective monitoring* of the new arrangement, and only later, building on a history of equity and goodwill, to close the loopholes by introducing reliable *enforcement mechanisms*.

But practice sometimes has a way of outrunning theory. As much as states and global corporations will resist encroachments on their authority, breakthroughs do occur that create precedents and interesting possibilities for the future of international law and institutions. The Indian government's brief seizure of Union Carbide's top officer after the Bhopal tragedy is one such precedent. Another is India's (failed) attempt to bring its case before a U.S. court. Imagine the prospect of several Scandinavian villages whose lakes have been poisoned by acid rain taking the British government to court. Or the citizens of two different countries, such as Canada and the United States, joining in a collective suit against a polluting industry. Nor should the possibility be excluded that an enforceable code of behavior to which TNCs and host countries subscribe will evolve. Companies, economies, and persons could mutually benefit from an agreement, under international auspices, that guaranteed the security of foreign investments in return for assurances of a reasonable return on profits, of fair economic, health, and safety practices, and of environmental protections for the community.[67]

Another prospect is that national courts may act where the ICJ cannot and governments will not. In 1985, for example, a federal appeals court in Washington, D.C., put pressure on Japan to respect a worldwide ban on the killing of whales by ordering the United States to impose sanctions on Japanese fishermen. The court's decision scuttled a U.S.–Japan agreement that would have allowed the Japanese whaling industry to keep killing sperm whales for three additional years. In the not-too-distant future, protectors of the environment as well as victims of state and corporate actions may become plaintiffs more often. And their arguments may be based not on personal but on global injury, an expanded version of the Nuremberg Principle to cover large-scale violations of the ecosystem and human rights.

In the meantime, it will be up to citizens and their global-minded representatives to keep the pressure on governments to use international law, organizations, and nongovernmental mechanisms (such as mediation and people-to-people exchanges) whenever possible. *Governments need to be educated to lawfulness* and constantly prompted to practice what they preach about justice. Hence the importance, once more, of popular movements. But we should also keep in mind that citizen action against oppression has up until now not been at the global level. Rebellions, revolutions, and secessions have been the norm. And whether these have toppled governments or led to the creation of new territories, they have all accepted the state as the appropriate vehicle for their rule.[68] Consequently, we see that among the obstacles to a new globalism is not only the absence of global consciousness and recourse to law by state leaderships, but also a continuing identification with the state even by those who feel oppressed by it.

THE PROSPECTS FOR HUMANITY

Ultimately, the future of the planet rests with individuals—those who, in their daily struggles to survive, create positive examples of courage and self-sacrifice that will empower others; and those who use the fact of not having to struggle as a privileged opportunity to work for human betterment. Both kinds of persons reflect the best of human values and the best hope for humanity.

If it is true, as Richard Falk says, that "the most revealing world order statement each of us makes is with his or her life,"[69] then we are fortunate to have plenty of examples of people who have made the planet a better place—and in the process demonstrated that individuals do make a difference. In an age when personal power exercised on behalf of humanity is infrequently applauded in the global media, we would do well to remind ourselves of those who have fought and are fighting for human rights; of the enormous strides that have been made in a very short time by the women's, environmental, civil rights, and liberation theology movements; of the worldwide support for calls to restore ecological rationality and end the arms race, and the prominent place of religious institutions in catalyzing such support. Just a few concerned citizens were enough to inspire transforming events such as the UN's International Year of Cooperation, the Partial Test Ban, and the Bilateral Nuclear Freeze initiative. In short, world politics is too important to be left to diplomats; as "Star Trek's" Mr. Spock observed, "We must acknowledge that the purpose of diplomacy is to prolong a crisis."

Positive developments such as these reflect one kind of individual empowerment: people acting to make both their communities and the world more secure. Another kind has to do with a potentially far-reaching shift in individual values. In the United States, where this shift has been documented,[70] it seems to be occurring across the political and social spectrum. Its most remarkable feature in world-political terms is that it displays a turn away from many prominent Realist and Corporate-Globalist values (such as competition, materialism, quantity, individualism, and power) and toward many Global-Humanist values (such as cooperation, spirituality, enoughness, community, and personal growth). Although too much can be made of the political direction and scope of this values shift, neither can it be considered spurious or ephemeral. When large numbers of people from all walks of life simplify their lifestyles (their "needs") and change their values (their "wants"), and when they begin to participate in recreating the substance of their communities, national, and eventually global, politics must also change. The emphasis on growth and expansion that has always characterized state and corporate politics will have to be redefined, as "national security" is pressured to more directly serve "human security" needs.

When and whether such a dramatic transformation—and the prospects for universalizing it—will occur may finally depend on people's beliefs and attitudes at least as much as on their energies. For the global crisis is as much psychological as it is material, and it starts with us. How much we believe in ourselves, whether or not we question our beliefs as well as others', how important we really believe the crisis is, and how seriously we believe in one person's ability to influence it—these, Roger Walsh eloquently tells us, are among the fundamental issues each of us must decide as we confront hunger, the arms race, and pollution.[71]

It takes great inner strength in times of fear and uncertainty to hold to a positive vision of the future. Yet positiveness and hopefulness are essential to creating a humane world. As Patricia Mische perceptively pointed out to an audience of peace workers:

> Many of us are not successful in our efforts for peace because secretly
> we don't really believe it can happen. Secretly, we don't even know if
> we want it to happen. And if we do want it to happen, we don't know
> what a peace system would look like. We know what it is we're work-
> ing against, but we don't know what it is we want to create. Our im-
> ages of the future serve like magnets. If we walk around only with
> images of destruction, we [may] use our energies to bring about the
> very destruction we fear.[72]

The struggle for dominion that takes place at every level of human activity will surely remain with us for a very long time. But not necessarily forever, in the same forms, or with the same intensities or doomsday
potential. Global Humanism contends that it is realistic to be optimistic, for we can stave off worldwide collapse by calling forth the best
that is within each of us.

The bottom line is that our age is but another phase in the universal evolutionary process. Like all ages that preceded it and all that will
follow, this one holds out new opportunities for tapping the human
potential. It is demonstrably true that everyone can achieve a fulfilling
life, and that the earth can be kept green and blue—just as true as humanity's ability to explore distant planets. The real question is whether
enough of us will believe in that prospect and will dedicate our "lives
and sacred fortunes" to realizing it.

The opening pages of this study quoted the warning of the UN
Secretary-General U Thant about an impending planetary crisis brought
on by the arms race and underdevelopment. U Thant's plea was that
people develop a "dual allegiance . . . to the human race as well as to
our local community or nation." "I even believe," he concluded, "that
the mark of the truly educated and imaginative person facing the
twenty-first century is that he feels himself to be a planetary citizen."[73]
Perhaps the best argument on behalf of space travel is that every astro-
naut and cosmonaut who has gazed at the planet from the moon and
deep space has moved toward that dual allegiance. The last word belongs to one of them, Edgar Mitchell:

> No man I know of has gone to the moon that has not been affected in
> some way that is similar. It is what I prefer to call instant global con-
> sciousness. Each man comes back with a feeling that he is no longer
> only an American citizen; he is a planetary citizen. He doesn't like
> things the way they are, and he wants to improve them.

Notes

PREFACE

1. In Richard A. Falk, *A Study of Future Worlds* (1975), pp. xvii–xviii.
2. A rare exception is Glenn D. Paige, "On Values and Science: *The Korean Decision* Reconsidered," *American Political Science Review*.

CHAPTER ONE

1. Address of May 9, 1969, "Ten Crucial Years," *United Nations Monthly Chronicle*, p. ii.
2. On water, see Ruth Leger Sivard, ed., *World Military and Social Expenditures 1983: An Annual Report on World Priorities*, p. 14; Richard J. Barnet, *The Lean Years: Politics in the Age of Scarcity*, p. 195; Willy Brandt et al., *North-South, A Program for Survival*, p. 55. This last source, the Brandt Report, adds (again, p. 55): "Between 20 and 25 million children below the age of five die every year in developing countries, and a third of these deaths are from diarrhoea caught from polluted water."
   On hunger, see Brandt et al., p. 55; and Gerald O. Barney, ed. *The Global 2000 Report to the President: Entering the Twenty-First Century*, vol. 1, p. 17.
3. Brandt et al., p. 58.
4. Andre Gunder Frank, *Crisis: In the World Economy*, p. 13; Barnet, p. 258.
5. Brandt et al., pp. 50–51; Kim Carney, "Development Aid: An Economist's Perception," *International Journal on World Peace*, p. 7; Sivard, *World Priorities*, p. 14.
6. Barney, *Global 2000: Twenty-First Century*, pp. 8-9.
7. Barney, *Global 2000: Twenty-First Century*, p. 36 (on forests) and p. 38 (on species losses). See also Edward C. Wolf, *On the Brink of Extinction: Conserving the Diversity of Life*, pp. 11, 14; and Lester R. Brown, *Building a Sustainable Society*, p. 96 (on food supplies).
8. Lester R. Brown et al., *State of the World 1986: A Worldwatch Institute Report on Progress Toward a Sustainable Society*, p. 196 (on military spending); Sivard, *World Priorities*, p. 18 (on nuclear arsenals); and United Nations Centre for Disarmament, Department of Political and Security Council Affairs, *The United Nations Disarmament Yearbook*, vol. 6 (1981), p. 353 (on scientists). The figure of 20 percent represents about 500,000 people in the 1970s.
9. Sivard, *World Priorities*, pp. 10–11.

10. Sivard, *World Priorities*, p. 5; Brandt et al., p. 14.

11. Humane values and norms, as key elements in the Global-Humanist (or "world order") perspective, are discussed in the following major works: Richard A. Falk, *A Study of Future Worlds* (the introduction to which includes discussion of the World Order Models Project); Richard A. Falk, Samuel S. Kim, and Saul H. Mendlovitz, eds., *Toward a Just World Order*, vol. 1; Samuel S. Kim, *The Quest for a Just World Order*; Saul H. Mendlovitz, ed., *On the Creation of a Just World Order*; and Johan Galtung, *The True Worlds: A Transnational Perspective*.

12. There are several different emphases to "international political economy," reflecting narrower or broader understandings of what "politics" comprises. For a sense of the diversity, see R. Dan Walleri, "The Political Economy Literature on North-South Relations: Alternative Approaches and Empirical Evidence," *International Studies Quarterly*; James Petras, *Critical Perspectives on Imperialism and Social Class in the Third World*, ch. 1; and Robert J. Gilpin, *U.S. Power and the Multinational Corporations*, ch. 1.

13. Kissinger, quoted in Charles W. Kegley, Jr. and Eugene R. Wittkopf, *World Politics: Trend and Transformation*, p. 29.

CHAPTER TWO

1. Among the most influential Realist writings are Edward H. Carr, *The Twenty-Years' Crisis, 1919–1939: An Introduction to the Study of International Relations*; George F. Kennan, *Realities of American Foreign Policy*; and Hans J. Morgenthau, *Politics Among Nations: The Struggle for Power and Peace*, 5th rev. ed. For brief reviews of the literature, see Kegley and Wittkopf, pp. 19–22; and Ray Maghroori, "Introduction: Major Debates in International Relations," in Ray Maghroori and Bennett Ramberg, eds., *Globalism Versus Realism: International Relations' Third Debate*, pp. 9–22.

2. *Non*capitalist systems should also be considered to have their Corporate Globalists, however. They would be key figures in socialist and communist parties, state trading companies, and similar powerful bureaucracies that operate transnationally. Like their capitalist counterparts, these highly centralized organizations are also propelled by globalist ideas: the spread of socialist economic models, political institutions, and culture. Examples of the Corporate-Globalist world view are in Maghroori and Ramberg, *Globalism Versus Realism*; Richard J. Barnet and Ronald E. Müller, *Global Reach: The Power of the Multinational Corporations*, part 1; and Stephen Guisinger, ed., *Private Enterprise and the New Global Economic Challenge*.

3. As President Lyndon B. Johnson said in 1966: "There are 3 billion people in the world and we have only 200 million of them. We are outnumbered 15 to 1. If might did make right, they would sweep over the United States and take what we have. We have what they want." Quoted in Richard J. Barnet, *Intervention and Revolution: The United States in the Third World*, p. 25.

4. Richard J. Barnet, *Roots of War*, pp. 95–96.

5. Henry A. Kissinger, *Nuclear Weapons and Foreign Policy*, p. 244.

6. Kissinger, quoted in James Petras and Morris Morley, *The United States and Chile: Imperialism and the Overthrow of the Allende Government*, p. vii.

7. Henry A. Kissinger, *White House Years*, p. 673. This, despite the U.S. ambassador's predictably paranoid admission that "Chile voted calmly to have a Marxist-Leninist state, the first nation in the world to make this choice freely and knowingly."

8. Morgenthau, p. 274.

9. Seymour M. Hersh, *The Price of Power: Kissinger in the Nixon White House*, p. 263.

10. Kissinger, interviewed in *Trialogue*, p. 3.

11. Huan Xiang, "China Is Its Own Master in Foreign Affairs," in Zhou Guo, ed., *China and the World*, vol. 3, pp. 46–47.

12. Truman, quoted in Noam Chomsky, *American Power and the New Mandarins*, p. 268.

13. Figures are from Dexter F. Baker, "Foreign Investment—A Two-way Street," *Vital Speeches of the Day*, vol. 48, no. 14 (May 1, 1982), pp. 446–448; John M. Stopford and John H. Dunning, eds., *The World Directory of Multinational Enterprises, 1982–83: Company Performance and Global Trends*, table 1.2, p. 5; David H. Blake and Robert S. Walters, *The Politics of Global Economic Relations*, p. 79.

14. *International Herald Tribune*, March 22, 1983.

15. On the Trilateral Commission's origins and development, see Holly K. Sklar, ed., *Trilateralism: The Trilateral Commission and Elite Planning for World Management*, chs. 2–4; and Laurence Shoup, *The Carter Presidency*, ch. 2.

16. Rockefeller, quoted in Thomas Ferguson and Joel Rogers, "Another Trilateral Election?" *The Nation*, June 28, 1980, p. 784.

17. These surpluses, as Robert J. Gilpin reminds us in *U.S. Power and the Multinational Corporations*, p. 157, are quite apart from income and from portfolio investments—stocks, bonds, and the like—which amount to several times the receipts from direct investments.

18. John Cavanagh and Frederick Clairmonte, "The Transnational Economy: Transnational Corporations and Global Markets," table 6, p. 25.

19. Stopford and Dunning, p. 1.

20. Cavanagh and Clairmonte, p. 17.

21. Kegley and Wittkopf, p. 132.

22. Stopford and Dunning, table 1.2, p. 5.

23. Stopford and Dunning, table 1.3, p. 6.

24. *Los Angeles Times*, April 8, 1981, 4/p. 1.

25. Figures are from Cheryl Payer, *The World Bank: A Critical Analysis*, p. 15; and Charles F. Meissner, "Debt: Reform Without Governments," *Foreign Policy*, p. 90.

26. Figures: Carney, table 3, p. 11. The remainder comes from voluntary agencies (2%) and various credits (9%).

27. Convincing cases are presented in Teresa Hayter, *Aid As Imperialism*, ch. 4; Payer, *World Bank*, pp. 19–21; and Cheryl Payer, *The Debt Trap: The IMF and the Third World*, ch. 10.

28. Darrell Delamaide, *Debt Shock: The Full Story of the World Credit Crisis*, pp. 131–132.

29. See Delamaide, pp. 112, 227–228. As Meissner comments (p. 89), the efforts of Third World governments to restructure (postpone) their debts involves them in an elaborate "game." It can only work if, in return for the governments' opening up their economies to foreign investments and increased trade, the transnational banks greatly liberalize lending policies, including a cap on interest rates. So far, only the debtors have been playing the game.

30. Baker, p. 446.

31. Mahbub ul Haq, "Negotiating the Future," *Foreign Affairs*, p. 416.

32. Barnet and Müller, pp. 14–15.

33. Barnet and Müller, p. 15.

34. See Anthony Smith, *The Geopolitics of Information: How Western Culture Dominates the World*, pp. 73–77.

35. Herbert I. Schiller, *Who Knows: Information in the Age of the Fortune 500*, pp. 30–33. U.S.-based data banks hold about two-thirds of all organized data bases (Schiller, p. 36).

36. Smith, p. 73.

37. Smith, ch. 2.

38. For example, Gulf Oil (owned by Chevron) has for many years operated a refinery in Cabinda Bay, Angola, a socialist country. Despite pressure from U.S. conservatives to pull out of Angola, where the United States is assisting rebel forces seeking to overthrow its government, Gulf has stayed on. As the board chair and chief executive officer of Gulf Oil, James E. Lee, has said: "The experience of Gulf Oil in Angola underscores the fact that ideological commitments—whether Marxist, Centrist, or Capitalist—can co-exist with a quite responsible and pragmatic approach to business relationships" ("To Live in Interesting Times," in *Vital Speeches of the Day*, vol. 48, no. 24 [October 1, 1982], p. 743).

39. Quoted in Delamaide, p. 81.

40. See Michael J. Crozier, Samuel P. Huntington, and Joji Watanuki, *The Crisis of Democracy: Report on the Governability of Democracies to the Trilateral Commission* pp. 113–115, on the need for greater "moderation" of democratic processes, including press freedom.

41. IBM's leadership, for instance, once made the case for business sovereignty in South Africa this way: "We feel we should be able to do business where and with whom the law allows, where we judge the risks and returns to be acceptable, and where we can remain faithful to our policies and beliefs." With convoluted logic, in a mimeograph on "IBM Operations in South Africa," the corporation argued further that for it to reduce or eliminate its role in South Africa would be to "set a precedent which no thoughtful American should welcome: a precedent of taking foreign policy out of the hands of government and putting it into the hands of corporations." In other words, you (in government) do your business and let us do ours. In 1986, however, IBM joined with other major U.S. companies in pulling out of South Africa.

42. See Frederick B. Dent, "The Multinational Corporation—Toward a World Economy," *Financial Executive*, pp. 42–47.

43. On economic nationalism, see Petras, ch. 6; and Frank, p. 284.

44. Tom Farer, "The United States and the Third World: A Basis for Accommodation," *Foreign Affairs*, pp. 79–97.

45. This account of postwar planning is largely based on Fred Block, *The Origins of International Economic Disorder: A Study of United States International Monetary Policy from World War II to the Present*; Gabriel and Joyce

Kolko, *The Limits of Power: The World and United States Foreign Policy, 1945–1954*, chs. 1–6 and 12–13; Alan Wolfe, *America's Impasse: The Rise and Fall of the Politics of Growth*, esp. pp. 9–31; Laurence H. Shoup and William Minter, "Shaping a New World Order: The Council on Foreign Relations' Blueprint for World Hegemony," in Sklar, part 3, ch. 1; and John Lewis Gaddis, *Strategies of Containment: A Critical Appraisal of Postwar American National Security Policy*, pp. 60–65.

46. Wolfe, p. 114.

47. Byrnes, quoted in Kolko, p. 23. See similar quotes by Cordell Hull and Dean Acheson in Block, p. 40.

48. Quoted in Kolko, p. 24.

49. Truman to Byrnes, January 5, 1946, in Glenn Paige, *The Korean Decision: June 24–30, 1950*, p. 54.

50. Quoted in Barnet, *Roots of War*, p. 100.

51. Quoted in Walter Millis, ed., *The Forrestal Diaries*, pp. 251–252.

52. NSC-68 is reproduced in full in John P. Glennon et al., eds., *Foreign Relations of the United States 1950*; vol. 1: *National Security Affairs, Foreign Economic Policy*. The quoted portions are from pp. 262, 258–259, 262–263 in that order.

53. On Eisenhower's foreign economic policy, see Blanche Wiesen Cook, *The Declassified Eisenhower: A Divided Legacy of Peace and Political Warfare*, pp. 293–309.

54. Quoted in Holly K. Sklar, "Trilateralism and the Management of Contradictions: Concluding Perspectives," in Sklar, p. 564.

CHAPTER THREE

1. William P. Bundy, "Elements of Power," *Foreign Affairs*, p. 26.

2. ul Haq, p. 417.

3. Brandt, et al., pp. 8–11.

4. Roy Preiswerk, "Could We Study International Relations As If People Mattered?" in Falk, Kim, and Mendlovitz, pp. 175–197.

5. Sakamoto, "The Global Crisis and Peace Research," *International Peace Research Newsletter*, pp. 4–7.

6. On these values, see the introduction to Falk, Kim, and Mendlovitz, pp. 1–9. For the application of these values to Latin American political development, see Gustavo Lagos, "The Revolution of Being: A Preferred World Model," in Heraldo Muñoz, ed., *From Dependency to Development: Strategies to Overcome Underdevelopment and Inequality*, pp. 123–160.

7. Richard Falk, "World Order Values: Secular Means and Spiritual Ends."

8. These documents have been collected in U.S. Department of State, Bureau of Public Affairs, Selected Documents no. 5, *Human Rights*. On the record of ratification by governments, see Kim, *Just World Order*, table 6.4, p. 232.

9. See Gerald and Patricia Mische, *Toward a Human World Order: Beyond the National Security Straitjacket*, pp. 21–22 and 30–33, on the Tasadays in the Philippines and the Iks in Uganda. Also relevant are the Bushmen

of southern Africa. See, for example, Laurens van der Post, *The Lost World of the Kalahari*.

10. Carl Rogers (*On Personal Power*, ch. 7) offers many insights from person-centered therapy that he has pioneered concerning communication among racially, economically, and politically different persons and groups. He refers, for instance, to the importance of perceiving others as humans, not symbols; of the unconditional acceptance of others' feelings; of listening closely as others express deep-seated rage. "It is being human which dissolves the barriers and brings closeness," he concludes.

11. Richard A. Falk, "Contending Approaches to World Order," in Falk, Kim, and Mendlovitz, p. 154.

12. Richard A. Falk, "On Invisible Oppression and World Order," in Falk, Kim, and Mendlovitz, p. 44.

13. Fouad Ajami, *Human Rights and World Order Politics*. Also see Hazel Henderson's discussion of "flat-earth economics," which she contends is common to modern-day capitalist and socialist thought, in *The Politics of the Solar Age: Alternatives to Economics*, pp. 22–26.

14. Barnet, *Lean Years*, p. 299.

15. See Johan Galtung, "A Structural Theory of Imperialism," *Journal of Peace Research*, pp. 81–117.

16. The pastoral letter appears in "The Challenge of Peace: God's Promise and Our Response," *Origins*, p. 322.

17. Preiswerk, in Falk, Kim, and Mendlovitz, p. 179.

18. Paolo Friere, *Pedagogy of the Oppressed*, trans. Myra Bergman Ramos, p. 74.

19. Ajami, pp. 1–8.

20. Ajami, pp. 28–29.

21. Richard A. Falk, "Comparative Protection of Human Rights in Capitalist and Socialist Third World Countries," in Falk, Kim, and Mendlovitz, pp. 424–425.

22. See, for example, Edward S. Herman and Frank Brodhead, *Demonstration Elections: U.S.–Staged Elections in the Dominican Republic, Vietnam, and El Salvador*; and Raymond Bonner, *Weakness and Deceit: U.S. Policy and El Salvador*.

23. Eqbal Ahmad, "The Neo-Fascist State: Notes on the Pathology of Power in the Third World," in Falk, Kim, and Mendlovitz, pp. 74–83.

24. For examples on the U.S. side of the preference for "stability" in Third World politics, see Melvin Gurtov and Ray Maghroori, eds., *Roots of Failure: United States Policy in the Third World*, pp. 198–202.

25. For example, see Kim, *Just World Order*, pp. 102–116.

26. Sivard, *World Priorities*, tables I and II, pp. 32 and 33.

27. Sivard, *World Priorities*, p. 23.

28. Sivard, *World Priorities*, p. 23.

29. Brandt et al., p. 14.

30. Sivard, *World Priorities*, p. 24.

31. Barnet, *Lean Years*, p. 229.

32. *United Nations Disarmament Yearbook* (1981), p. 353.

33. Sivard, *World Priorities*, p. 6.

34. Sivard, *World Priorities*, p. 19; Kegley and Wittkopf, p. 381.

35. Kim, *Just World Order*, pp. 105–106. Another, perhaps more concrete, way to ponder the almost unimaginable threat to human life posed by

nuclear weapons is to consider the following: A single U.S. Navy Trident D-class nuclear submarine (of which there are already seven deployed and several more planned for deployment), armed with twenty-four Trident intercontinental ballistic missiles, each of which carries ten independently targetable (MIRV'd) warheads (for a total of 240 warheads), by itself can deliver the explosive power of over 18,000 Hiroshimas.

36. *Newsweek*, October 11, 1982, pp. 117–118; *Los Angeles Times*, June 27, 1984, 6/p. 10.

37. Amory B. Lovins, L. Hunter Lovins, and Leonard Ross, "Nuclear Power and Nuclear Bombs," *Foreign Affairs*, p. 1175.

38. Arthur H. Westing and E. W. Pfeiffer, "The Cratering of Indochina," *Scientific American*, pp. 21–29. Another summary of the ecological devastation is in Raphael Littauer and Norman Uphoff, eds., *The Air War in Indochina*, rev. ed., pp. 245–261.

39. The jury is, however, still out on yellow rain: see Erik Guyot, "The Case Is Not Proved," *The Nation*. In fact, some researchers have advanced evidence that U.S. charges against the Soviet Union are politically motivated and contrary to the actual findings in Southeast Asia. See *International Herald Tribune*, September 1, 1987, p. 6.

40. On nuclear winter, see Carl Sagan, "Nuclear War and Climatic Catastrophe," *Foreign Affairs*, pp. 257–292. Subsequently, an international research team reported that the worst long-term consequence of nuclear winter would probably be mass starvation: anywhere from 1 to 4 *billion* people might die as huge clouds of soot blot out the sun, bringing on global famine (*Los Angeles Times*, September 13, 1985, p. 5).

41. About 99 percent of all high-level radioactive waste in the United States comes from military reactors. The Defense Department produces roughly 400,000 tons a year of nuclear waste. See Joel S. Hirschhorn, "Toxic Waste," *Los Angeles Times*, October 10, 1983, 2/p. 5; David E. Kaplan and Ida Landauer, "Radioactivity for the Oceans," *The Nation*; and "Military Nuclear Wastes: The Hidden Burden of the Nuclear Arms Race," *The Defense Monitor* 10, no. 1 (1981), pp. 1–8.

42. Osvaldo Sunkel, "Development Styles and the Environment: An Interpretation of the Latin American Case," in Muñoz, pp. 93–114.

43. Muñoz, p. 99.

44. The principal source on pesticide dumping is David Weir and Mark Schapiro, *Circle of Poison: Pesticides and People in a Hungry World*. The *Multinational Monitor* reports an estimate of Oxfam International that "375,000 pesticide poisonings, 6,700 of which are fatal, occur each year in the Third World" (in Robert Engler, "Technology Out of Control," *The Nation*, p. 489).

45. On the Bhopal tragedy, see Engler, pp. 488–500.

46. Cited in Fritjof Capra and Charlene Spretnak, *Green Politics*, p. 33.

47. Irene L. Gendzier, *Managing Political Change: Social Scientists and the Third World*. The role of the major U.S. foundations in transmitting values and institutions to the Third World is well documented in Robert F. Arnove, *Philanthropy and Cultural Imperialism: The Foundations at Home and Abroad*, especially the essay by Edward H. Berman, "Educational Colonialism in Africa: The Role of American Foundations, 1910–1945," pp. 179–202.

48. Fernando Henrique Cardoso, "Towards Another Development," in Muñoz, pp. 298–300.

49. Gandhi's concept is elaborated in Louis Fischer, ed., *The Essential Gandhi: His Life, Work, and Ideas*, p. 93.

50. Kim, *Just World Order*, p. 139. If the income floor is $500 a year, the number living in absolute poverty is more like 2 billion people (Sivard, *World Priorities*, p. 26).

51. Mao Zedong, *Selected Readings from the Works of Mao Tsetung*, p. 500.

52. Edgar Snow, *Red Star Over China*, pp. 128–130.

53. Amilcar Cabral, *Revolution in Guinea: Selected Texts*, trans. Richard Handyside, pp. 62–63.

54. V. S. Naipaul, *India: A Wounded Civilization*, pp. 20–21.

55. Naipaul, p. 23.

56. Naipaul, p. 189.

57. Malcolm X, with Alex Haley, *The Autobiography of Malcolm X*, pp. 159–160.

58. Excerpted from Steve Biko, *I Write What I Like* (1978), in Falk, Kim, and Mendlovitz, pp. 25, 27, 31.

59. Mao Zedong, *Mao Zedong xuan ji*, 1, pp. 31–32.

60. Ruth Leger Sivard, ed., *Women: A World Survey*, p. 5.

61. Domitila Barrios de Chungara, with Moema Viezzer, *Let Me Speak! Testimony of Domitila, A Woman of the Bolivian Mines*, trans. Victoria Ortiz, pp. 40–41.

62. See Annette Fuentes and Barbara Ehrenreich, *Women in the Global Factory*, p. 13.

63. Fuentes and Ehrenreich, p. 20.

64. Fuentes and Ehrenreich, p. 16.

65. "Speech, Stockholm, Sweden, December 9, 1982, on the Occasion of Receiving the Alternative Peace Prize."

66. In Saul K. Padover, ed., *Nehru on World History*, pp. 109, 111–112.

67. Fanon, *The Wretched of the Earth*, trans. Constance Farrington, pp. 44–45, 210–211.

68. In Bernard B. Fall, ed., *Ho Chi Minh on Revolution: Selected Writings, 1920-66*, p. 141.

69. E. M. Forster, *A Passage to India*, p. 322.

70. Fouad Ajami, "The Fate of Nonalignment," *Foreign Affairs*, p. 383.

71. Ngugi wa Thiong'o, *Petals of Blood*, pp. 163–164.

72. Luis Inacio Da Silva, speech of August 28, 1982, in Sao Paolo State, taped by Ronald Chilcote; trans. Claudia Pompan.

73. Ngugi, p. 88.

74. Ali Shariati, "Reflections of a Concerned Muslim: On the Plight of Oppressed Peoples," in Falk, Kim, and Mendlovitz, pp. 20–22.

75. This section relies on Penny Lernoux, *Cry of the People: The Struggle for Human Rights in Latin America—The Catholic Church in Conflict with U.S. Policy*, especially pp. 37–39, 463–470, and (concerning the CIA) ch. 8.

76. Lernoux, p. xviii.

77. Leonardo Boff, *Church: Charism and Power; Liberation Theology and the Institutional Church*, trans. John W. Diercksmeier, pp. 7–10.

78. Jacobo Timerman, *Prisoner Without a Name, Cell Without a Number*, trans. Toby Talbot, pp. 155, 157.

79. Manlio Argueta, *One Day of Life*, pp. 193–194.

80. Sivard, *World Priorities*, p. 19. She adds that "in an additional 35 [countries], the practice occurs but less frequently." Kim (*Just World Order*, table 6.2, p. 222) writes that—based on an Amnesty International report—in 1981, 48 of 117 governments practiced torture.

81. "Charter 77: Czech Group's Plea for Human Rights," in Falk, Kim, and Mendlovitz, pp. 34–35.

82. "Manifesto of the Alliance for Human Rights in China," Falk, Kim, and Mendlovitz, pp. 401–404.

83. "Interview: Kim Dae Jung—Democracy and Dissidence in South Korea," *Journal of International Affairs*, pp. 181–191.

84. In T. C. McLuhan, ed., *Touch the Earth: A Self-Portrait of Indian Existence*, p. 169.

85. "Haudenosaunee Statement to the World, May 1979," *Akwesasne Notes*.

86. Solzhenitsyn, *The Gulag Archipelago, 1918–1956: An Experiment in Literary Investigation*, trans. Thomas P. Whitney, pp. 177–178. Solzhenitsyn's reference in the quoted matter is to the Soviet failure to prosecute Nazi war criminals.

CHAPTER FOUR

1. See George Marotta, "The Third World: Threat or Opportunity?" *Agenda* (Agency for International Development), pp. 23–26; address by Richard L. McCall, assistant secretary of state for international organization affairs, October 14, 1980, in U.S. Department of State, *Current Policy*, no. 235, same date; and testimony of Secretary of State George Shultz, February 16, 1983, *Current Policy*, no. 454, same date.

2. For background, see Frank, ch. 5. On the full range of the NIEO agenda, see Frank, pp. 273–274.

3. World Bank, *World Development Report 1984*, p. 6. By comparison, in 1900, underdeveloped countries represented 66 percent of world population and 19 percent of world production. In 1950 the figures were 67 percent and 17 percent. If we focus on the poorest countries, in 1980 they accounted for 47 percent of world population but only 5 percent of world production.

4. World Bank, p. 6.

5. Frank, pp. 266–269.

6. See Rupert Emerson, "The Fate of Human Rights in the Third World," *World Politics*, pp. 201–226 on the denial by Third World spokespersons of ethnic and democratic rights in their own countries.

7. Frank, p. 271.

8. Fouad Ajami, "The Fate of Nonalignment," p. 370.

9. Fifteen TNCs—and in most cases only three to six of those—control international trade in food, agricultural raw materials, and minerals. See Cavanagh and Clairmonte, table 4, p. 17; and, with respect to oil, Barnet, *Lean Years*, p. 40.

10. Lagos, in Muñoz, p. 130.

11. On Brazil's income (for 1972), see World Bank, table 28, p. 273.

12. Americas Watch Committee and American Civil Liberties Union, *Report on Human Rights in El Salvador*, pp. 19–20. A similar situation exists elsewhere in Central America. See Billie R. DeWalt, "The Agrarian Bases of Conflict in Central America," in Kenneth M. Coleman and George C. Herring, eds., *The Central American Crisis: Sources of Conflict and the Failure of U.S. Policy*, p. 50.

13. A. Kent MacDougall, "In Third World, All but the Rich are Poorer," *Los Angeles Times*, November 4, 1984, 6/pp.1–3.

14. Mark Sheperd, Jr., "National Regulation of the International Economy: A Business Perspective," in Guisinger, p. 85.

15. Frank, p. 13. It is also true that many kinds of work, especially by women and children, are *not* counted in official statistics.

16. On Brazil's Northeast, see Josué de Castro, *Death in the Northeast*, pp. 82–84.

17. Barnet, *Lean Years*, p. 259.

18. Barnet, *Lean Years*, p. 262.

19. Oxfam America, "Special Report: Women in Development," pp. 1–8.

20. See Susan J. Pharr, *Political Women in Japan: The Search for a Place in Political Life,* pp. 174–177.

21. Roderic A. Camp, "Women and Political Leadership in Mexico: A Comparative Study of Female and Male Political Elites," *Journal of Politics*, p. 440.

22. For analyses of the Green Revolution, see: Susan George, *How the Other Half Dies: The Real Reasons for World Hunger*, esp. ch. 5; Betsy Hartmann and James K. Boyce, *Needless Hunger: Voices from a Bangladesh Village*, pp. 48–54. Kusum Nair's study *In Defense of the Irrational Peasant: Indian Agriculture After the Green Revolution* recounts the different results of the Green Revolution for inefficient rich land owners and efficient small farmers.

23. World Bank, fig. 1.2, p. 5.

24. World Bank, table 23, pp. 262–263. Figures are for 1982.

25. *Riverside Press-Enterprise*, December 8, 1983, p. A2.

26. World Bank, table 25, pp. 266–267.

27. World Bank, table 24, pp. 264–265 (concerning doctors and health).

28. On meat consumption, see Brown, *Building a Sustainable Society*, table 5–5, p. 106. Concerning caloric intake, see Charles Garvin and Greg Rosenbaum, *World Without Plenty: A Basic Overview of World Resources*, table 4.2, p. 151.

29. Barnet, *Lean Years*, p. 196.

30. For a brief review of the evidence on overpopulation and underdevelopment, see Garvin and Rosenbaum, pp. 18–25. Cultural factors, of course, such as the status gained from having more children, also are among the reasons behind large families.

31. MacDougall, p. 3.

32. The politics of birth control in the Third World is treated by Mark Dowie, "The Corporate Crime of the Century," *Mother Jones*, pp. 23–38.

33. Frank, pp. 183–190.

34. An excellent case study of denationalization caused by TNC takeovers of local firms is by Richard S. Newfarmer, "TNC Takeovers in Brazil: The

Uneven Distribution of Benefits in the Market for Firms," *World Development*, pp. 25–43.

35. Figures on the extensive TNC role in Latin American exports are in David Blond, "The Future Contribution of Multinational Corporations to World Growth—A Positive Appraisal," *Business Economics*, pp. 81–82.

36. Brown, *Building a Sustainable Society*, pp. 92–94.

37. See Robert H. Bates, *Markets and States in Tropical Africa: The Political Basis of Agricultural Policies*.

38. See Barnet, *Lean Years*, pp. 153, 156, 169. A U.S. Department of State publication notes: "The US accounts for more than 65% of world coarse grain trade, 50% of world wheat trade, and about 60% of trade in soybeans and soybean products, and is an important factor in the world market in meat, poultry, and fruits and vegetables" ("Agriculture in US Foreign Economic Policy," *GIST*, November 1981, p. 1.)

39. Barnet, *Lean Years*, pp. 152–153. In some of the richest countries, as much as three-quarters of all grain is fed to livestock. So is an increasing amount of soybeans. That makes meat an extremely expensive source of protein, and one that literally takes food out of the mouths of the poor. See Brown, *Building a Sustainable Society*, pp. 105–107.

40. On the corruption, inefficiency, and politics that bedevil food aid programs, see George, ch. 8; Frances Moore Lappé and Joseph Collins, *Food First: Beyond the Myth of Scarcity*, pp. 328–339; and Barnet, *Lean Years*, p. 155.

41. Brown, *Building a Sustainable Society*, pp. 36–40.

42. On the Amazon, see Brown et al., *State of the World 1985*, pp. 12–13, and Barnet, *Lean Years*, p. 75. The loss of species is documented in Wolf, p. 14.

43. On TNC clear-cutting operations, see Norman Myers, "The Conversion of Tropical Forests," *Environment*, pp. 6–13.

44. See David Weir, "The Boomerang Crime," *Mother Jones*, pp. 40–49.

45. Sunkel, in Muñoz, pp. 99–109.

46. Althea L. Duersten and Arpad von Lazar, "The Global Poor," in Daniel Yergin and Martin Hillenbrand, eds., *Global Insecurity: A Strategy for Energy and Economic Renewal*, pp. 266–267.

47. World Bank, table 16, pp. 248–249.

48. World Bank, table 16, pp. 248–249. Updated figures are in Brown, *State of the World 1986*, table 1–1, p. 7.

49. Summaries from country studies of the IMF in action may be found in Hayter, pp. 154–162; and Payer, *Debt Trap*, pp. 41–42.

50. For example, see the report on the World Bank's impact on small businesses in Chile, in Cynthia Brown, "The High Cost of Monetarism in Chile," *The Nation*.

51. On capital flight, see James Henry, "Where the Money Went," *The New Republic*. World Bank profits are reported in *Los Angeles Times*, September 22, 1986, p. 2. The matter of net transfers is in *Los Angeles Times*, June 30, 1986, 4/p. 4.

52. Michael T. Klare has written on both Soviet and U.S. arms sales to the Third World. See "Soviet Arms Transfers to the Third World," *Bulletin of the Atomic Scientists*; and Michael T. Klare and Cynthia Arnson, *Supplying Repression: U.S. Support for Authoritarian Regimes Abroad*.

53. Nicole Ball, "Military Expenditure and Socio-Economic Development," *International Social Science Journal*.

54. On state and class in Iran, see Fred Halliday, *Iran: Dictatorship and Development*; and Frances FitzGerald, "Giving the Shah Everything He Wants," *Harper's*.

55. Sivard, *World Priorities*, p. 11.

56. Sivard, *World Priorities*, p. 19.

57. The *Annals* of the American Association of Political and Social Science, vol. 467 (May 1983), contains a comprehensive survey of the worldwide refugee issue. See in particular Earl E. Huyck and Leon F. Bouvier, "The Demography of Refugees," pp. 39–61. Their article draws extensively from the annual *World Refugee Survey* published by the U.S. Committee for Refugees.

By the time of publication of this book, the accepted figure on the world's refugees had become 10 million.

58. Concerning El Salvador, see Americas Watch and ACLU, p. xxviii.

59. Address by James N. Purcell, Jr., director of the State Department's Bureau for Refugee Programs, *Current Policy*, no. 693, April 17, 1985.

60. In Mao, p. 321.

61. Lucien Bianco, *Origins of the Chinese Revolution 1915–1949*, trans. Muriel Bell, p. 95.

62. For an eyewitness account, see A. Doak Barnett, *China On the Eve of Communist Takeover*, esp. pp. 111–118.

63. William Hinton, *Fanshen: A Documentary of Revolution in a Chinese Village*, p. xii.

64. 1980s figures from World Bank, tables 23–25, pp. 262, 264, 266.

65. *Beijing Review*, vol. 30, no. 27 (July 6, 1987), p. 24.

66. Brown et al., *State of the World 1986*, pp. 18 ff.

67. Ding Chen, "The Economic Development of China," *Scientific American*, p. 154. The income gap has, however, widened somewhat since that 1:4 ratio was reported in 1978.

68. Victor Li, *Law Without Lawyers*.

69. See, for example, Amnesty International, *Political Imprisonment in the People's Republic of China*.

70. Shen Baoxiang et al., "Human Rights in the World Arena," in Zhou Guo 3, pp. 48–63.

71. On the discriminatory laws under apartheid, see Lawrence Litvak, Robert DeGrasse, and Kathleen McTigue, *South Africa: Foreign Investment and Apartheid*, pp. 19–24.

72. The origins of apartheid are treated in Phyllis MacRae, "Race and Class in Southern Africa," *The African Review*, pp. 237–258; and Stanley B. Greenberg, *Race and State in Capitalist Development: Comparative Perspectives*, pp. 34–37.

73. Greenberg, pp. 6–12, 393–394.

74. Quoted in L. E. Neame, *The History of Apartheid: The Story of the Colour War*, p. 73.

75. Resistance efforts are briefly reviewed in Mike Calabrese and Mike Kendall, "The Black Agenda for South Africa," *The Nation*, pp. 393, 406–409.

76. On white reformism, see Greenberg, pp. 26–27 ff.; and Litvak, DeGrasse, and McTigue, pp. 34–36.

77. See, for example, Gavin W. H. Relly, "South Africa: A Time for Patriotism," *Washington Post Weekly Edition*, October 7, 1985, p. 29. Relly chairs the Anglo-American Corporation of South Africa.

78. See Ann Seidman and Neva Seidman, *South Africa and U.S. Multinational Corporations*, p. 6; and Desaix Myers, *Labor Practices of U.S. Corporations in South Africa*.

79. Litvak, DeGrasse, and McTigue, pp. 43–61.

80. U.S. policy is reviewed by Kevin Danaher, *In Whose Interest? A Guide to U.S.–South Africa Relations*, pp. 80–83.

81. During the Nixon and Ford administrations, for example, human rights in South Africa—the "racial issue," as it was termed—were only considered important "because other countries have made it so" and because apartheid could lead to violence "and greater involvement of the communist powers." See Mohamed A. El-Khawas and Barry Cohen, eds., *The Kissinger Study of Southern Africa: National Security Study Memorandum 39*, p. 89. The quotations are from the once secret memorandum.

82. The historical background of U.S. involvement is in Walter LaFeber, *Inevitable Revolutions: The United States in Central America*, pp. 64–69, 160–164.

83. Social and economic conditions under Somoza are described in Richard Harris and Carlos M. Vilas, eds., *Nicaragua: A Revolution Under Siege*, pp. 299–302.

84. The class system is documented in Peter Rosset and John Vandermeer, eds., *The Nicaragua Reader: Documents of a Revolution Under Fire*, pp. 122–127; DeWalt, in Coleman and Herring, pp. 50–51; and Carlos M. Vilas, *The Sandinista Revolution: National Liberation and Social Transformation in Central America*, pp. 56–81, 101–116, on rural and urban conditions. Nicaragua's underdevelopment did *not*, however, include significant foreign investment (Vilas, pp. 81–83).

85. See Rosset and Vandermeer, pp. 341–346. On the social and economic character and nature of the Sandinistan program, see Harris and Vilas.

86. Joseph Collins et al., *What Difference Could a Revolution Make? Food and Family in the New Nicaragua*. See pp. 4–5 for a brief recounting of Nicaragua's post-1979 accomplishments in food policy.

87. Collins et al., pp. 111–113.

88. See Mike Conroy, "U.S. Observers Report: Legitimate Elections Despite U.S. Interference," *Nicaraguan Perspectives*, pp. 27–29.

89. Sister Maria was interviewed by the author in April 1985 at the University of California, Riverside.

90. Teodore A. Agoncillo, *A Short History of the Philippines*, p. 219.

91. Robert A. Manning, "The Philippines in Crisis," *Foreign Affairs*, p. 397.

92. Charles W. Lindsey, "The Philippine Economy," *Monthly Review*, p. 35.

93. Lindsey, p. 36. After Marcos's overthrow, investigations by members of the U.S. Congress and Aquino's own commission uncovered between $5 billion and $10 billion in overseas real estate and bank holdings.

94. On the nuclear deal, see Walden Bello, Peter Hayes, and Lyuba Zarsky, " '500-Mile Island': The Philippine Nuclear Reactor Deal," *Pacific Research*, p. 2. The Westinghouse reactor, built on the side of an active volcano, cost the Philippines over $2 billion, not to mention a $10 million commission

paid to Marcos's crony to solidify the deal and over $300,000 a day in interest on the loan for it. See *Los Angeles Times*, April 10, 1986, p. 14; and June 12, 1986, pp. 12–13.

95. Permanent Peoples' Tribunal Session on the Philippines, *The Philippines: Repression and Resistance*, p. 266.

96. Torture and other abuses are documented by Amnesty International, *Human Rights in the Philippines: Hearing before the Subcommittee on International Organizations of the Committee on International Relations, House of Representatives*, pp. 4, 17; and Lawyers' Committee for Human Rights, *"Salvaging" Democracy: Human Rights in the Philippines*.

97. *Los Angeles Times*, April 20, 1986, pp. 8–9.

98. Sidney G. Sillinian, "The Philippines in 1983: Authoritarianism Beleaguered," *Asian Survey*, p. 150.

99. *The Nation*, August 31, 1985, p. 136.

100. Jack Donnelly, "Human Rights and Development: Complementary or Competing Concerns?" *World Politics*, pp. 264–265.

101. Gavan McCormack, "The South Korean Economy: GNP Versus the People," in McCormack and Mark Selden, eds., *Korea North and South: The Deepening Crisis*, pp. 103–104. See also Parvez Hasan and D. C. Rao, *Korea: Policy Issues for Long-Term Development*.

102. World Bank, table 22, p. 261.

103. Kim Dae Jung, *Mass-Participatory Economy*, pp. 36–37.

104. Michael A. Launis, "The State and Industrial Labor in South Korea," *Bulletin of Concerned Asian Scholars*, p. 9.

105. Launis, p. 4.

106. World Bank, table 16, p. 249, for 1982; Launis, p. 4, for 1984.

107. Launis, p. 4.

108. Kim Dae Jung, pp. 38–39.

109. For example, Donnelly, pp. 280–281.

CHAPTER FIVE

1. *USA Today*, August 19, 1985, p. 2.

2. Quoted by Inga Thorsson, "Study on Disarmament and Development," *Bulletin of the Atomic Scientists*, p. 41.

3. Sivard, *World Priorities*, p. 6.

4. Sivard, *World Priorities*, pp. 7, 9. Sivard estimates total U.S. and Soviet forces stationed abroad (not including naval personnel) at 461,130 and 700,880 respectively.

5. Quoted in Milton Leitenberg, "The Numbers Game or 'Who's on First?'" *Bulletin of the Atomic Scientists*, p. 27.

6. Quoted in P. Edward Haley, David M. Keithly, and Jack Merritt, eds., *Nuclear Strategy, Arms Control, and the Future*, p. 166.

7. Two recent studies offer excellent case histories of how political priorities, values, and assumptions have determined the development of nuclear technology: Greg Herken's *The Winning Weapon: The Atomic Bomb in the Cold War, 1945–1950*; and Jonathan Stein's *From H-Bomb to Star Wars: The Politics of Strategic Decision Making*.

8. Jonathan Schell, *The Fate of the Earth*, pp. 189–193.

9. Eric Chivian et al., eds., *Last Aid: The Medical Dimensions of Nuclear War*, p. 304.

10. See Sagan, pp. 252–292; Paul R. Ehrlich, "North America After the War," *Natural History*, pp. 4–8; and *Los Angeles Times*, September 13, 1985, p. 5.

11. Quoted in Haley, Keithly, and Merritt, pp. 79–80.

12. Quoted in Haley, Keithly, and Merritt, p. 234.

13. *Los Angeles Times*, August 25, 1983, p. 4.

14. Tactical nuclear weapons are estimated in Nigel Calder, *Nuclear Nightmares: An Investigation into Possible Wars*, pp. 26–27, and *Los Angeles Times*, June 14, 1985, p. 8, summarizing findings in William M. Arkin and Richard W. Fieldhouse, *Nuclear Battlefields*.

15. Sivard, *World Priorities*, p. 15, lists British and French nuclear arsenals.

16. See "U.S.–Soviet Military Facts," *The Defense Monitor* 13, no. 6 (1984) p. 1; and R. Jeffrey Smith, "Soviets Drop Farther Back in Weapons Technology," *Science*, pp. 1300–1301. This U.S. research lead extends to areas critical to space-based systems. See "Star Wars: Vision and Reality," *The Defense Monitor*, no. 2 (1986), p. 7.

17. Roy A. and Zhores A. Medvedev ("Nuclear Samizdat," *The Nation*, pp. 38–50) give a Russian perspective that is particularly interesting, since it comes from two dissidents. Former U.S. Secretary of Defense Robert S. McNamara, in an interview with the *Los Angeles Times* (April 8, 1982, p. 13), confirmed the wide U.S. missile advantage of the early 1960s. He said that "by 1962 [the Russians] had under way a plan to substantially build up their nuclear forces. One possible explanation of their action . . . is that . . . they thought we were trying to achieve a first-strike capability." The U.S. Air Force in fact sought to persuade President Kennedy to acquire such a capability.

18. Sivard, *World Priorities*, p. 14.

19. *Los Angeles Times*, January 14, 1985, p. 10.

20. Glenn H. Snyder, *Deterrence and Defense: Toward A Theory of National Security*, p. 6.

21. For evidence of past Soviet belief in nuclear victory, see the selections in Haley, Keithly, and Merritt, pp. 138–157. On the U.S. side, see the quotations in Robert Scheer, *With Enough Shovels: Reagan, Bush and Nuclear War*, e.g., pp. 253, 261–262; *Los Angeles Times*, August 15, 1982, p. 1 (on the Pentagon's secret nuclear-war plans); and "Preparing for Nuclear War: President Reagan's Program," *The Defense Monitor* 10, no. 8 (1982), p. 2.

22. Brezhnev's 1981 statement is in Haley, Keithly, and Merritt, p. 168.

23. Desmond Ball, "Can Nuclear War Be Controlled?" in Haley, Keithly, and Merritt, pp. 107–113.

24. Bundy et al., p. 757.

25. *Los Angeles Times*, April 8, 1982, p. 13.

26. Daniel Ford, *The Button: The Pentagon's Strategic Command and Control System*, p. 17.

27. Dean Babst, Robert Aldridge and David Krieger, *Accidental Nuclear War Dangers of the "Star Wars" Proposal*, p. 3.

28. Robert C. Aldridge, "Fear Over U.S. 'War' Computers," *San Francisco Chronicle*, June 14, 1980, p. 34.

29. David Pearson, "K.A.L. 007: What the U.S. Knew and When We Knew It," *The Nation*. Pearson's article on the August 1983 event presents a plausible case for the thesis that the airliner "made a deliberate, carefully planned intrusion into Soviet territory with the knowledge of U.S. military and intelligence agencies," in order to test Soviet radar and air defense responsiveness. But Soviet reactions proved extremely slow, even incompetent, and they evidently mistook the flight for something more dangerous. Moreover, the United States may have electronically jammed their radar. Another careful study by Seymour M. Hersh (" 'The Target Is Destroyed': What Really Happened to Flight 007," *The Atlantic*) rejects Pearson's conspiracy thesis but adds to the evidence that the shooting down was a case of mistaken identity that U.S. leaders knew about but chose to exploit for propaganda advantages. All this suggests how unforeseen accidents can occur, and the next one may involve substantially more than the 269 lives that were lost over the Sea of Japan when flight 007 went down.

30. Aldridge, p. 34.

31. The Pentagon's list of "Broken Arrows" was first published by Stephen Talbot, "The H-Bombs Next Door," *The Nation*, p. 145.

32. *Time*, July 29, 1985, pp. 52–53.

33. Lovins et al., p. 1146 (their emphasis).

34. Walter C. Patterson, *The Plutonium Business and the Spread of the Bomb*, pp. 156–157.

35. Kim, *Just World Order*, p. 123.

36. These were krytrons, which are used in making nuclear triggers. See Charles William Maynes, "When Israel Jumped the Nuclear Firebreak," *Los Angeles Times*, June 9, 1985, 4/p. 2, and Harold Freeman, "Pakistan: Joining the Nuke Club," *Los Angeles Times*, December 1, 1985, 4/p. 2. Another case involving illegal nuclear technology exports to Pakistan broke in July 1987 and caused a rift in U.S.–Pakistani relations.

37. Kim, *Just World Order*, pp. 126–127; and Gurtov and Maghroori, pp. 42–44. The Reagan administration's support of nuclear sales was concisely summarized by a senior State Department official: "To achieve our nonproliferation goals, we must also maintain a position as a leading and reliable nuclear exporter" (U.S. Department of State, Bureau of Public Affairs, *Current Policy*, no. 434, November 17, 1982, p. 2). Such support, as evidenced in the Philippines case, has included substantial loans to Third World countries to finance nuclear-plant construction—for instance, $5.8 billion from the U.S. Export-Import Bank as of 1982 (*Los Angeles Times*, April 5, 1982, 4/p. 1).

38. William Walker and Man Lönnroth, "Proliferation and Nuclear Trade: A Look Ahead," *Bulletin of the Atomic Scientists*, pp. 29–33.

39. Fred Charles Iklé, "Nuclear Strategy: Can There Be a Happy Ending?" *Foreign Affairs*, p. 824.

40. Among the numerous sources consulted for this evaluation of Star Wars, see William E. Burrows, "Ballistic Missile Defense: The Illusion of Security," *Foreign Affairs*; "Star Wars: Vision and Reality," *The Defense Monitor*, pp. 1-8; Gary L. Guertner, "What Is Proof?" *Foreign Policy*, pp. 73–84; Babst, Aldridge and Krieger, p. 3; *New York Times*, March 7, 1985, p. 1; and *Los Angeles Times*, September 22, 1985, p. 1. Illustrative of the pro-Star Wars position is Keith B. Payne and Colin S. Gray, "Nuclear Policy and the Defensive Transition," *Foreign Affairs*.

41. The best source is Gordon Adams, *The Iron Triangle: The Politics of Defense Contracting*. See also Gurtov and Maghroori, pp. 35–36.

42. The point of Soviet and U.S. similarities is made in a special supplement to the *Los Angeles Times*, "Servants or Masters? Revisiting the Military-Industrial Complex," July 10, 1983, p. 4.

43. Sivard, *World Priorities*, p. 7.

44. Sivard, *World Priorities*, p. 9.

45. The combined U.S.–USSR share of arms exports has dropped from about 74 percent in 1963 to 67.5 percent in 1979 and to 54.6 percent on average between 1980 and 1984 (U.S. Arms Control and Disarmament Agency, *World Military Expenditures and Arms Transfers 1985*, p. 20).

46. See *Los Angeles Times*, April 10, 1985, p. 1, which further reports that research and development in the United States for classified military programs accounts for about 20 percent of total Defense Department spending.

47. Thomas R. Cusack and Michael Don Ward, "Military Spending in the United States, the Soviet Union, and the People's Republic of China," *Journal of Conflict Resolution*, pp. 435–438.

48. *World Military Expenditures*, p. 15.

49. The costs of major strategic weapons are given in "More Bang, More Bucks: $450 Billion for Nuclear War," *The Defense Monitor* 12, no. 7 (1983), p. 9.

50. William Hartung and Rosy Nimroody, "Cutting Up the Star Wars Pie," *The Nation*, p. 201. See also *Washington Post*, October 20 and 21, 1985, p. 1.

51. *Los Angeles Times*, January 21, 1982, p. 2.

52. Sources on U.S. "atomic diplomacy" include Herken, pp. 259–262; Daniel Ellsberg, "Introduction: Call to Mutiny," in E. P. Thompson and Dan Smith, eds., *Protest and Survive*, pp. v–vii; Gurtov and Maghroori, p. 39; *Time*, July 29, 1985, pp. 52–53; and Hersh, *The Price of Power*, p. 124.

53. President Truman, for example, twice privately considered using the bomb against the USSR and China in 1952, during the Korean conflict (*Riverside Press-Enterprise*, August 30, 1980, p. 1). Nixon and Kissinger in 1969 ordered studies on using tactical nuclear weapons in Vietnam, according to Hersh, *The Price of Power*, pp. 120–129. For other instances, see Ellsberg, in Thompson and Smith, pp. v–vii; and Walter Pincus, "U.S. Repeatedly Considered Use of N-Bombs," *The Oregonian* (Portland), July 29, 1985, p. 2.

54. Zbigniew Brzezinski, "How the Cold War Was Played," *Foreign Affairs*, p. 204. Brzezinski was President Carter's special assistant for national security affairs.

55. See Pincus, p. 2, on service competition.

56. The memorandum is quoted in Pincus, p. 2.

57. See Robert C. Johansen, *The National Interest and the Human Interest*, pp. 38–56; and "SALT II: One Small Step for Mankind," *The Defense Monitor* 8, no. 5 (July 1979), pp. 7–8.

58. McNamara, "The Military Role of Nuclear Weapons: Perceptions and Misperceptions," *Foreign Affairs*, p. 79 (emphasis in original).

59. Quoted in Kegley and Wittkopf, p. 344.

60. Frances Fukuyama, "Gorbachev and the Third World," *Foreign Affairs*, p. 718.

61. This overview is based on John P. Hardt and Donna Gold, "Andropov's Economic Future," *Orbis*.

62. World Bank, table 9, p. 235.

63. Brown, *Building a Sustainable Society*, pp. 94, 106–107; and Brown et al., *State of the World 1985*, p. 31.

64. Brown, *Building a Sustainable Society*, p. 97.

65. See Brown et al., *State of the World 1985*, pp. 51, 55 (on water); p. 106 (on air pollution); pp. 151-154 (on industrial inefficiency).

66. Daniel Singer, *The Road to Gdansk: Poland and the USSR*, pp. 78–80, 115–117.

67. Ralph S. Clem, "Ethnicity and Its Implications," *Bulletin of the Atomic Scientists*, p. 54.

68. On Soviet women, see Singer, pp. 109–110.

69. The problem of alcoholism is discussed in *Los Angeles Times*, June 2, 1985, p. 25.

70. Frank, p. 182.

71. Frank, p. 318.

72. Frank, pp. 6, 185–186, 188.

73. Timothy J. Colton, *The Dilemma of Reform in the Soviet Union*, p. 92.

74. Colton, p. 94.

75. Frank, p. 194.

76. Frank, p. 217.

77. Frank, pp. 194–204, 209–210.

78. The main features of Gorbachev's program are drawn from press reports; from Professor Stephen F. Cohen's "Sovieticus" columns in *The Nation* (in particular the issue of May 31, 1986, p. 750); and from Robert C. Tucker, "Where Is the Soviet Union Headed?" *World Policy Journal*.

79. *Los Angeles Times*, August 3, 1984, p. 5; and May 23, 1985, p. 1.

80. *Los Angeles Times*, October 4, 1984, 4/p. 2.

81. Illiteracy has most recently been explored by Jonathan Kozol, *Illiterate America*. Kozol proposes that 25 million Americans cannot read (a more commonly used figure is about 10 million) and another 35 million can read only at a level below the ninth grade.

82. *Riverside Press-Enterprise*, December 19, 1983, p. A-3.

83. On toxic waste, see, e.g., *Los Angeles Times*, April 28, 1983, 2/p. 1. It is commonly estimated that $40 billion is required to clean up U.S. toxic waste dumps.

84. See *Los Angeles Times*, February 27, 1985, p. 10, concerning a report by a twenty-seven-member Physician Task Force on Hunger.

85. The report was followed by another in May 1986—by the Carnegie Forum on Education and the Economy—that called for an equally dramatic national effort to attract and retain the best teachers.

86. On the crime rate, see *Los Angeles Times*, April 28, 1985, 4/p. 3.

87. Nikki Meredith, "The Murder Epidemic," *Science '84*, excerpted in *Utne Reader*, no. 8 (February-March 1985), p. 80.

88. *In These Times*, February 24-March 9, 1982, p. 5.

89. *U.S. News & World Report*, March 21, 1983, p. 75.

90. "In at least one of the first three years of the Reagan Administration, more than half of the 250 largest and most profitable corporations paid no Federal income tax. Over that period, the profits of just 128 of those corporations totaled $57.1 billion" (Christopher Hitchens, "Minority Report," *The Nation*).

91. Bob Rebitzer, "Repeal of Unitary Tax: Giveaway to Big Business?" *The Economic Democrat.*

92. Farm figures are from Deborah Lanner, "A Farm Bill for Farmers," *The Nation.*

93. *International Herald Tribune,* March 22, 1983. The folding of some large banks, such as Continental Illinois, was in part attributable to poor lending practices in the Third World.

94. Quoted in Delamaide, p. 157.

95. Charles R. Morris, "The Soaring Dollar: Up, Up . . . and No One Really Knows Why," *Los Angeles Times,* February 24, 1985, 5/p. 1.

96. Sidney Lens, "Will It Be the Crash Next Time?" *The Nation.*

97. Lester C. Thurow, "America's Economy 'Ain't Broke,' but Creeping Rust is Taking Its Toll," *Los Angeles Times,* March 17, 1985, 5/p. 3.

98. Paul Murphy, "The Military Tax Bite 1986."

99. Brown et al., *State of the World 1986,* p. 200. Between 1980 and 1985, U.S. military expenditures grew by about $110 billion (in current dollars), whereas health payments increased about $11 billion and agricultural subsidies about $15 billion.

100. "The Pentagon Spending Juggernaut: Will Congress Put On the Brakes?" *The Defense Monitor* 14, no. 4 (1985), p. 3.

101. Seymour Melman, "Profits Without Production: Deterioration in the Industrial System," in Suzanne Gordon and Dave McFadden, eds., *Economic Conversion: Revitalizing America's Economy,* pp. 19–32.

102. "Military Research and the Economy: Burden or Benefit," *The Defense Monitor* 14, no. 1 (1985), p. 2.

103. Quoted in *The Defense Monitor* 14, no. 1 (1985), p. 6.

104. *Los Angeles Times,* supplement, July 10, 1983, p. 3.

105. Quoted in *Los Angeles Times,* supplement, July 10, 1983, p. 12.

106. "Military Research and the Economy," *The Defense Monitor* 14, no. 1 (1985), pp. 2–3; Robert W. DeGrasse, Jr., "The Military Economy," in Gordon and McFadden, pp. 7–8; Marion Anderson, "The Empty Pork Barrel: Unemployment and the Pentagon Budget"; *Los Angeles Times,* supplement, July 10, 1983, p. 13 (citing a 1983 study by the Council on Economic Priorities).

107. "Military Research and the Economy," *The Defense Monitor* 14, no. 1 (1985), pp. 5–7; DeGrasse, in Gordon and McFadden, p. 12.

108. *Los Angeles Times,* August 27, 1982, p. 12.

CHAPTER SIX

1. Figures from Sivard, *World Priorities,* p. 9 and table II, pp. 33 ff.; and from *World Military Expenditures,* p. 10.

2. Sivard, *World Priorities,* p. 7.

3. Sivard, *World Priorities,* p. 7.

4. Block, pp. 134–163.

5. World Bank, tables 2.2, 2.4, pp. 16, 17.

6. Frank, pp. 28, 32.

7. Kegley and Wittkopf, p. 172.

8. The figure, from a statement by the Canadian secretary of state for external affairs, is cited in Gerald O. Barney et al., *Global 2000: Implications for Canada*, p. 58.

9. See Frank, pp. 34–35, and David P. Calleo, "Inflation and American Power," *Foreign Affairs*.

10. See World Bank, table 2.5, p. 18, for comparisons of nontariff barriers to imports from developed and developing countries.

11. Stopford and Dunning, tables 1.2, 1.4, pp. 5, 7.

12. DeGrasse, in Gordon and McFadden, p. 14.

13. Melman, in Gordon and McFadden, ch. 2; Shepherd, in Guisinger, ch. 4.

14. World Bank, table 2.5, p. 17.

15. Sivard, *World Priorities*, pp. 36–39.

16. Wallace J. Thies, "The Atlantic Alliance, Nuclear Weapons and European Attitudes: Reexamining the Conventional Wisdom," p. 50.

17. McNamara, pp. 68–69.

18. George M. Seignious II and Jonathan Paul Yates, "Europe's Nuclear Superpowers," *Foreign Policy*.

19. Quoted in McNamara, p. 59.

20. McNamara, pp. 70–71. The most recent estimate is by Prof. Henry Kendall of the physics department at the Massachusetts Institute of Technology. He calculates that a nuclear war in Europe in which 1,000 one-megaton weapons were exploded would cause over 200 million fatalities directly and would contaminate several million square miles—*not* counting the Soviet Union. See "Nuclear War in Europe," *The Defense Monitor* 10, no. 7 (1981), p. 6.

21. *Los Angeles Times*, August 30, 1981, p. 2.

22. Thies, pp. 3–16.

23. Robert English, "Eastern Europe's Doves," *Foreign Policy*, p. 44.

24. Dave Elliott and Hilary Wainwright, "The Lucas Plan: The Roots of the Movement," in Gordon and McFadden, pp. 89–107.

25. Suzanne Gordon, "Economic Conversion Activity in Western Europe," pp. 108–129.

26. Gordon, in Gordon and McFadden, p. 116.

27. See Kiyoshi Kojima, *Japan and the New World Economic Order*, pp. 120–124.

28. Robert S. Ozaki, "Introduction: The Political Economy of Japan's Foreign Relations," in Robert S. Ozaki and Walter Arnold, eds., *Japan's Foreign Relations: A Global Search for Economic Security*, pp. 2–5; Kenneth B. Pyle, "In Pursuit of a Grand Design: Nakasone Betwixt the Past and the Future," in Pyle, ed., *The Trade Crisis: How Will Japan Respond?* pp. 7–9.

29. See Robert O. Keohane, *After Hegemony: Cooperation and Discord in the World Political Economy*, table 9.4, p. 202; and Ronald A. Morse, "Introduction: Japan's Energy Policies and Options," in Ronald A. Morse, ed., *The Politics of Japan's Energy Strategy: Resources—Diplomacy—Security*, p. 3.

30. Robert S. Ozaki, *The Control of Imports and Foreign Capital in Japan*, chs. 4–5.

31. Stopford and Dunning, tables 1.7 and 1.10, pp. 12, 15.

32. Terutomo Ozawa, *Multinationalism, Japanese Style: The Political Economy of Outward Dependency*, ch. 7.

33. The debate is covered by Kei Wakaizumi, "Japan's Dilemma: To Act or Not to Act," *Foreign Policy*. See also Pyle, in Pyle, ed., pp. 13–32.

34. Charles K. Ebinger, "U.S.–Japanese Nuclear Energy Relations: Prospects for Cooperation/Conflict"; and Daniel K. Chapman, "USSR–Japan Energy Cooperation in Siberia: Implications for U.S.–Japanese Relations," both in Charles K. Ebinger and Ronald A. Morse, eds., *U.S.–Japanese Energy Relations: Cooperation and Competition*, pp. 147–162 and 229–239.

35. Teruyasu Murakami, "The Remarkable Adaptation of Japan's Economy," in Yergin and Hillenbrand, pp. 142–143.

36. Richard J. Samuels, "The Politics of Alternative Energy Research and Development in Japan," in Morse, pp. 134–162.

37. Joji Watanuki, "Japanese Society and the Limits of Growth," in Yergin and Hillenbrand, pp. 173, 178–182.

38. Barney et al., *Global 2000: Implications for Canada*, p. 50.

39. *Los Angeles Times*, October 29, 1985, p. 18.

40. Jacob Kaplan, "U.S. Resource Policy: Canadian Connections," in Carl E. Beigie and Alfred O. Hero, Jr., eds., *Natural Resources in U.S.–Canada Relations*, vol. 1: *The Evolution of Policies and Issues*, p. 104.

41. The dependence argument is made, for instance, by Jim Laxer, "Introduction to the Political Economy of Canada," in Robert Laxer, ed., *(Canada) Ltd.: The Political Economy of Dependency*, pp. 28–29. Jim Laxer argues that Canadian capitalism has been shaped by foreign rather than native industrialists, creating a class of people who need dependence to maintain their social and economic position.

42. Quoted in Kari Levitt, *Silent Surrender: The Multinational Corporation in Canada*, pp. 1–2.

43. Stopford and Dunning, table 1.10, p. 15.

44. Daniel Drache and Arthur Kroker, "Labyrinth of Dependency," *Canadian Journal of Political and Social Theory*, p. 16.

45. Drache and Kroker, p. 16.

46. Levitt, p. 140. See also p. 118 ff. for discussion of the limitations on Canadian sovereignty.

47. Levitt, p. 3.

48. See Barney, *Global 2000: Implications for Canada*, p. 44.

49. For further discussion of possible future issues, see Paul Daniel and Richard Shaffner, "Lessons from Bilateral Trade in Energy Resources," in Beigie and Hero, pp. 322–332.

50. John E. Carroll, *Environmental Diplomacy: An Examination and a Prospective of Canadian–U.S. Transboundary Environmental Relations*, table 2, pp. 22–23.

51. The discussion of acid rain relies on Carroll, ch. 11. Documentation is in Jurgen Schmandt and Hilliard Roderick, eds., *Acid Rain and Friendly Neighbors: The Policy Dispute Between Canada and the United States*.

52. *Los Angeles Times*, August 18, 1984, p. 10.

53. Paul M. Sweezy, "The Suppression of the Polish Workers Movement," *Monthly Review*, p. 28.

54. *Los Angeles Times*, February 12, 1986, p. 1.

55. The report is quoted in Jerzy Milewski et al., "Poland: Four Years After," *Foreign Affairs*, p. 345.

56. Wladyslaw Majkowski, *People's Poland: Patterns of Social Inequality and Conflict*, pp. 126–129.

57. Quoted in Majkowski, p. 173.

58. The background to Solidarity is in Singer, pp. 157–238.

59. Based on a poll taken by the Polish Academy of Sciences; see Milewski, p. 342.

60. Wendy Cooper, "The Economic Consequences of Intervention," *The Nation*, p. 672.

61. This and related quotes from international bankers are in Jeff Frieden, "Why the Big Banks Love Martial Law," *The Nation*.

62. Milewski, pp. 342–343.

63. See the Poland sections of *Amnesty International Report 1980*, pp. 283–288; *1981*, pp. 308–312; and *1982*, pp. 280–285.

64. Milewski, p. 343.

65. Milewski, p. 346.

CHAPTER SEVEN

1. James Robertson, *The Sane Alternative: A Choice of Futures*, pp. 16–29, 80–81.

2. Brandt et al., p. 8.

3. Richard Rosecrance, *The Rise of the Trading State: Commerce and Conquest in the Modern World*.

4. Quoted in Marcus G. Raskin, "Progressive Liberalism for the '80s," *The Nation*, p. 591.

5. On the essentially domestic sources of Soviet and American security, see John W. Burton, *Global Conflict: The Domestic Sources of International Crisis*.

6. Lappé and Collins, pp. 328–339.

7. Bruce Stokes, *Helping Ourselves: Local Solutions to Global Problems*, p. 96.

8. "Let's Get Tiny Loans to the World's Poor," *New Options*, no. 37 (March 30, 1987), p. 1.

9. Paul Harrison, *The Greening of Africa: Breaking Through in the Battle for Land and Food*, pp. 89–91.

10. Oxfam is headquartered in London; Oxfam America, its U.S. affiliate, is in Boston. Church World Service, in New York, is part of the National Council of Churches of Christ. Grassroots International is located in Cambridge, Massachusetts. The Plenty Project, which has won international recognition for its self-help teachings in Guatemala (and the South Bronx), is sponsored by The Farm in Tennessee, the largest intentional community in the United States. See Lillie Wilson, "The Plenty Project: Inside the Hippie Peace Corps," *New Age*.

11. For example, Soviet and U.S. scientists have made important advances in plant pathology and biotechnologies that could be more widely shared. So could energy conserving skills—and in fact at least one private firm (the International Institute for Energy Conservation, based in Boston) is doing just that, under contract with the People's Republic of China.

12. Quoted in Duane Elgin, *Voluntary Simplicity: Toward a Way of Life That is Outwardly Simple, Inwardly Rich*, p. 190.

13. Land conservation programs are outlined in a study by the American Farmland Trust, "Future Policy Directions for American Agriculture," pp. 90–92. Brown et al., *State of the World 1985*, pp. 135–139, notes promising research currently being done on plants and crops to increase food yields, develop new strains, and improve hardiness. The Eugene (Oregon) *Register-Guard* of August 2, 1985, p. 2c, reports on new developments in hydroponics—growing food without soil. Plants thrive by being suspended in fertilizer solutions, and herbicides are not applied.

14. The UN claims to have already saved the lives of 1 million children (*Los Angeles Times*, December 12, 1985, pp. 1, 36).

15. Harrison, pp. 261–271.

16. The Andes program is reported in *Los Angeles Times*, February 16, 1985, p. 1.

17. Amory B. Lovins, *Soft Energy Paths: Toward a Durable Peace*.

18. Good, concise discussions of "soft path" technologies are in Lovins, pp. 38–46; John J. Berger, *Nuclear Power: Unviable Option*, rev. ed., part II; Brown et al., *State of the World 1985*, ch. 8; and Brown, *Building a Sustainable Society*, ch. 9. Emphasis on small-scale energy technologies is also beginning to appear in U.S. aid programs: see the issue of *Agenda* (A.I.D.), vol. 5, no. 1 (January-February 1982).

19. See, for example, Brown, *Building a Sustainable Society*, p. 215; and Harrison, pp. 210–215.

20. The economic, health, safety, and energy costs of the nuclear option are briefly discussed in Berger, chs. 3–7; Brown, *Building a Sustainable Society*, pp. 73–81; and Lovins, Lovins, and Ross, pp. 1149–1153. Less frequently noted are the potentially astronomical costs (not to mention safety hazards) of decommissioning nuclear plants and disposing of their waste products and equipment. One recent study by Cynthia Pollock ("Decommissioning: Nuclear Power's Missing Link") observes that over 350 nuclear plants will need to be decommissioned worldwide by 2020; the average lifetime of each is only about thirty-one years. That cost alone could be anywhere from $50 million to $3 billion per plant.

21. See the extensive discussion by Carlos F. Dìaz-Alejandro, "Delinking North and South: Unshackled or Unhinged?" in Albert Fishlow et al., *Rich and Poor Nations in the World Economy*, pp. 105–144. On Third World transnational firms, see the study by Sanjaya Lall, *The New Multinationals: The Spread of Third World Enterprises*.

22. Estimate in Brown, *Building a Sustainable Society*, table 10-1, p. 249.

23. See *Los Angeles Times*, April 30, 1986, p. 5 for a table on electricity supplied by nuclear plants around the world.

24. On nuclear power in the Third World, see Brown, *Building a Sustainable Society*, pp. 76–77. The main customers are Argentina, Brazil, Taiwan, and South Korea.

25. On coal as a transitional fuel, see Brown, *Building a Sustainable Society*, pp. 81–85.

26. Brown, *Building a Sustainable Society*, p. 82.

27. Kellogg and Schware, p. 1108.

28. William U. Chandler, in Brown et al., *State of the World 1985*, p. 149.

29. Brown et al., *State of the World 1985*, pp. 149–150.

30. *Los Angeles Times*, February 19, 1986, p. 21.

31. See "A *Practical* Alternative to Mindless Growth?" *New Options*, no. 15 (April 8, 1985), pp. 1–2.

32. *Los Angeles Times*, February 4, 1985, pp. 1, 16.

33. Kellogg and Schware, p. 1104; Maranto, p. 49.

34. See Elisabeth Mann Borgese, "The Law of the Sea," *Scientific American*, pp. 42–49.

35. The Japanese proposal is in Yoichi Kaya et al., "Management of Global Environmental Issues," *World Futures*, pp. 223–231.

36. Kirkpatrick Sale, *Dwellers in the Land: The Bioregional Vision*.

37. The antipollution conventions are briefly discussed by Armin Rosencranz, "The Problem of Transboundary Pollution," *Environment*, pp. 16–17.

38. See *Utne Reader*, no. 15 (April-May 1986), pp. 24–33.

39. Karl W. Deutsch et al., *Political Community and the North Atlantic Area: International Organization in the Light of Historical Experience*, p. 5.

40. See Robert C. Johansen, "Toward An Alternative Security System: Moving Beyond the Balance of Power in the Search for World Security," pp. 33–36.

41. Patricia Mische, "Re-Visioning National Security: Toward a Viable World Security System," in Carolyn M. Stephenson, ed., *Alternative Methods for International Security*, pp. 82–84.

42. Louis Henkin, *How Nations Behave: Law and Foreign Policy*, p. 113.

43. Roger Fisher and William L. Ury, *Getting to YES: Negotiating Agreement Without Giving In*.

44. George F. Kennan, "On Nuclear War," *New York Review of Books*, p. 10. Also see Donald Keys, "The Neglected 'Software' Aspects of Disarmament," in Ervin Laszlo and Donald Keys, eds., *Disarmament: The Human Factor*, p. 19.

45. R. Jeffrey Smith, "Scientists Fault Charges of Soviet Cheating," *Science*. For a contrary view, see the U.S. State Department's "Soviet Noncompliance with Arms Control Agreements."

46. See Jozef Goldblat, "Charges of Treaty Violations," *Bulletin of the Atomic Scientists*.

47. William L. Ury, *Beyond the Hotline: How We Can Prevent the Crisis that Might Bring on a Nuclear War*.

48. Council on Foreign Relations, *Blocking the Spread of Nuclear Weapons: American and European Perspectives*, p. 10.

49. McGeorge Bundy, George F. Kennan, Robert S. McNamara, and Gerard Smith, "Nuclear Weapons and the Atlantic Alliance," *Foreign Affairs*, pp. 766–777.

50. Patterson, p. 197.

51. The perseverance of a few individuals has kept the idea of a "Peacesat" system alive. One of them is Howard G. Kurtz, co-founder of War Control Planners in Washington, D.C. He publishes a newsletter, *Checkpoint*, for those who wish to keep up-to-date on international satellites.

52. See Alexander L. George, "Crisis Prevention Reexamined," in Alexander L. George, ed., *Managing U.S.–Soviet Rivalry: Problems of Crisis Prevention*, pp. 379–382.

53. Johansen, "Toward An Alternative Security System," p. 45.

54. Discussions with John Marks, executive director of Search for Common Ground, Washington, D.C., April 1986.

55. The conversion (or more usually, diversification) of military industrial plants has a disputed record in the United States. A Pentagon study based
mainly on conversion experiences in three communities perhaps predictably
found no compelling reasons for establishing a national office to promote or
facilitate shifts to nonmilitary production (U.S. Department of Defense, Office
of the Assistant Secretary of Defense, Office of Economic Adjustment, and
President's Economic Adjustment Committee, *Economic Adjustment/Conver-
sion*). Patricia Mische (in Stephenson, p. 81), on the other hand, cites another
Defense Department study of successful conversions in sixty-one U.S. communities. Both the problems and the opportunities presented by military conversion are clearly outlined in a case study by Joel S. Yudken, "Conversion in
the Aerospace Industry: The McDonnell-Douglas Project," in Gordon and
McFadden, pp. 130–143.

Western European experiences are more promising: see Elliott and Wainwright, pp. 89–107; and Gordon, pp. 108–129, both in Gordon and Mc-
Fadden. A conversion "menu" is offered by Elise Boulding, "A Post-Military
Agenda for the Scientific Community," *International Social Science Journal*,
pp. 163–199.

56. Mische, in Stephenson, pp. 75–76; Robert Muller, "A World Core
Curriculum," *Education Network News*.

57. The widening interest in peace and global studies is reflected in Bar-
bara J. Wien, ed., *Peace and World Order Studies*, 4th ed.; Robert Woito, *To
End War: A New Approach to International Conflict*; and "Teaching for
Peace," *Christian Science Monitor* supplement, January 31, 1986.

58. Figures on NFZs are courtesy of Brian Moucka and Jeanne Tenase,
Nuclear Free Zone Registry, Lake Elsinore, California. Texts of the first three
NFZ treaties are in Arms Control and Disarmament Agency, *Arms Control and
Disarmament Agreements: Texts and Histories of Negotiations*. The fourth,
the Treaty of Rarotonga, was endorsed by the twelve countries of the South
Pacific Forum on August 7, 1985. It bans nuclear testing, waste disposal, reex-
ports, and production, but leaves to each government the matter of transits by
nuclear ships. The zone extends east and south to touch the Latin American
NFZ and Antarctica. It includes the French Polynesian territories where nuclear testing is continuing, which explains France's opposition to the treaty.

59. The many ways in which to "think globally, act locally" can be
understood, theoretically and practically, by consulting Elgin; Stokes; Harry C.
Boyte, *The Backyard Revolution: Understanding the New Citizen Movement*;
Margo Adair, *Working Inside Out: Tools for Change*; Joan Bodner, ed., with the
American Friends Service Committee, *Taking Charge of Our Lives: Living Responsibly in a Troubled World*; and Corinne McLaughlin and Gordon Davidson, *Builders of the Dawn: Community Lifestyles in a Changing World*.

60. On nonviolent defense, see Gene Sharp, "Making the Abolition of
War A Realistic Goal," in Severyn T. Bruyn and Paula M. Rayman, eds., *Nonviolent Action and Social Change*.

61. *Los Angeles Times*, February 16, 1986, p. 19.

62. Global Education Associates of East Orange, New Jersey, is one organization that seeks to forge a transnational network. Patricia Mische, cited
above, is its co-founder. Most of the other organizations listed can be found in
Woito, pp. 539–604.

63. On the Greens, consult Capra and Spretnak.

64. Sivard, *Women: A World Survey*, pp. 29–34; Brandt et al., pp. 59–62.

65. Shuman, pp. 29–35.

66. Jan F. Triska and Robert M. Slusser, *The Theory, Law, and Policy of Soviet Treaties*, pp. 394–395.

67. See Blond, pp. 86–90 for suggestions of a code of TNC conduct.

68. Hedley Bull, "The State's Positive Role in World Affairs," *Daedalus*.

69. Richard A. Falk, introduction to Falk, Kim, and Mendlovitz, p. 14.

70. A useful general discussion of a values shift is in Brown, *Building a Sustainable Society*, pp. 349–361. That a shift is taking place in the United States is established in different ways by several writers. See, e.g., Daniel Yankelovich, *New Rules: Searching for Self-Fulfillment in a World Turned Upside Down*, public opinion poll results; Arnold Mitchell, "Changing Values and Lifestyles"; Alvin Toffler, *The Third Wave*; and Marilyn Ferguson, *The Aquarian Conspiracy: Personal and Social Transformation in the 1980s*.

The *necessity* of a values shift is cogently argued in an expanding number of books, notably: Brown, *Building a Sustainable Society*, pp. 349–361; Mark Satin, *New Age Politics: Healing Self and Society*; Theodore Roszak, *Person/Planet: The Creative Disintegration of Industrial Society*; and Robert N. Bellah et al., *Habits of the Heart*. Finally, nothing illuminates better than personal experiences of changed values and attitudes. Norie Huddle's *Surviving: The Best Game on Earth* contains a number of interviews with both well-known and not so well-known people (including a few from outside the United States) on the critical question of redefining national security.

71. Roger Walsh, *Staying Alive: The Psychology of Human Survival*, ch. 11.

72. *Los Angeles Times*, September 26, 1984, 5/p. 1.

73. U Thant, *View from the UN*, p. 454.

Bibliography

BOOKS

Adair, Margo. *Working Inside Out: Tools for Change.* East Haven, Conn.: Inland, 1984.

Adams, Gordon. *The Iron Triangle: The Politics of Defense Contracting.* New York: Council on Economic Priorities, 1981.

Agoncillo, Teodoro A. *A Short History of the Philippines.* New York: New American Library, 1969.

Americas Watch Committee and American Civil Liberties Union. *Report on Human Rights in El Salvador.* New York: Vintage, 1982.

Amnesty International. *Political Imprisonment in the People's Republic of China.* London: AI, 1978.

Argueta, Manlio. *One Day of Life.* New York: Vintage, 1983.

Arnove, Robert F. *Philanthropy and Cultural Imperialism: The Foundations at Home and Abroad.* Bloomington: Indiana University Press, 1982.

Barnet, Richard J. *Intervention and Revolution: The United States in the Third World.* Cleveland: World, 1968.

———. *Roots of War.* New York: Atheneum, 1972.

———. *The Lean Years: Politics In The Age of Scarcity.* New York: Touchstone/Simon and Schuster, 1980.

———, and Ronald E. Müller. *Global Reach: The Power of the Multinational Corporations.* New York: Simon and Schuster, 1974.

Barnett, A. Doak. *China On The Eve of Communist Takeover.* New York: Praeger, 1963.

Barney, Gerald O. et al. *Global 2000: Implications for Canada.* Toronto: Pergamon, n.d.

———, ed. *The Global 2000 Report to the President: Entering the Twenty-First Century.* Vol. 1. Harmondsworth, Middlesex, England: Penguin, 1982.

Bates, Robert H. *Markets and States in Tropical Africa: The Political Basis of Agricultural Policies.* Berkeley: University of California Press, 1981.

Beigie, Carl E., and Alfred O. Hero, Jr., eds. *Natural Resources in U.S.–Canada Relations: Vol. 1: The Evolution of Policies and Issues.* Boulder, Colo.: Westview, 1980.

Bellah, Robert N. et al. *Habits of the Heart: Individualism and Commitment in American Life.* New York: Harper and Row, 1985.

Berger, John J. *Nuclear Power: The Unviable Option.* Rev. ed. Palo Alto, Calif.: Ramparts, 1977.

Bianco, Lucien. *Origins of the Chinese Revolution, 1915–1949.* Trans. Muriel Bell. Stanford, Calif.: Stanford University Press, 1971.

Blake, David H., and Robert S. Walters. *The Politics of Global Economic Relations.* Englewood Cliffs, N.J.: Prentice-Hall, 1976.

Block, Fred L. *The Origins of International Economic Disorder: A Study of United States International Monetary Policy from World War II to the Present.* Berkeley: University of California Press, 1977.

Bodner, Joan, ed., with the American Friends Service Committee. *Taking Charge of Our Lives: Living Responsibly in a Troubled World.* New York: Harper and Row, 1984.

Boff, Leonardo. *Church: Charism and Power; Liberation Theology and the Institutional Church.* Trans. John W. Diercksmeier. New York: Crossroad, 1985.

Bonner, Raymond. *Weakness and Deceit: U.S. Policy and El Salvador.* New York: Times Books, 1984.

Boyte, Harry C. *The Backyard Revolution: Understanding the New Citizen Movement.* Philadelphia: Temple University Press, 1980.

Brandt, Willy et al., *North-South, A Program for Survival: Report of the Independent Commission on International Development Issues.* Cambridge, Mass.: MIT Press, 1980.

Brown, Lester R. *Building a Sustainable Society.* New York: Norton, 1981.

———et al. *State of the World 1985: A Worldwatch Institute Report on Progress Toward a Sustainable Society.* New York: Norton, 1985.

———et al. *State of the World 1986: A Worldwatch Institute Report on Progress Toward a Sustainable Society.* New York: Norton, 1986.

Bruyn, Severyn T., and Paula M. Rayman, eds. *Nonviolent Action and Social Change.* New York: Irvington, 1979.

Burton, John W. *Global Conflict: The Domestic Sources of International Crisis.* Brighton, Sussex, England: Wheatsheaf, for the Center for International Development, 1984.

Cabral, Amilcar. *Revolution in Guinea: Selected Texts.* Trans. Richard Handyside. New York: Monthly Review, 1969.

Capra, Fritjof, and Charlene Spretnak. *Green Politics.* New York: Dutton, 1984.

Calder, Nigel. *Nuclear Nightmares: An Investigation into Possible Wars.* Harmondsworth, Middlesex, England: Penguin, 1981.

Carr, Edward H. *The Twenty-Years' Crisis, 1919–1939: An Introduction to the Study of International Relations.* London: Macmillan, 1939.

Carroll, John E. *Environmental Diplomacy: An Examination and a Prospective of Canadian–U.S. Transboundary Environmental Relations.* Ann Arbor, Mich.: University of Michigan, 1983.

Chivian, Eric et al., eds *Last Aid: The Medical Dimensions of Nuclear War.* San Francisco: W. H. Freeman, 1982.

Chomsky, Noam. *American Power and the New Mandarins.* New York: Pantheon, 1967.

Coates, Gary J., ed. *Resettling America: The Movement Toward Local Self-Reliance.* Andover, Mass.: Brick House, 1982.

Cole, Paul M., and William J. Taylor, Jr., eds. *The Nuclear Freeze Debate: Arms Control Issues for the 1980s.* Boulder, Colo.: Westview, 1983.

Coleman, Kenneth M., and George C. Herring, eds. *The Central American Crisis: Sources of Conflict and the Failure of U.S. Policy.* Wilmington, Del.: Scholarly Resources, 1985.

Collins, Joseph et al. *What Difference Could a Revolution Make? Food and Family in the New Nicaragua.* San Francisco: Institute for Food and Development Policy, 1982.

Colton, Timothy J. *The Dilemma of Reform in the Soviet Union*. New York: Council on Foreign Relations, 1984.

Cook, Blanche Wiesen. *The Declassified Eisenhower: A Divided Legacy of Peace and Political Warfare*. New York: Penguin, 1984.

Council on Foreign Relations. *Blocking the Spread of Nuclear Weapons: American and European Perspectives*. New York: CFR, 1986.

Crozier, Michael J., Samuel P. Huntington, and Joji Watanuki. *The Crisis of Democracy: Report on the Governability of Democracies to the Trilateral Commission*. New York: New York University Press, 1975.

Danaher, Kevin. *In Whose Interest? A Guide to U.S.–South Africa Relations*. Washington, D.C.: Institute for Policy Studies, 1984.

de Castro, Josué. *Death in the Northeast*. New York: Vintage, 1969.

Delamaide, Darrell. *Debt Shock: The Full Story of the World Credit Crisis*. Garden City, N.Y.: Doubleday, 1984.

Deutsch, Karl W., et al. *Political Community and the North Atlantic Area: International Organization in the Light of Historical Experience*. Princeton, N.J.: Princeton University Press, 1957.

Domitila Barrios de Chungara, with Moema Viezzer. *Let Me Speak! Testimony of Domitila, A Woman of the Bolivian Mines*. Trans. Victoria Ortiz. New York: Monthly Review, 1978.

Ebinger, Charles K., and Ronald A. Morse, eds. *U.S.– Japanese Energy Relations: Cooperation and Competition*. Boulder, Colo.: Westview, 1984.

Elgin, Duane. *Voluntary Simplicity: Toward a Way of Life That is Outwardly Simple, Inwardly Rich*. New York: William Morrow, 1981.

El-Khawas, Mohamed A., and Barry Cohen, eds. *The Kissinger Study of Southern Africa: National Security Study Memorandum 39*. Westport, Conn.: Lawrence Hill, 1976.

Falk, Richard A. *A Study of Future Worlds*. New York: Free Press, 1975.

———, Samuel S. Kim, and Saul H. Mendlovitz, eds. *Toward a Just World Order*. Vol. 1. Boulder, Colo.: Westview, 1980.

Fall, Bernard B., ed. *Ho Chi Minh on Revolution: Selected Writings, 1920–66*. New York: Praeger, 1967.

Fanon, Frantz. *The Wretched of the Earth*. Trans. Constance Farrington. New York: Grove, 1963.

Ferguson, Marilyn. *The Aquarian Conspiracy: Personal and Social Transformation in the 1980s*. Los Angeles: J. P. Tarcher, 1980.

Fischer, Louis, ed. *The Essential Gandhi: His Life, Work, and Ideas*. New York: Vintage, 1962.

Fisher, Roger, and William L. Ury. *Getting to YES: Negotiating Agreement Without Giving In*. New York: Penguin, 1981.

Fishlow, Albert et al. *Rich and Poor Nations in the World Economy*. New York: McGraw-Hill, for the Council on Foreign Relations, 1978.

Ford, Daniel. *The Button: The Pentagon's Strategic Command and Control System*. New York: Simon and Schuster, 1985.

Forster, E. M. *A Passage to India*. New York: Harcourt, Brace and World, 1952.

Frank, Andre Gunder. *Crisis: In the World Economy*. New York: Holmes and Meier, 1980.

Friere, Paolo. *Pedagogy of the Oppressed*. Trans. Myra Bergman Ramos. New York: Herder and Herder, 1972.

Fuentes, Annette, and Barbara Ehrenreich. *Women in the Global Factory*. Boston: South End, 1983.

Gaddis, John Lewis. *Strategies of Containment: A Critical Appraisal of Postwar American National Security Policy*. New York: Oxford University Press, 1982.

Galtung, Johan. *The True Worlds: A Transnational Perspective*. New York: Free Press, 1980.

Garvin, Charles, and Greg Rosenbaum. *World Without Plenty: A Basic Overview of World Resources*. Skokie, Ill.: National Textbook, 1975.

Gendzier, Irene L. *Managing Political Change: Social Scientists and the Third World*. Boulder, Colo.: Westview, 1984.

George, Alexander L., ed. *Managing U.S.–Soviet Rivalry: Problems of Crisis Prevention*. Boulder, Colo.: Westview, 1983.

George, Susan. *How the Other Half Dies: The Real Reasons for World Hunger*. Montclair, N.J.: Allanheld, Osmun, 1977.

Gilpin, Robert J. *U.S. Power and the Multinational Corporations*. New York: Basic Books, 1975.

Gordon, Suzanne, and Dave McFadden, eds. *Economic Conversion: Revitalizing America's Economy*. Cambridge, Mass.: Ballinger, 1984.

Greenberg, Stanley B. *Race and State in Capitalist Development: Comparative Perspectives*. New Haven, Conn.: Yale University Press, 1980.

Grossman, Karl. *Nicaragua: America's New Vietnam? Sag Harbor, N.Y.: Permanent Press, 1984.*

Guisinger, Stephen, ed. *Private Enterprise and the New Global Economic Challenge*. Indianapolis: Bobbs-Merrill, 1979.

Gurtov, Melvin, and Ray Maghroori, eds. *Roots of Failure: United States Policy in the Third World*. Westport, Conn.: Greenwood, 1984.

Haley, P. Edward, David M. Keithly, and Jack Merritt, eds. *Nuclear Strategy, Arms Control, and the Future*. Boulder, Colo.: Westview, 1985.

Halliday, Fred. *Iran: Dictatorship and Development*. Harmondsworth, Middlesex, England: Penguin, 1979.

Halliday, Jon, and Gaven McCormack. *Japanese Imperialism Today: Co-Prosperity in Greater Asia*. New York: Monthly Review, 1973.

Harris, Richard, and Carlos M. Vilas, eds. *Nicaragua: A Revolution Under Siege*. London: Zed, 1985.

Harrison, Paul. *The Greening of Africa: Breaking Through in the Battle for Land and Food*. Harmondsworth, Middlesex, England: Penguin, 1987.

Hartmann, Betsy, and James K. Boyce. *Needless Hunger: Voices from a Bangladesh Village*. San Francisco: Institute for Food and Development Policy, 1979.

Hasan, Parvez, and D. C. Rao. *Korea: Policy Issues for Long-Term Development*. Baltimore, Md.: Johns Hopkins University Press, for the World Bank, 1979.

Hayter, Teresa. *Aid As Imperialism*. Harmondsworth, Middlesex, England: Penguin, 1971.

Henderson, Hazel. *The Politics of the Solar Age: Alternatives to Economics*. New York: Doubleday Anchor, 1981.

Henkin, Louis. *How Nations Behave: Law and Foreign Policy*. New York: Columbia University Press, 1979.

Herken, Gregg. *The Winning Weapon: The Atomic Bomb in the Cold War, 1945–1950*. New York: Vintage, 1982.

Herman, Edward S., and Frank Brodhead. *Demonstration Elections: U.S.– Staged Elections in the Dominican Republic, Vietnam, and El Salvador*. Boston: South End, 1984.

Hersh, Seymour M. *The Price of Power: Kissinger in the Nixon White House*. New York: Summit, 1983.

Hinton, William. *Fanshen: A Documentary of Revolution in a Chinese Village*. New York: Vintage, 1966.

Huddle, Norie. *Surviving: The Best Game on Earth*. New York: Schocken, 1984.

Johansen, Robert C. *The National Interest and the Human Interest: An Analysis of U.S. Foreign Policy*. Princeton, N.J.: Princeton University Press, 1980.

Kegley, Charles W., Jr., and Eugene R. Wittkopf. *World Politics: Trend and Transformation*. New York: St. Martin's, 1981.

Kennan, George F. *The Nuclear Delusion: Soviet–American Relations in the Atomic Age*. New York: Pantheon, 1982.

———. *Realities of American Foreign Policy*. Princeton, N.J.: Princeton University Press, 1954.

Keohane, Robert O. *After Hegemony: Cooperation and Discord in the World Political Economy*. Princeton, N.J.: Princeton University Press, 1984.

Kidron, Michael, and Ronald Segal, eds. *The State of the World Atlas*. London: Pan, 1981.

Kim Dae Jung. *Mass-Participatory Economy: A Democratic Alternative for Korea*. Lanham, Md.: University Press of America and Center for International Affairs, Harvard University, 1985.

Kim, Samuel S. *The Quest for a Just World Order*. Boulder, Colo.: Westview, 1984.

Kissinger, Henry A. *Nuclear Weapons and Foreign Policy*. Garden City, N.Y.: Doubleday Anchor, 1968.

———. *White House Years*. Boston: Little, Brown, 1979.

Klare, Michael T., and Cynthia Arnson. *Supplying Repression: U.S. Support for Authoritarian Regimes Abroad*. Washington, D.C.: Institute for Policy Studies, 1981.

Kojima, Kiyoshi. *Japan and a New World Economic Order*. London. Croom Helm, 1977.

Kolko, Joyce, and Gabriel Kolko. *The Limits of Power: The World and United States Foreign Policy, 1945–1954*. New York: Harper and Row, 1972.

Kozol, Jonathan. *Illiterate America*. Garden City, N.Y.: Doubleday Anchor, 1985.

LaFeber, Walter. *Inevitable Revolutions: The United States in Central America*. New York: Norton, 1984.

Lagos, Gustavo, and Horacio H. Godoy. *Revolution of Being: A Latin American View of the Future*. New York: Free Press, 1977.

Lall, Sanjaya. *The New Multinationals: The Spread of Third World Enterprises*. Chichester, N.Y.: John Wiley, 1983.

Lappé, Frances Moore, and Joseph Collins. *Food First: Beyond the Myth of Scarcity*. Boston: Houghton Mifflin, 1977.

Laszlo, Ervin, and Donald Keys, eds. *Disarmament: The Human Factor*. New York: Pergamon, 1981.

Lawyer's Committee for Human Rights. *"Salvaging" Democracy: Human Rights in the Philippines*. New York: LCHR, December 1985.

Laxer, Robert, ed. *(Canada) Ltd.: The Political Economy of Dependency.* Toronto: McClelland and Stewart, 1973.

Lernoux, Penny. *Cry of the People: The Struggle for Human Rights in Latin America—The Catholic Church in Conflict with U.S. Policy.* Harmondsworth, Middlesex, England: Penguin, 1982.

Levitt, Kari. *Silent Surrender: The Multinational Corporation in Canada.* Toronto: Macmillan, 1970.

Li, Victor. *Law Without Lawyers.* Boulder, Colo.: Westview, 1978.

Littauer, Raphael, and Norman Uphoff, eds. *The Air War in Indochina.* Rev. ed. Boston: Beacon, 1971.

Litvak, Lawrence, Robert DeGrasse, and Kathleen McTigue. *South Africa: Foreign Investment and Apartheid.* Washington, D.C.: Institute for Policy Studies, 1978.

Lovins, Amory B. *Soft Energy Paths: Toward a Durable Peace.* New York: Harper and Row, 1979.

Maghroori, Ray, and Bennett Ramberg, eds. *Globalism Versus Realism: International Relations' Third Debate.* Boulder, Colo.: Westview, 1982.

Majkowski, Wladyslaw. *People's Poland: Patterns of Social Inequality and Conflict.* Westport, Conn.: Greenwood, 1985.

Malcolm X, with Alex Haley. *The Autobiography of Malcolm X.* New York: Grove, 1969.

Mao Zedong. *Mao Zedong xuan ji* [Selected Works of Mao Zedong]. 5 vols. Beijing: People's Publishing House, 1969.

————. *Selected Readings from the Works of Mao Tsetung.* Beijing: Foreign Languages Press, 1971.

McCormack, Gavan, and Mark Selden, eds. *Korea North and South: The Deepening Crisis.* New York: Monthly Review, 1978.

McKean, Margaret A. *Environmental Protest and Citizen Politics in Japan.* Berkeley: University of California Press, 1981.

McLaughlin, Corinne, and Gordon Davidson. *Builders of the Dawn: Community Lifestyles in a Changing World.* Walpole, N.H.: Stillpoint, 1985.

McLuhan, T. C., ed. *Touch the Earth: A Self-Portrait of Indian Existence.* New York: Simon and Schuster, 1971.

Mendlovitz, Saul, ed. *On the Creation of a Just World Order.* New York: Free Press, 1975.

Millis, Walter, ed. *The Forrestal Diaries.* New York: Viking, 1951.

Mische, Gerald, and Patricia Mische. *Toward a Human World Order: Beyond the National Security Straitjacket.* New York: Paulist Press, 1977.

Morgenthau, Hans J. *Politics Among Nations: The Struggle for Power and Peace.* 5th rev. ed. New York: Knopf, 1978.

Morse, Ronald A., ed. *The Politics of Japan's Energy Strategy: Resources—Diplomacy—Security.* Berkeley: University of California, Institute of East Asian Studies, 1981.

Muñoz, Heraldo, ed. *From Dependency to Development: Strategies to Overcome Underdevelopment and Inequality.* Boulder, Colo.: Westview, 1981.

Myers, Desaix. *Labor Practices of U.S. Corporations in South Africa.* New York: Praeger, 1977.

Naipaul, V. S. *India: A Wounded Civilization.* New York: Vintage, 1977.

Nair, Kusum. *In Defense of the Irrational Peasant: Indian Agriculture After the Green Revolution.* Chicago: University of Chicago Press, 1979.

Neame, L. E. *The History of Apartheid: The Story of the Colour War in South Africa*. London: Pall Mall, 1962.

Nehru, Jawaharlal. *Nehru on World History*. Ed. Saul K. Padover. New York: John Day, 1960.

Ngugi wa Thiong'o. *Petals of Blood*. New York: Dutton, 1977.

Ozaki, Robert S. *The Control of Imports and Foreign Capital in Japan*. New York: Praeger, 1972.

———, and Walter Arnold, eds. *Japan's Foreign Relations: A Global Search for Economic Security*. Boulder, Colo.: Westview, 1985.

Ozawa, Terutomo. *Multinationalism, Japanese Style: The Political Economy of Outward Dependency*. Princeton, N.J.: Princeton University Press, 1979.

Paige, Glenn D. *The Korean Decision: June 24–30, 1950*. New York: Free Press, 1968.

Panofsky, Wolfgang K. H. *Arms Control and Salt II*. Seattle: University of Washington Press, 1979.

Patterson, Walter C. *The Plutonium Business and the Spread of the Bomb*. San Francisco: Sierra Club, 1984.

Payer, Cheryl. *The Debt Trap: The IMF and the Third World*. New York: Monthly Review, 1974.

———. *The World Bank: A Critical Analysis*. New York: Monthly Review, 1982.

Permanent Peoples' Tribunal Session on the Phillipines. *The Phillipines: Repression and Resistance*. N.p.: Komite ng Sambayanang Pilipino, 1981.

Petras, James. *Critical Perspectives on Imperialism and Social Class in the Third World*. New York: Monthly Review, 1978.

———, and Morris Morley. *The United States and Chile: Imperialism and the Overthrow of the Allende Government*. New York: Monthly Review, 1975.

Pharr, Susan J. *Political Women in Japan: The Search for a Place in Political Life*. Berkeley: University of California Press, 1981.

Pyle, Kenneth B., ed. *The Trade Crisis: How Will Japan Respond?* Seattle: Society for Japanese Studies, 1987.

Robertson, James. *The Sane Alternative: A Choice of Futures*. St. Paul, Minn.: River Basin, 1979.

Rogers, Carl R. *On Personal Power*. New York: Delta, 1977.

Rosecrance, Richard. *The Rise of the Trading State: Commerce and Conquest in the Modern World*. New York: Basic, 1986.

Rosset, Peter, and John Vandermeer, eds. *The Nicaragua Reader: Documents of a Revolution Under Fire*. New York: Grove, 1983.

Roszak, Theodore. *Person/Planet: The Creative Disintegration of Industrial Society*. Garden City, N.Y.: Doubleday Anchor, 1978.

Sale, Kirkpatrick. *Dwellers in the Land: The Bioregional Vision*. San Francisco: Sierra Club, 1985.

Satin, Mark. *New Age Politics: Healing Self and Society*. New York: Delta, 1979.

Scheer, Robert. *With Enough Shovels: Reagan, Bush and Nuclear War*. New York: Vintage, 1983.

Schell, Jonathan. *The Fate of the Earth*. New York: Knopf, 1982.

Schiller, Herbert I. *Who Knows: Information in the Age of the Fortune 500*. Norwood, N.J.: Ablex, 1981.

Schmandt, Jurgen, and Hilliard Roderick, eds. *Acid Rain and Friendly Neighbors: The Policy Dispute Between Canada and the United States*. Durham, N.C.: Duke University Press, 1986.

Seidman, Ann, and Neva Seidman. *South Africa and U.S. Multinational Corporations*. Westport, Conn.: Lawrence Hill, 1977.

Servan-Schreiber, Jean-Jacques. *The World Challenge*. New York: Simon and Schuster, 1980.

Shoup, Laurence. *The Carter Presidency*. Palo Alto, Calif.: Ramparts, 1980.

Singer, Daniel. *The Road to Gdansk: Poland and the USSR*. New York: Monthly Review, 1981.

Sivard, Ruth Leger, ed., *Women: A World Survey*. Washington, D.C.: World Priorities, 1985.

————, ed. *World Military and Social Expenditures 1983: An Annual Report on World Priorities*. Washington, D.C.: World Priorities, 1983.

Sklar, Holly K., ed. *Trilateralism: The Trilateral Commission and Elite Planning for World Management*. Boston: South End, 1980.

Smith, Anthony. *The Geopolitics of Information: How Western Culture Dominates the World*. New York: Oxford University Press, 1980.

Snow, Edgar. *Red Star Over China*. New York: Grove, 1944.

Snyder, Glenn H. *Deterrence and Defense: Toward a Theory of National Security*. Princeton, N.J.: Princeton University Press, 1961.

Solzhenitsyn, Aleksandr I. *The Gulag Archipelago, 1918–1956: An Experiment in Literary Investigation*. Trans. Thomas P. Whitney. New York: Harper and Row, 1973.

Stein, Jonathan B. *From H-Bomb to Star Wars: The Politics of Strategic Decision Making*. Lexington, Mass.: Lexington, 1984.

Stephenson, Carolyn M., ed. *Alternative Methods for International Security*. Lanham, Md.: University Press of America, 1982.

Stokes, Bruce. *Helping Ourselves: Local Solutions to Global Problems*. New York: Norton, 1981.

Stopford, John M., and John H. Dunning, eds. *The World Directory of Multinational Enterprises, 1982–83: Company Performance and Global Trends*. 2nd ed. Detroit: Gale Research Company, 1983.

Stover, William James. *Information Technology in the Third World: Can It Lead to Humane National Development?* Boulder, Colo.: Westview, 1984.

Thompson, E. P., and Dan Smith, eds. *Protest and Survive*. New York: Monthly Review, 1981.

Timerman, Jacobo. *Prisoner Without a Name, Cell Without a Number*. Trans. Toby Talbot. New York: Vintage, 1982.

Toffler, Alvin. *The Third Wave*. New York: William Morrow, 1980.

Triska, Jan F., and Robert M. Slusser. *The Theory, Law, and Policy of Soviet Treaties*. Stanford, Calif.: Stanford University Press, 1962.

Tunstall, Jeremy. *The Media Are American: Anglo-American Media in the World*. London: Constable, 1977.

Ury, William L. *Beyond the Hotline: How We Can Prevent the Crisis that Might Bring Nuclear War*. Boston: Houghton Mifflin, 1985.

U Thant. *View From the UN*. Garden City, N.Y.: Doubleday, 1978.

van der Post, Laurens. *The Lost World of the Kalahari*. Harmondsworth, Middlesex, England: Penguin, 1958.

Vasconcellos, John. *A Liberating Vision: Politics for Growing Humans*. San Luis Obispo, Calif.: Impact, 1979.

Vilas, Carlos M. *The Sandinista Revolution: National Liberation and Social Transformation in Central America*. Trans. Judy Butler. New York: Monthly Review, 1986.

Walsh, Roger. *Staying Alive: The Psychology of Human Survival*. Boulder, Colo.: New Science Library, 1984.
Weir, David, and Mark Schapiro. *Circle of Poison: Pesticides and People in a Hungry World*. San Francisco: Institute for Food and Development Policy, 1981.
White, Richard Alan. *The Morass: The United States' Intervention in Central America*. New York: Harper and Row, 1984.
Wien, Barbara J., ed. *Peace and World Order Studies*. 4th ed. New York: World Policy Institute, 1984.
Woito, Robert S. *To End War: A New Approach to International Conflict*. New York: Pilgrim Press, 1982.
Wolfe, Alan. *America's Impasse: The Rise and Fall of the Politics of Growth*. Boston: South End, 1981.
Yankelovich, Daniel. *New Rules: Searching for Self-Fulfillment in a World Turned Upside Down*. New York: Random House, 1981.
Yergin, Daniel. *Shattered Peace: The Origins of the Cold War and the National Security State*. Boston: Houghton Mifflin, 1977.
————, and Martin Hillenbrand, eds. *Global Insecurity: A Strategy for Energy and Economic Renewal*. Boston: Houghton Mifflin, 1982.
Zhou Guo, ed. *China and the World*. 4 vols. Beijing: Beijing Review, 1982–1983.

ARTICLES AND PAPERS

Ajami, Fouad. "Human Rights and World Order Politics." Working paper no. 4. New York: Institute for World Order, 1978.
————. "The Fate of Nonalignment." *Foreign Affairs* 59 (Winter 1980–81): 366–385.
Aldridge, Robert C. "Fear Over U.S. 'War' Computers." *San Francisco Chronicle*, June 14, 1980, 34.
Amcrican Farmland Trust. "Future Policy Directions for American Agriculture." Washington, D.C.: A.F.T., November 1984.
Anderson, Marion. "The Empty Pork Barrel: Unemployment and the Pentagon Budget." Lansing, Michigan: 1978. Mimeo.
Babst, Dean, Robert Aldridge, and David Krieger. *Accidental Nuclear War Dangers of the "Star Wars" Proposal*. Santa Barbara: Nuclear Age Peace Foundation, 1985.
Ball, Nicole. "Military Expenditure and Socio-Economic Development." *International Social Science Journal*, no. 95 (1983): 81–97.
Bello, Walden, Peter Hayes, and Lyuba Zarsky. " '500-Mile Island': The Philippine Nuclear Reactor Deal." *Pacific Research* 10 (First Quarter 1979): 1–29.
Blond, David. "The Future Contribution of Multinational Corporations to World Growth—A Positive Appraisal." *Business Economics* (May 1978): 80–95.
Borgese, Elisabeth Mann. "The Law of the Sea." *Scientific American* (March 1983): 42–49.
Boulding, Elise. "A Post-Military Agenda for the Scientific Community." *International Social Science Journal*, no. 95 (1983): 163–199.

Brown, Cynthia. "The High Cost of Monetarism in Chile." *The Nation*, September 27, 1980, 271–275.

Brzezinski, Zbigniew. "How the Cold War Was Played." *Foreign Affairs* 51 (October 1972): 181–209.

Bull, Hedley. "The State's Positive Role in World Affairs." *Daedalus* 108 (Fall 1979): 111–123.

Bundy, McGeorge, George F. Kennan, Robert S. McNamara, and Gerard Smith. "Nuclear Weapons and the Atlantic Alliance." *Foreign Affairs* 60 (Spring 1982): 753–768.

Bundy, William P. "Elements of Power," *Foreign Affairs* 56 (October 1977): 1–26.

Burrows, William E. "Ballistic Missile Defense: The Illusion of Security." *Foreign Affairs* 62 (Spring 1984): 843–856.

Calabrese, Mike, and Mike Kendall. "The Black Agenda for South Africa." *The Nation*, October 27, 1985, 393, 406–409.

Calleo, David P. "Inflation and American Power." *Foreign Affairs* 59 (Spring, 1981): 781–812.

Camp, Roderic A. "Women and Political Leadership in Mexico: A Comparative Study of Female and Male Political Elites." *Journal of Politics* 41 (May 1979): 417–441.

Carney, Kim. "Development Aid: An Economist's Perception." *International Journal on World Peace* 2 (July–September 1985): 3–18.

Cavanagh, John, and Frederick Clairmonte. "The Transnational Economy: Transnational Corporations and Global Markets." Washington, D.C.: Institute for Policy Studies, 1982.

"The Challenge of Peace: God's Promise and Our Response." *Origins* 12 (October 28, 1982): 305–328.

Clem, Ralph S. "Ethnicity and Its Implications." *Bulletin of the Atomic Scientists* 38 (June 1982): 53–58.

Conroy, Mike. "U.S. Observers Report: Legitimate Elections Despite U.S. Interference." *Nicaraguan Perspectives*, no. 10 (Spring–Summer 1985): 27–29.

Cooper, Wendy. "The Economic Consequences of Intervention." *The Nation*, December 20, 1980, 668–672.

Cusack, Thomas R., and Michael Don Ward. "Military Spending in the United States, the Soviet Union, and the People's Republic of China." *Journal of Conflict Resolution* 25 (September 1981): 429–469.

Dent, Frederick B. "The Multinational Corporation—Toward a World Economy." *Financial Executive*, February 1974, 42–47.

Ding Chen. "The Economic Development of China." *Scientific American*, September 1980, 153–165.

Donnelly, Jack. "Human Rights and Development: Complementary or Competing Concerns?" *World Politics* 36 (January 1984): 255–283.

Dowie, Mark. "The Corporate Crime of the Century." *Mother Jones*, November 1979, 23–38.

Drache, Daniel, and Arthur Kroker. "Labyrinth of Dependency." *Canadian Journal of Political and Social Theory* 7 (Fall 1983): 5–24.

Ehrlich, Paul R. "North America After the War." *Natural History* 93 (March 1984): 4–8.

Emerson, Rupert. "The Fate of Human Rights in the Third World." *World Politics* 27 (January 1975): 201–226.

Engler, Robert. "Technology Out of Control." *The Nation*, April 27, 1985, 488–500.

English, Robert. "Eastern Europe's Doves." *Foreign Policy*, no. 56 (Fall 1984): 44–60.

Falk, Richard A. "World Order Values: Secular Means and Spiritual Ends." New York: Planetary Citizens, n.d.

Farer, Tom. "The United States and the Third World: A Basis for Accommodation." *Foreign Affairs* 54 (October 1975): 79–97.

Ferguson, Thomas, and Joel Rogers. "Another Trilateral Election?" *The Nation*, June 28, 1980, 770, 783–787.

FitzGerald, Frances. "Giving the Shah Everything He Wants." *Harper's*, November 1974, 55–82.

Freeman, Harold. "Pakistan: Joining the Nuke Club." *Los Angeles Times*, December 1, 1985, 4/p. 2.

Frieden, Jeff. "Why the Big Banks Love Martial Law." *The Nation*, January 23, 1982, 65, 81–84.

Fukuyama, Frances. "Gorbachev and the Third World." *Foreign Affairs* 64 (Spring 1986): 715–731.

Galtung, Johan. "A Structural Theory of Imperialism." *Journal of Peace Research*, no. 8 (1971): 81–117.

———. "The New International Economic Order and the Basic Needs Approach." *Alternatives* 4 (March 1979): 455–476.

Goldblat, Jozef. "Charges of Treaty Violations." *Bulletin of the Atomic Scientists* 40 (May 1984): 33–36.

Guertner, Gary L. "What is Proof?" *Foreign Policy*, no. 59 (Summer 1985): 73–84.

Guyot, Erik. "The Case Is Not Proved." *The Nation*, November 10, 1984, 465, 478–484.

Hardt, John P., and Donna Gold. "Andropov's Economic Future." *Orbis* 27 (Spring 1983): 11–20.

Hartung, William, and Rosy Nimroody. "Cutting Up the Star Wars Pie." *The Nation*, September 14, 1985, 200–202.

"Haudenosaunce Statement to the World, May 1979." *Akwesasne Notes*, Spring 1979, p. 7.

Hawk, David. "The Killing of Cambodia." *New Republic*, November 15, 1982, 17–21.

Henry, James. "Where the Money Went." *The New Republic*, April 14, 1986, 20–23.

Hersh, Seymour M. "'The Target Is Destroyed': What Really Happened to Flight 007." *The Atlantic*, September 1986, 47–69.

Hirschhorn, Joel S. "Toxic Waste." *Los Angeles Times*, October 10, 1983, 2/p. 5.

Hitchens, Christopher. "Minority Report." *The Nation*, November 3, 1984, 438.

Huyck, Earl E., and Leon F. Bouvier. "The Demography of Refugees." *The Annals* 467 (May 1983): 39–61.

Iklé, Fred Charles. "Nuclear Strategy: Can There Be a Happy Ending?" *Foreign Affairs* 63 (Spring 1985): 810–826.

International Business Machines. "IBM Operations in South Africa." Armonk, N.Y.: February 1982. Mimeo.

"Interview: Kim Dae Jung—Democracy and Dissidence in South Korea," *Journal of International Affairs* 38 (Winter 1985): 181–191.

Johansen, Robert C. "Toward an Alternative Security System: Moving Beyond the Balance of Power in the Search for World Security." New York: World Policy Institute, no. 24, 1983.

Kaplan, David E., and Ida Landauer. "Radioactivity for the Oceans." *The Nation*, October 9, 1982, 336–339.

Kaya, Yoichi et al. "Management of Global Environmental Issues." *World Futures* 19 (1984), pp. 223–231.

Kellogg, William W., and Robert Schware. "Society, Science and Climate Change." *Foreign Affairs* 60 (Summer 1982): 1076–1109.

Kennan, George F. "On Nuclear War." *New York Review of Books*, January 21, 1982, 8–12.

Klare, Michael T. "Soviet Arms Transfers to the Third World." *Bulletin of the Atomic Scientists* 40 (May 1984): 26–32.

Lanner, Deborah. "A Farm Bill for Farmers." *The Nation*, July 6–13, 1985, 19–20.

Launis, Michael A. "The State and Industrial Labor in South Korea." *Bulletin of Concerned Asian Scholars* 16 (October–December 1984): 2–10.

Leitenberg, Milton. "The Numbers Game or 'Who's on First?' " *Bulletin of the Atomic Scientists* 38 (June 1982): 27–32.

Lens, Sidney. "Will It Be the Crash Next Time?" *The Nation*, June 22, 1985, 764–766.

Lindsey, Charles W. "The Philippine Economy." *Monthly Review* 36 (April 1985): 28–41.

Lovins, Amory B., L. Hunter Lovins, and Leonard Ross. "Nuclear Power and Nuclear Bombs." *Foreign Affairs* 58 (Summer 1980): 1137–1177.

MacDougall, A. Kent. "In Third World, All but the Rich are Poorer." *Los Angeles Times*, November 4, 1984, 4/pp. 1, 3.

MacRae, Phyllis. "Race and Class in Southern Africa." *The African Review* 4 (1974): 237–258.

Macy, Joanna Rogers. "How to Deal with Despair." *New Age*, June 1979, 40–45.

Manning, Robert A. "The Philippines in Crisis." *Foreign Affairs* 63 (Winter 1984–85): 392–410.

Maranto, Gina. "Are We Close to the Road's End?" *Discover* 7 (January 1986): 28–50.

Marotta, George. "The Third World: Threat or Opportunity?" *Agenda* (U.S. Agency for International Development), January–February 1980, pp. 23–26.

Maynes, Charles William. "When Israel Jumped the Nuclear Firebreak." *Los Angeles Times*, June 9, 1985, 4/p. 2.

McNamara, Robert S. "The Military Role of Nuclear Weapons." *Foreign Affairs* 62 (Fall 1983): 59–80.

Medvedev, Roy A., and Zhores A. Medvedev. "Nuclear Samizdat." *The Nation*, January 16, 1982, 38–50.

Meissner, Charles F. "Debt: Reform Without Governments." *Foreign Policy*, no. 56 (Fall 1984): 81–93.

Milewski, Jerzy et al. "Poland: Four Years After." *Foreign Affairs* 64 (Winter 1985–86): 337–359.

Mitchell, Arnold. "Changing Values and Lifestyles." Palo Alto, Calif.: Stanford Research Institute, n.d.

Morris, Charles R. "The Soaring Dollar: Up, Up . . . and No One Really Knows Why." *Los Angeles Times*, February 24, 1985, 5/pp. 1–2.

Muller, Robert. "A World Core Curriculum." *Education Network News* 1 (November 1982): 1–4.

Murphy, Paul. "The Military Tax Bite 1986." Washington, D.C.: Military Spending Research Services, March 1986.

Myers, Norman. "The Conversion of Tropical Forests." *Environment* 22 (July–August 1980): 6–13.

Newfarmer, Richard S. "TNC Takeovers in Brazil: The Uneven Distribution of Benefits in the Market for Firms." *World Development* 7 (January 1979): 25–43.

Oxfam America. "Special Report: Women in Development." Winter 1985, 1–8.

Paige, Glenn D. "On Values and Science: *The Korean Decision* Reconsidered." *American Political Science Review* 71 (December 1977): 1603–1609.

Payne, Keith B., and Colin S. Gray. "Nuclear Policy and the Defensive Transition." *Foreign Affairs* 62 (Spring 1984): 820–842.

Pearson, David. "K.A.L. 007: What the U.S. Knew and When We Knew It." *The Nation*, August 18–25, 1984, 105–124.

Pincus, Walter. "U.S. Repeatedly Considered Use of N-Bombs." *The Oregonian*, July 29, 1985, p. 2.

"The Politics of Human Rights." *Trialogue*, no. 19 (Fall 1978): 1–36.

Pollock, Cynthia. "Decommissioning: Nuclear Power's Missing Link." Washington, D.C.: Worldwatch Institute, April 1986.

Prescott, James W. "Body Pleasure and the Origins of Violence." *The Futurist*, April 1975, 64–74.

Raskin, Marcus G. "Progressive Liberalism for the '80s." *The Nation*, May 17, 1980, 577, 587–596.

Rebitzer, Bob. "Repeal of Unitary Tax: Giveaway to Big Business?" *The Economic Democrat*, March 1985, 3.

Rosencranz, Armin. "The Problem of Transboundary Pollution." *Environment* 22 (June 1980): 15–20.

Sagan, Carl. "Nuclear War and Climatic Catastrophe." *Foreign Affairs* 62 (Winter 1983–84): 257–292.

Sakamato, Yoshikazu. "The Global Crisis and Peace Research." *International Peace Research Newsletter* 21 (1983): 4–7.

Seignious, George M., II, and Jonathan Paul Yates. "Europe's Nuclear Superpowers." *Foreign Policy*, no. 55 (Summer 1984): 40–53.

Sharp, Gene. "Making the Abolition of War A Realistic Goal." New York: Institute for World Order, 1980.

Shuman, Michael Harrison. "International Institution Building: The Missing Link for Peace." Center for Innovative Diplomacy, June 1984.

Sillinian, Sidney G. "The Philippines in 1983: Authoritarianism Beleaguered." *Asian Survey* 24 (February 1984): 149–158.

Smith, R. Jeffrey. "Scientists Fault Charges of Soviet Cheating." *Science* 220 (May 13, 1983): 695–697.

———. "Soviets Drop Farther Back in Weapons Technology." *Science* 219 (March 18, 1983): 1300–1301.

Sommer, Mark. "Beating Our Swords into Shields: Forging a Preservative Defense." Miranda, Calif.: Center for a Preservative Defense, 1983.

Sweezy, Paul M. "The Suppression of the Polish Workers Movement." *Monthly Review* 34 (January 1983): 27–30.

Talbot, Stephen. "The H-Bombs Next Door." *The Nation*, February 7, 1981, 129, 143–148.

"Teaching for Peace." *Christian Science Monitor* supplement, January 31, 1986.

Thies, Wallace J. "The Atlantic Alliance, Nuclear Weapons and European Attitudes: Reexamining the Conventional Wisdom." Berkeley: Institute of International Studies, no. 19, University of California, 1983.

Thorsson, Inga. "Study on Disarmament and Development." *Bulletin of the Atomic Scientists* 38 (June 1982): 41–44.

Thurow, Lester C. "America's Economy 'Ain't Broke,' But Creeping Rust is Taking Its Toll." *Los Angeles Times*, March 17, 1985, 5/p. 3.

Tucker, Robert C. "Where is the Soviet Union Headed?" *World Policy Journal* 4 (Spring 1987): 179–206.

ul Haq, Mahbub. "Negotiating the Future." *Foreign Affairs* 59 (Winter 1980–81): 398–417.

U Thant. "Ten Crucial Years." *United Nations Monthly Chronicle* 6 (July 1969): i–v.

Vogel, Ezra F. "Pax Nipponica?" *Foreign Affairs* 64 (Spring 1986): 752–767.

Wakaizumi, Kei. "Japan's Dilemma: To Act or Not to Act." *Foreign Policy*, no. 16 (Fall 1974): 30–47.

Walker, William, and Mans Lönnroth. "Proliferation and Nuclear Trade: A Look Ahead." *Bulletin of the Atomic Scientists* 40 (April 1984): 29–33.

Walleri, R. Dan. "The Political Economy Literature on North-South Relations: Alternative Approaches and Empirical Evidence." *International Studies Quarterly* 22 (December 1978): 587–623.

Weir, David. "The Boomerang Crime." *Mother Jones*, November 1979, 40–49.

Westing, Arthur H., and E. W. Pfeiffer. "The Cratering of Indochina." *Scientific American*, May 1972, 21–29.

Wilson, Lillie. "The Plenty Project: Inside the Hippie Peace Corps." *New Age*, July 1981, 18–26.

Wolf, Edward C. "On the Brink of Extinction: Conserving the Diversity of Life." New York: Worldwatch Institute (no. 78), 1987.

DOCUMENTS AND OTHER PRIMARY SOURCES

Amnesty International. *Human Rights in the Philippines: Hearing before the Subcommittee on International Organizations of the Committee on International Relations, House of Representatives, Ninety-fourth Congress.* 2nd ed. Washington, D.C.: AI, September 15, 1976.

———. *Amnesty International Report 1980.* London: AI, 1980.

———. *Amnesty International Report 1981.* London: AI, 1981.

———. *Amnesty International Report 1982.* London: AI, 1982.

Glennon, John P. et al., eds. *Foreign Relations of the United States 1950. Vol. 1: National Security Affairs; Foreign Economic Policy.* Washington, D.C.: U.S. Government Printing Office, 1977.

International Solidarity Front for the Defense of the Iranian People's Democratic Rights. "The Crimes of Khomeini's Regime: A Report on the Violations of Civil and Political Rights by the Islamic Republic of Iran." N.p.: ISF-Iran, 1982.

Kelly, Petra Karin. "Speech, Stockholm, Sweden, December 9, 1982, on the Occasion of Receiving the Alternative Peace Prize." Mimeo.

United Nations Centre for Disarmament. Department of Political and Security Council Affairs. *The United Nations Disarmament Yearbook* 6, 1981.

U.S. Arms Control and Disarmament Agency. *Arms Control and Disarmament Agreements: Texts and Histories of Negotiations.* Washington, D.C.: ACDA, 1982.

———. *World Military Expenditures and Arms Transfers, 1985.* Washington, D.C.: ACDA, 1985.

U.S. Department of Defense. Office of the Assistant Secretary of Defense, Office of Economic Adjustment, and President's Economic Adjustment Committee. *Economic Adjustment/Conversion.* Washington, D.C.: The Pentagon, July 1985.

U.S. Department of State. *Human Rights.* Selected Documents no. 5. Washington, D.C.: U.S. Government Printing Office, 1977.

———. *Human Rights and Foreign Policy: Commemoration of the Universal Declaration of Human Rights.* Selected Documents no. 22. Washington, D.C.: U.S. Government Printing Office, December 1983.

———. *Soviet Noncompliance with Arms Control Agreements.* Special Report no. 122, February 1, 1985.

———. Bureau of Public Affairs. *Current Policy.* 1975–1985.

———. Bureau of Public Affairs. *Special Report: Human Rights in the Republic of Korea.* September 1974.

World Bank. *World Development Report 1984.* New York: Oxford University Press, 1984.

Index

Acid rain, 10, 21, 178, 180, 181, 195; in dispute between U.S. and Canada, 164–165; in Germany, 56
AEG Telefunken, 33
Afghanistan, 19, 52, 54, 76, 81, 88, 135; Soviet invasion of, 116
Africa, 19, 80, 84, 88, 99, 176, 189, 192; ecological destruction in, 55; health care in, 176; military coups in, 88; refugees in, 88; underdevelopment in, 55. *See* also Hunger; Third World; Underdevelopment.
African National Congress (ANC), 96, 97
Agence France-Presse, 28
Agent Orange, 54
Ahmad, Eqbal, 52
Aid, 26, 56, 76, 84, 102, 138, 171, 174, 175, 177; development, 87; military, 29, 75; people-to-people, 174; programs, 55, 173. *See* also Third World; World Bank; and individual countries.
Ajami, Fouad, 50, 51, 65
Albania, 153, 156
Algeria, 27, 64
Allende, Salvador, 18, 19
Alliance for Human Rights in China, 69
Amnesty International, 11, 106, 168, 192
Anglican Church, 188
Angola, 98, 99, 135, 202*n*
Antarctic Treaty, 185, 189
Anti-ballistic Missile (ABM), 127, 133

Anti-Ballistic Missile Treaty, 128, 185, 186
Antinuclear movement, 11, 20, 48
Antisatellite weapons, 127, 187
ANZUS (Australia, New Zealand, and the United States), 21, 156
Apartheid, 94–99. *See* also South Africa, Republic of.
Aquino, Benigno, 71, 104
Aquino, Corazon, 104, 106
Argueta, Manlio, 68
Argentina, 6, 58, 67, 85, 88, 125, 126, 177, 191; health programs in, 176; military rule in, 52, 68
Arms control, 115, 116, 132, 139, 170, 182, 186, 192; agreements, 123, 148, 183, 186; negotiations, 121, 147, 185–188; U.S.–Soviet, 133
Arms expenditures, 5, 117, 144; and economic performance, 150; costs of, 115; in Third World, 87. *See* also under country entries.
Arms race, 9, 18, 45, 52, 76, 115, 118, 125, 126, 127, 129, 133, 183, 187, 191, 194; conversion of, 155–156, 172, 188; costs and effects of, 19, 114, 134–148; and employment, 53; and refugees, 53; strategic, 114, 115, 116, 119–121. *See* also Arms expenditures; Nuclear weapons; Nuclear war; Soviet Union; Third World; United States.

Arms sales, 49, 114; and underdeveloped countries, 52–53, 76
Asia, 25, 35, 64, 76, 83, 109, 189
Asian Development Bank, 26, 159
Associated Press, 28
AT&T, 28
Australia, 17, 149, 150, 152
Authoritarianism, 49, 103

Balance-of-Power, 17, 20, 45, 52
Balance of terror, 115
Ball, Desmond, 122, 123
Bangladesh, 125, 174
Bank of America, 25
Barnet, Richard, 17, 27, 28, 47
Baruch Plan, 132
Basic needs, 18, 47, 49, 51, 54, 56, 58, 76, 81–82, 114, 170, 171, 172, 173
Bechtel Corp., 126
Belgium, 119, 150
Berlin crisis, 131
Bhopal, India, 5, 56, 180. *See* also Union Carbide.
Biko, Steve, 60, 61, 63, 95
Birth control, 10
Block, Fred, 37
Blumenthal, Michael, 22
Boeing, 130
Boff, Leonardo, 67
Bolivia, 67, 177
Bolshevik Revolution, 134
Boulding, Elise, 193
Boulding, Kenneth, 44
Brain drain, 89
Brandt, Willy, 155
Brandt Commission, 14, 41, 80, 170
Brazil, 67, 74, 76, 79, 107, 109, 144, 152, 162, 177, 178, 191; deforestation

About the Book
and the Author

Traditional studies of world politics emphasize the struggle for power between states as they search for national security. But the sources of power have changed, making real security more elusive than ever. As Professor Gurtov demonstrates, Third World underdevelopment, the declining influence of the superpowers, the economic strength of Japan and Western Europe, and global economic and ecological interdependence have transformed the world political agenda. Students and scholars alike, therefore, need new tools for understanding the threats and the opportunities posed by this transformation.

Global Politics in the Human Interest provides these tools. Addressing four interrelated global problems—underdevelopment, human rights violations, the arms race, and environmental destruction—it offers a planetary perspective on how world politics are being reshaped. The book utilizes a global-humanist framework of values and ideas for analyzing world political economy; and concludes with a thought-provoking redefinition of international security and specific ways that it might be achieved.

Gurtov's thoughtful critique of traditional approaches to international politics underlines the crucial role of transnational corporations in world political economy and gives considerable attention to the underdeveloped world, not merely to the superpowers. The book has a very practical bent: it tries to convey how global politics affects the quality and content of people's lives throughout the world.

Mel Gurtov is professor of political science and director of the International Studies Program at Portland State University.